THE SCOTS COLLEGE ROME
1600–2000

Scots College Rome Quatercentenary. Painting by Patricia Hakim.
Reproduced by kind permission of the artist.

The Scots College Rome
1600–2000

Edited by
Raymond McCluskey

John Donald
Edinburgh

Published in 2000 by
John Donald, an imprint of
Birlinn Limited
8 Canongate Venture
5 New Street
Edinburgh
EH8 8BH

ISBN 0 85976 524 5

British Library Cataloguing-in-Publication Data
A catalogue record for this book is available from the British Library

Typeset and origination by Textype Typesetters, Cambridge
Printed and bound by Redwood Books, Trowbridge

Contents

The Scots College Rome Quatercentenary   vii
    Cardinal Thomas J. Winning

Four Hundred Years   ix
    Christopher J. McElroy

Abbreviations   x

Preface   xi

Contributors   xiv

Introduction: Rome, the Papacy and the Foundation of National   1
    Colleges in the sixteenth and early seventeenth centuries
    Anthony D. Wright

1. Beginnings 1600–1707   19
    Mark Dilworth OSB

2. Development 1707–1820   43
    James F. McMillan

3. Tribulations 1820–1922   67
    Raymond McCluskey

4. Challenges 1922–2000   108
    John McIntyre

Appendix 1: A British College in Rome?   145
    Michael E. Williams

Appendix 2: Clement VIII's Bull of Foundation (1600)   151

Appendix 3: The Letters of Thomas Crumly   153

Appendix 4: Register of the Scots College Archives   164

Appendix 5: Cardinal Protectors of the Scottish Nation   168

Appendix 6: Rectors of the Scots College Rome   169

Index   171

The Scots College Rome Quatercentenary

His Eminence Cardinal Thomas J. Winning

One moment of my life etched for ever in my memory is when I was told I was going to Rome to continue my studies for the Priesthood. It was for me a blessing I have always cherished.

Later that year, 1945, as part of a small group of seminarians travelling to Rome by boat and train, I thought of other young men – some of them boys of twelve or thirteen years – who had made this same journey in the seventeenth, eighteenth and nineteenth centuries in very different and much more trying circumstances.

Coach, sailing vessel and more coach, running into weeks and even months of travel and all because they wished to become priests who would return one day to evangelise and bring the sacraments to the small remnant of Catholics in their homeland. I search for words to describe the Roman students of yesteryear: valiant? courageous? heroic? In the early days the *Collegio Romano* which the Scots attended provided secondary school preparation as well as the curriculum of a major seminary.

These youngsters must have felt the tug of home, family and friends as they set about their studies for as many as twelve or thirteen years. No telephone; no internet; no radio; no TV; no press: an erratic postal service and a huge dollop of faith in God kept them going.

They and their like are what the Pontifical Scots College is still about. Now as we celebrate its quatercentenary we realise more than ever the inestimable contribution this institution has made to the Catholic Church in Scotland.

The history of the College is a story of hardship, poverty, endeavour and achievement – a microcosm of 400 years of Catholic life in Scotland.

The best has yet to come!

Four Hundred Years

Very Rev Christopher J. McElroy

One of the first things the visitor sees in the Pontifical Scots College is a marble plaque with a list of names. These are the College rectors from inauguration to the present day, and in itself, therefore, this plaque is something of a historical record. While honoured to be the forty-ninth name on the list, and at the time of the College's 400th anniversary of foundation, I should point out that one has to go far beyond the front door to discover the true story of the Scots College. This book helps you to do just that, and to glimpse something of the personalities and emotions, the traditions and the customs which have made the College what it is today. The College community is truly grateful to the editor and contributors for this book that helps us to be proudly aware of our past and challenges us to follow the example of sacrifice and dedication by so many who have been here before us.

The story of the College is a story of faith, faith in God and in His call, and faith in the gift to respond to His call. It is a story of faith meeting culture in a city which bears the unique testimony of ancient civilisation and Christian history, and of generations of young men returning home with renewed faith and vision for the work of preaching the Gospel of Jesus Christ. For four centuries this College has been a part of Scotland in the heart of Rome: our hope is that it will continue to prosper and add a special quality to Church and society both in the Eternal City and in our native land.

ABBREVIATIONS

APF	Archive of Propaganda Fide, Rome
ARSI	*Archivum Romanum Societatis Iesu*
Gray	J. Gray (ed.), *The Scots College Rome. A Tribute to the Scots College Society* (London–Edinburgh, 1930)
CP	Congregazione Particolari [APF]
DNB	*Dictionary of National Biography*
GAA	Glasgow Archdiocesan Archives
IR	*The Innes Review. The Journal of the Scottish Catholic Historical Association*
MacPherson	W. J. Anderson (ed.), 'Abbé Paul MacPherson: History of the Scots College Rome', in *IR*, 12 (1961)
RSC	*Records of the Scots Colleges at Douai, Rome, Madrid, Valladolid and Ratisbon*, New Spalding Club (Aberdeen, 1906)
RSCHS	*Records of the Scottish Church History Society*
SCA	Scottish Catholic Archives, Columba House, Edinburgh
SCAR	Scots College Archives, Rome
SCD	*Scottish Catholic Directory*
TRHS	*Transactions of the Royal Historical Society*
Williams	Michael E. Williams, *The Venerable English College Rome* (London, 1979)

Preface

Raymond McCluskey

In 1930, by way of marking the first twenty-five years of the Scots College Society (founded in 1904 with a membership drawn from the College's alumni, friends and benefactors), Canon John Gray edited a volume entitled *The Scots College Rome.* Prepared for the private enjoyment of the Society, the book was never meant for a wide audience. Only 750 copies were printed and each volume was numbered as a matter of bibliographical record. The contents – historical essays and memoirs – pre-supposed an intimate familiarity with the College. The contributors seamlessly weaved Italian terms such as *villeggiatura, carrozzabile, tinello,* and *coretto* into their narratives. Translation was redundant; such words had become part of the natural vocabulary of the College's ex-students and represented a shared identity amongst the largely clerical readership. They were badges of *romanità* and transports to a longing nostalgia for priests now engaged in serving the Scottish Mission.

Seventy years on from John Gray's publication, the 400th anniversary of the foundation of the Scots College Rome by Pope Clement VIII in 1600 occasions the appearance of yet another history of the institution. However, in less than a century, times have changed dramatically. The Second World War and the Second Vatican Council (1962–65) have been major backdrops to transformations in the life of the College, not least the move to a new site in 1964. Yet, perhaps even more importantly for a volume such as this present one, the practice of history-writing in Scotland has moved on, especially in the area of Scottish Catholic studies. The publication of the Scottish Catholic Historical Association's journal *The Innes Review* since 1950 and the establishment of the Scottish Catholic Archives in Columba House, Edinburgh, in 1959 have resulted in an increasing number of scholars researching in the field whose work is marked by the highest standards of academic rigour. That community of ideas and half-century of critical and analytical research which *The Innes Review*, to date, represents was simply not available to the distinguished historian, W. E. Brown, when he penned his essay on the College's history for Gray's volume. There is no such excuse for authors at the dawn of the twenty-first century. The marriage which once existed between scholarship and apologetic has been annulled.

The College's quatercentenary, then, may have served as the pretext for the commissioning of this new book but its *raison d'être* emerges out of a more complex response to the demands of modern Scottish historiography. The Scots College in Rome has a strong claim to being the oldest extant Scottish institution on the continent of Europe. It is no mere cliché, therefore, to assert that its place in the annals of Scottish history is unique. Its history can no longer be considered the precious property of only a limited number of alumni and well-wishers; rather, its history belongs to the entire population of the devolved, pluralist, and increasingly secularist nation which is Scotland today. Consequently, this book aims to make an important contribution to the continuing attempts by scholars to re-draft their understanding of Scottish culture, society and, ultimately, identity. The Scots who taught or studied in the Scots College Rome are illuminating *exempla* of the Scottish experience in Europe over the centuries and of the diverse layers of identity – Catholic-Scots-British-Lowlander-Highlander-Irish-Roman-Italian-European – which were brought back to their homeland. This experience can no longer be sidelined, as it once might have been in 1930, as a variant experience of little significance to mainstream Scottish culture. Scholars now appreciate more than ever that to talk of a monolithic, homogeneous Scottish culture is to perpetuate a myth. Scotland is a melting-pot of *cultures* and always has been.

Even a book has a history. This particular one began life with a phonecall from Cardinal Thomas Winning, Archbishop of Glasgow, to the editor in the autumn of 1997. As a former student in the 1940s and spiritual director at the College in the early 1960s, the cardinal's interest has been both personal and constant, though always in the background. The book finally made the transition from proposal to going concern after the first meeting in February 1998 in the Scots College Rome of the Quatercentenary Committee specially set up to co-ordinate events in 2000. The hospitality of the rector, staff and students of the College was most welcoming and very much appreciated. The membership of that Committee was: Rt Rev Mario Conti, Bishop of Aberdeen (the chairman); Mgr John McIntyre (former rector of the College); Mgr Charles Burns, OBE (formerly of the Vatican Archives); Mgr Hugh Boyle (archivist of the Archdiocese of Glasgow); Professor Jos Janssens SJ (Head of the Department of Ecclesiastical History in the Gregorian University, Rome); Fr Christopher McElroy (present rector of the College); Dr Raymond McCluskey (St Aloysius' College, Glasgow). All members of the Committee must be thanked for their unfailing support and encouragement. Bishop Conti's enthusiastic advocacy of a new history was irrepressible and the Committee responded accordingly in the affirmative.

However, the production of a history of the College, to be prepared in the short time available before publication in 2000, seemed something of a tall order. That this book has, nonetheless, made it into print is largely thanks to several people, not least the contributors. Each of the principal contributors had to agree to a chronological approach to their chapters as the book aims to provide – for the first time – both the specialist and the general reader with a basic, well-informed narrative of the College's past. This requirement was graciously met by all the contributors. Hopefully, the chronological method provides the book with a unity which multi-authored books often lack. The editor's gratitude to all of the contributors is sincere and profound. They will not mind a special note of pleasure being expressed at the willingness of Fr Michael Williams, the author of a distinguished history of the English College Rome, to contribute to the volume. His appendix stands as a symbol of the respect and friendship which characterises relations between the two ecclesiastical institutions in the Eternal City spawned by the island of Britain.

Many have given the editor support in the preparation of this volume, not all of whom can be mentioned here. Mr Bernard Aspinwall, Fellow of the Research Centre in Scottish History at the University of Strathclyde, was spontaneous in his advice and encouragement. The editor is in his debt. No one has done more than Mr Aspinwall to forward the study of Scottish Catholic history in the modern period. Dr John Durkan, Senior Honorary Research Fellow in the Department of Scottish History, University of Glasgow, was, as ever, a major source of information and inspiration. The Vicar General of the Diocese of Galloway, Mgr Joseph Boyd, graciously allowed the editor not only to read the remarkable correspondence written by his great-uncle, Thomas Crumly, who attended the College in the 1870s, but also to publish an edited selection (see Appendix 3). These letters are an invaluable supplement to our knowledge of that distinctive era – the only student's account of the period of *risorgimento* and the fall of Rome to have survived. Fr Christopher McElroy, rector of the Scots College, was an ever attentive e-mail correspondent. His efforts on the editor's behalf were legion. Words cannot sufficiently convey the editor's gratitude. Mention must also be made of the vice-rector, Fr Raymond Breslin, for help at a particularly crucial stage. Fr Adrian Porter SJ, Head Master of St Aloysius' College, Glasgow, generously gave the editor leave to attend meetings in Rome and Glasgow; it is also due to his kind permission that the editor will be able to attend and speak at the November 2000 conference in the Scots College which is based on this book.

Mgr John McIntyre's contribution to this book is much more than just his splendid chapter on the modern College. A former student and rector of the College, he has long believed that a revised history is required and he has actively campaigned on its behalf. While this volume is not the single-author work of long gestation which is Mgr McIntyre's ultimate goal, it does represent an answer to his prayers that a worthy volume might be produced for the quatercentenary. Though far from being comprehensive in its treatment of the College's long history, the editor joins with Mgr McIntyre in hoping that this collection of studies will stimulate the interest of the scholarly community and, especially, of a future research student who might find in the abundant archive material enough for a doctoral thesis and eventual monograph. In the meantime, it remains for the editor of the present work to thank Mgr McIntyre for his support which has been so generous in the provision of vital information, photocopies and books. This particular book would not have been possible without him.

Finally, a word of thanks to the publishers, John Donald, and to the editor's successive contacts, Hugh Andrew, Andrew Simmons, Russell Walker and Donald Morrison, for professional advice and guidance. It is good to be associated with a publisher which has done so much to forward the cause of Scottish history in recent years.

CONTRIBUTORS

Rt Rev Dr Mark Dilworth OSB — Titular Abbot of Iona; formerly Abbot of St Benedict's Abbey, Fort Augustus; past Keeper of the Scottish Catholic Archives and former Editor of *The Innes Review*.

Dr Raymond McCluskey — Teacher of History, St Aloysius' College, Glasgow; author of *St Joseph's Kilmarnock 1847–1997: A Portrait of a Parish Community* (Kilmarnock, 1997); editor of *The See of Ninian: A History of the Medieval Diocese of Whithorn and the Diocese of Galloway in Modern Times* (Ayr, 1997).

Very Rev Christopher J. McElroy — Rector of the Scots College Rome since 1995.

Rt Rev Monsignor John McIntyre — Parish Priest of St Bridget's, Baillieston; former rector of Blairs College, Aberdeen, and the Scots College Rome.

Professor James F. McMillan — Richard Pares Professor of History in the University of Edinburgh; Convener of the Scottish Catholic Historical Association.

Rev Dr Michael E. Williams — Honorary Research Fellow, Trinity and All Saints' College, University of Leeds; author of *The Venerable English College Rome* (London, 1979) and *St Alban's College, Valladolid* (London, 1986).

Cardinal Thomas J. Winning — Archbishop of Glasgow since 1974; created Cardinal Priest in 1994.

Dr Anthony D. Wright — Senior Lecturer in the School of History, University of Leeds; General Editor of the *Longman History of the Papacy* series.

Rome, The Papacy and The Foundation of National Colleges in the Sixteenth and early Seventeenth Centuries

Anthony D. Wright

The Counter-Reformation papacy saw the recovery for Catholicism of European territories affected by Protestantism as one of its obvious priorities. In this sense 'mission', within Western Europe itself, was certainly involved, even if that term needs here to be used with greater care than it has perhaps sometimes been, with reference for example to early English Catholic Recusancy[1] Moreover the centrality, in every sense, of Rome was undoubtedly reasserted in the Catholic Church of the Counter-Reformation. This was possible not least because the papacy had emerged from the Council of Trent (1545–63) with its powers potentially strengthened, despite challenges to those powers throughout the course of the Council. One of the most innovative achievements of the Council was the decision that a new type of training institution for diocesan clergy should be created, the seminary, distinct from existing schools and universities. The Conciliar decrees stated that ideally each diocese should have its own seminary, and detailed provisions for the funding of such establishments were added, even though these were often not easy for bishops to fulfil, and in many parts of Catholic Europe progress in creating seminaries was so slow as to be measured in centuries rather than just years or decades.[2] The innovative concept of the seminary derived from the response of Cardinal Pole to the peculiar difficulties he faced in the Catholic restoration, short-lived as it proved, in the English kingdom under Mary Tudor.[3] That episode is an immediate reminder that the Conciliar plan for diocesan seminaries was naturally an impossibility in territories under Protestant control, where Catholic communities continued only under penal proscription. To provide further generations of Catholic priests for such communities appropriate education would have to be provided elsewhere, at locations within Catholic lands. Such 'foreign' seminaries thus came to be founded in Spain, France and the Netherlands for the training of priests who might serve in Britain and Ireland. Similarly an attempt was made to train priests for Scandinavia within German Catholic territory.[4] The founding and funding of such institutions was neither consistently nor uniquely the result of papal initiative, though papal involvement, alongside that of Catholic rulers and prelates, was common. In Rome, however, a more confident papacy was pursuing, after the Council of Trent, a programme of architectural regeneration and urban replanning, epitomized by the reordering of routes across the city by Pope Sixtus V (1585–90). Monumental new housing was provided by 1584 for the chief Jesuit educational establishment in Rome, the *Collegio Romano*, founded in 1551. But it is important to note that this famous institution, which drew male students, mainly upper-class, from areas of Italy and Europe far beyond the city's immediate surroundings, was not itself a seminary. Future clerics certainly studied there, but some pupils, as in other Jesuit colleges elsewhere, were destined for lay life, as rulers, statesmen, or urban magistrates for example. The conservation and promotion of Catholicism in a religiously divided Europe needed the support and protection of leading laity as well as prelates.

Seminaries

For the same reason the German College, founded in Rome itself by Gregory XIII (1572–85), was intended to provide a securely Catholic education for young men, especially aristocrats, who would form the future leadership in Church and state within the territories of the Holy Roman Empire, where many bishops and abbots were indeed also the rulers of important lands. It was hoped similarly to train those who would be the leading prelates in other possessions of the Austrian Habsburgs, such as Hungary. Pope Gregory was also interested in schemes to establish suitable training within German Catholic territories themselves, and his favourable attitude towards the Society of Jesus encouraged him to see the Jesuits as suitable for the running of Catholic education, including that of future priests, not only in German lands but elsewhere too. So in Rome the direction of the German College was entrusted to the Jesuits.[5] By 1579 an English Hospice in the city, of medieval origin, was transformed into a seminary, the English College, to train priests to minister to the Catholic community in their native realm. But the handing over of direction to the Jesuits was not achieved with ease or instant agreement. Conflict over this was partly related to tension between the English and the Welsh within the institution. There was in the end to be no Welsh College in Rome, unlike those for the English, the Scots and the Irish. But the transformation from hospice to seminary was difficult for another reason as well. The initial, even if not the ultimate vision of a leading English Catholic exile, William Allen, had been not so much of a seminary abroad, as of a College in exile, a place of scholarship, where Catholic graduates could continue their studies until a hoped-for restoration of Catholic rule in England might allow this graduate elite to return to positions at the head of the Church and the universities there. The pristine vision of the future Cardinal Allen was obviously not to find its fulfilment. But from this strand of English Recusant thought came the involvement of a figure like Gregory Martin in the great achievement of an English Catholic translation of the Bible, the Rheims–Douai version.[6] A parallel is suggested by the case of the Scot, Thomas Dempster, born probably in 1579, who after study, unusually, perhaps, at Cambridge, moved to Paris and then Louvain, before an academic career spent almost exclusively in continental Catholic Europe as a layman, not a cleric.[7]

Clement VIII

Clement VIII (1592–1605) was arguably one of the great popes of the Counter-Reformation. Even if, for non-specialists, he has remained less famous than Pius V (1566–72) or Sixtus V, for example, his stature was clearly recognized by Gregory XV (1621–23), after the intervening pontificate of Paul V, and by Urban VIII (1623–44). He did not share the enthusiasm of Gregory XIII (or Gregory XV in fact) for the Society of Jesus, however. It was symptomatic that he removed the Jesuits from direction of the Greek College in Rome, and the Society was only later reinstated in control of this institution for the training of Greek-rite priests loyal to Rome. The Jesuit scholar, Cardinal Bellarmine, found himself required to reside outside Rome, on appointment as archbishop of Capua. The controversial English Jesuit, Robert Persons, was also eventually encouraged not to return to Rome from a visit to Bellarmine at Capua.[8] Clement's reserve about some members of the Society, at least, reflected in part his exasperation at the continued internal conflicts among the Jesuits, over their constitution and purpose, their organization and activities. This domestic disharmony, at least among some of the Spanish Jesuits, had already been evident by the time of the first non-Spanish General of the Society, Mercurian, between 1573 and 1580, but it was still disturbing the tenure of that office by Acquaviva, during Clement's pontificate. Moreover by this time doctrinal dispute between Jesuit and other Catholic theologians, initially in Spain and the Netherlands, had become so intense that Clement felt it necessary to try by the exercise of papal authority to determine the contested issues at Rome itself, by setting up the commission *De Auxiliis*, on the Means of Grace, though he died without giving public judgement. By contrast Clement was much influenced by the Oratorians, under their virtual founder, Philip Neri, and after Neri's death in 1595 he continued to pay much attention to the advice of the Oratorian scholar, Cardinal Baronius. The Roman, as opposed to the Neapolitan Oratorians, were clearly determined to preserve their status as secular clergy of the Rome diocese, not regulars. This complemented Clement's conspicuous care for episcopal reform, on Tridentine lines, within the diocese, pursued from the start of his pontificate, chiefly by means of canonic visitation. The pope also promoted visual expression of Catholic restoration and papal leadership, as with work at the cathedral of Rome, the Lateran basilica. Such programmes also related to the Jubilee of 1600 as a celebration of Catholic unity and Roman authority.[9] Previous popes, since the beginning of the Council of Trent, had encouraged the growing grandeur of the Jubilees, as in 1575. But Oratorian involvement in the care of pilgrims in Rome reached a climax in the Jubilee of 1600. Such pious celebration, for the city and the wider Catholic world, was thus the context of Clement's founding of the Scots College in Rome in December 1600.

It can also be understood why the Scots College, once it opened in 1602, was not initially under Jesuit direction. The Society only succeeded to that direction in 1615, under Paul V, even though he too had had moments of reserve about some aspects of Jesuit activity. The clarification from 1616 that the College was precisely a seminary, for priestly formation, can also be seen as part of a reordering of identity. The Scots Jesuit William Crichton had originally envisaged that Catholic students would move from the Scots universities to continue their studies in Catholic territories abroad, once suitable educational foundations had been established. But his vision, parallel to Allen's initial assumptions in the case of English Catholics, was not in this sense to achieve even the partial fulfilment of Allen's scheme.[10] From 1593 Crichton was responsible for the Scots College at Douai, in the Netherlands.[11] But when the pope sought to secure the opening of the Rome College, which began with less than a dozen students, the four sent by Crichton to Rome included Thomas Dempster, whose subsequent career proved to be that of a lay scholar. In the event, though Dempster's stay in Rome was financed by the pope, a recurrence of his ill health necessitated his return to Douai to resume his studies there with the support of a Spanish pension. It was not surprising that in the interval between 1600 and 1602 the pope was still concerned about the lack of priests for Scotland.[12] From 1602 to 1615 the Scots students in Rome attended the lectures of the Jesuits at the *Collegio Romano*, intended as these were for future clerics and future laymen alike. But the lack of prospective students from Scotland in the Scots educational foundations in Catholic Europe did not simply reflect the cumulative effects of proscription at home, already clear by the 1590s.[13] Financial support was also obviously a crucial but problematic issue.

Scots Colleges

The Scots College originally, perhaps, at Tournai and, subsequently, at Douai eventually had lost its initial financial maintenance after the deaths of Gregory XIII and Mary, Queen of Scots. After his succession to the papal throne Clement VIII appealed for benefactions for this foundation, in 1593, and at Crichton's instigation he directed his appeal in 1597 specifically to Archduke Albert, the Habsburg ruler in the Netherlands. By 1601 the pope was also urging on Henri IV – the new Bourbon and newly Catholic king of France – the idea that the ancient Scots College in Paris should be resurrected precisely as a seminary. This aspect of the renewed French interest in Scotland, after the eclipse of the Guises and the end of the Valois royal line, had been prompted by a suggestion of Cardinal Allen who, by the end of his life, was almost as involved in manoeuvres about the English succession to Elizabeth I as the pro-Spanish and Jesuit Persons was.[14] In 1580, indeed, a new version of a Scots College in Paris had been set up, endowed by Mary Queen of Scots and others, under a secular not a Jesuit president. But the following year this institution was transferred to Pont-à-Mousson, where Guise patronage had fostered a Catholic College which became effectively of university status and, by 1580, a Jesuit-directed foundation. Crichton and his fellow Jesuit, the Italian, Possevino, obtained from the pro-Jesuit Gregory XIII an endowment for the transferred Scots College, granted in 1581 for fifteen years. A further grant in 1584, however, accompanied a requirement that the College admit Irish students too, and in that year there were thirty-six Scots and seven Irish seminarians in a College where Jesuit direction had also been established, seemingly from about the time of the transfer from Paris. Before this, at Queen Mary's instigation, Leslie, bishop of Ross, had been urging Pope Gregory to obtain the agreement of the Emperor, Rudolf, that ancient German monastic foundations of the 'Scots' should be turned into modern seminaries for Scots (as opposed to Irish). But such schemes had, as yet, no effects in the late 1570s. The death of the Scots queen in any case ended the royal pension for the Pont-à-Mousson Scots College, and Pope Sixtus V, who was intent on building up the financial reserves in Rome itself, stopped its papal grant as one of his economies. For two years the main Jesuit foundation at Pont-à-Mousson provided some funding for the Scots College there, but by 1590 the latter had closed. The situation at the start of Clement's pontificate, as far as Scots colleges in Catholic Europe were concerned, was thus distinctly unpromising.[15]

The personal initiative of Clement VIII in the Jubilee year of 1600, in founding and endowing a Scots College that was in Rome, not elsewhere in either French or Habsburg territory, and not under Jesuit direction, was therefore a bold measure taken in a political and religious context of great complexity. The pope understood, at the very start of his pontificate, that the fortunes of Catholicism in Western Europe were delicately poised. He was gradually persuaded, not least by Oratorian advice, that a great opportunity for independent papal action in defence of the interests of Catholicism and of Rome in particular existed, but this rare interval of opportunity was undoubtedly surrounded by grave challenges and dangers. Clement's pontificate certainly proved a turning-point for the Counter-Reformation Church, after the long period during which the collapse of France (as a result of internal religious conflict and a crisis over dynastic succession) had left the Spanish Habsburgs more dominant than ever in Catholic Europe and, above all, with regard to the papacy. Though it was obvious that Philip II, king of Spain and also, since 1580, king of Portugal, would not live for ever, the most pressing questions in the 1590s were the succession to the French throne and the succession to the Protestant Queen Elizabeth in England. Both successions necessarily affected Scotland and, therefore, the interests of Scots Catholics. But also involved were plans fostered specifically by certain Jesuits, and related conflicts between Jesuits and their opponents within the divided ranks of the English Catholics. In 1600 Clement VIII had already appointed a new Cardinal Protector of Scotland, Cardinal Borghese, his eventual successor as Pope Paul V, an Italian, and not obviously identified with either Habsburg or Bourbon interests.[16] This contrasted with papal refusal to appoint an English or Welsh successor to Allen as titular 'cardinal of the English' on the latter's death in 1594.

The political context

From his own earliest years, before the 1590s, King James of Scotland had been an object of great interest at Rome during previous pontificates. While political events developed in Scotland with a perplexing rapidity, the boy's location and the identity of those who gained custody of him were reported to Rome by the nuncios in France. As such custodians succeeded in ousting one another, the likely religious leanings of each were commented on via this channel and, despite inevitably slow communications, a surprisingly up-to-date knowledge of events at Stirling Castle, for example, was available to Rome. Before their eclipse the Guises had been interested in plans to involve the papacy in a Catholic 'enterprise' against Protestant leaders in Scotland, and possibly to try to gain custody of James himself, to secure his Catholic education. The dynastic crisis in France and the difficulty, after 1590, of identifying a plausible, native Catholic claimant to the French throne, threatened to disrupt any hopes of Catholic restoration in Scotland by such routes.[17] But, by contrast, James had been pursuing his own interest in the succession to the English throne and, at times, this necessitated him making advances to Catholics, from the pope downwards. Even with regard to his ability to develop and then maintain some personal control of his own kingdom, he was anxious to avoid papal excommunication, which Philip II had sought to persuade Sixtus V to pronounce.[18] After the execution of Mary Queen of Scots the prospect of a Spanish attempt to invade England or otherwise exclude any claims by James to the eventual succession to the English throne was yet more alarming. The possibility that James might embrace Catholicism was believed by some Catholics to be correspondingly real, even if very far from certain, and this hope survived the eclipse of the Guises, even without the example set in 1593 by Henri of Navarre in abjuring Protestantism and seeking papal reconciliation in his pursuit of the French succession. The Scots Jesuit, Crichton, had had a moment of optimism about the chances of James's conversion in 1587. As Clement VIII considered whether to allow Henri the reconciliation which would fit him for the French throne in the eyes of many more Catholics in France, and thereby effectively exclude the chance of Philip II realizing Spanish claims on behalf of his daughter, the Infanta, to that throne, he naturally faced intense Spanish pressure to refuse. But the pope also had to consider the effects of his decision for Catholics not only in France but in England too and also in Ireland. Cardinal Allen, as titular leader of the English Catholics, was asked at least to consider whether there might not be some merit in seeing the Spanish king secure the Scots in addition to the English succession, from this angle. King James had made overtures to the papacy, not least in the hope of subsidies, from the time of Gregory XIII, but renewed his approaches after the election of Clement VIII, without however giving up hope of securing a less obstructive attitude on the part of Spain. Pope Clement was also aware of the potential advantages if English Catholics were not forced to place all their trust for their own future prospects in the Spanish, and not only because of his willingness to pursue policies which would reduce the papacy's own dependence on Spain. Since among English Catholics, whose internal divisions were ably encouraged by the Elizabethan regime, Jesuits and their supporters tended to favour Spain, their opponents increasingly hoped that a Catholic but non-Habsburg France would give them support. After James's queen, Anne of Denmark, had become a Catholic, she too was anxious that such internal conflict, between Jesuits and other Catholics, should not damage the Scots Catholic community. This was not an unrealistic concern, for there were signs that by 1593 the English Jesuit, Persons, was seeking to establish his own direct communications with Scots Catholic leaders. The Scots Jesuit, Crichton, was still involved at the start of Clement's pontificate in plans for aristocratic Scots Catholics to co-operate with a renewed Spanish 'enterprise' against England. This was the context of an appeal for funds to the Duke of Parma in the Netherlands, not only for a Scots mission but also for the Scots College at Douai, seen as a college for young nobles, rather than as a seminary for priests.

The idea of Scots Catholic nobles securing custody again of King James resurfaced too. While some English Catholics increasingly distrusted the schemes of Persons and Allen about the English succession, even though the latter was not a Jesuit, Persons in fact was not in favour of using Scotland as a launching-pad for an 'enterprise' against England. Crichton, too, apparently wished to avoid a Spanish landing in Scotland but, despite intervals of pessimism, he had recovered his optimism about a possible conversion to Catholicism by King James in 1593. This reflected his belief that the king was himself anxious to evade the dominance of antagonistic nobles and was open to the influence of his queen. Such optimism, while it lasted, could even extend to thinking that Spain might be persuaded to approve an 'enterprise' by James himself to secure a Catholic succession in England. This was why in 1596 Crichton was at first hostile to Persons over the controversial publication on the English succession which had argued in favour of Philip II and the Infanta, against the claims of James VI. In 1599 James was still seeking to leave room for Pope Clement to believe that he might yet follow the example of Henri IV of France, whose reconciliation the pope had eventually allowed. The death of Philip II in 1598 had not diminished Spanish fury in the face of this final reversal of papal policy as pursued by Clement's predecessors. For Spanish statesmen, whether associated with the old king or seeking to establish themselves with Philip III, urged the new king to defend Spain's interests, despite the peace with France agreed earlier that year with papal encouragement. As a result jurisdictional conflicts in Spain, Portugal, their overseas empires, and Spanish-ruled Sicily, Naples and Milan increased rather than diminished.

The interval 1600–2, when Clement was founding and then securing the opening of the Scots College in Rome, entrusted to one of his own Italian officials, was thus marked by the ever more intense manoeuvring of the Scots king to obtain the English succession, with all the potential consequences for Catholics in England, Ireland and Scotland which that might seem to entail. It was thus the French ambassador, urged by the English Catholic opponents of the Jesuits, who sought to represent to Clement the French king's pleasure if Persons were not to return from Capua to Rome. For Henri IV certainly wished to exclude a Spanish succession in England, quite apart from traditional French support for the Scots monarchs. Since for other reasons Clement was willing to act with favour towards the new French king, now Catholic but not Spanish Habsburg, the pope's opportunity to do other than accept the eventual succession in England of the Scots king was distinctly limited.

In 1602, before the English monarch finally died, the Scots queen was once again being urged by the pope to try to work for James's conversion and for the Catholic education of Prince Henry, potentially heir to both the Scots and English crowns.[19] For Clement's position in defence of Catholicism must not be misunderstood. His concern at the Spanish dominance of Catholic Europe and the papacy, especially since Philip's succession to the Portuguese crown in 1580, was natural in the 1590s, when it still seemed as though a relaunched Spanish armada against England might succeed or that, instead (or, indeed, as well), a Catholic succession in France might prove to be a Spanish one. Yet the pope's help to the Austrian Habsburgs in their Hungarian campaigns against the Turks was generous, for he saw the interests of Catholic Christendom fundamentally at stake there. In France, under a Catholic Bourbon king, the privileges of the Huguenots had to be allowed, by the Edict of Nantes, and Henri never fulfilled his promise to secure legal reception in the kingdom of the decrees of the Council of Trent. But the French king adopted a favourable attitude when another succession crisis, this time nearer at hand, in the Italian peninsula itself, allowed the pope to annex the duchy of Ferrara to the Papal States in 1598. The Anglo-Spanish peace of 1604 was to extend to James as king of England the peaceful relations with Spain which he had succeeded in maintaining as king of Scotland. But Clement was aware that Spanish support for Irish Catholicism had already been halted. Since individual Jesuits had been in Scotland and Ireland occasionally, even if not continuously, earlier than their arrival in England, it was clear that even before the 1570s, let alone before 1580, the fortunes of Catholicism in Scotland and England were intertwined. The genius of Clement VIII was to secure by papal action, independent of Jesuit activity, a place at the Roman heart of Catholicism where a secular clergy for Scotland itself might be formed.

More widely still, Clement's vision in this relates to the initiatives during his pontificate for the promotion of a non-regular clergy, amenable to immediate Roman direction, for work in Catholic 'missions', whether in non-Catholic or non-Christian territories, initiatives which were to reach later fruition, under Gregory XV and Urban VIII, with the definitive creation of the Roman Congregation *De Propaganda Fide* and foundation of a related Roman seminary.[20] While Clement

VIII strenuously resisted suggestions that a move might be made to canonize Loyola, the founder of the Jesuits, he had his own vision of what was required in defence of Catholicism in Europe. By the end of his pontificate he had ensured that France remained an officially Catholic, but independent, kingdom and that the papacy was consequently not reliant on Habsburg power alone. His concern for the defence of Catholicism in England and Scotland was also expressed in policies which sought to maximise such advantages for the Catholic communities as might be secured in political circumstances of great complexity and rapid change. For the essential provision of priests for the Scots Catholic community his personal initiative revealed a pastoral concern which, as in the case of France, lay at the heart of his political responsibilities.

Rome in 1600

The year 1600 also saw the burning in Rome of the dissident Dominican, Giordano Bruno. Whatever the precise range of his activities while in Elizabethan England, Bruno could certainly be condemned in Rome as an obstinate heretic. Yet his case has often been misunderstood because of a confusion between his highly individual and mystical speculations and a more truly scientific mental discipline subsequently demonstrated, for example, in at least some of Galileo's work. Bruno's condemnation did mark in its way a watershed in the Counter-Reformation but not because it introduced any new Catholic antagonism to scientific method.[21] On the contrary, it was rather the conclusion of the process by which the last remnants of heresy had been eradicated in Counter-Reformation Italy, from the 1540s and 1550s onwards. This execution also followed that of Beatrice Cenci, which subsequent ages again took to be symptomatic of papal repression in Clement's pontificate. But, in the Romantic legend which grew around the death of a relatively young noblewoman accused of complicity in the murder of her father, lurid certainties came to replace confused complexities. For it is not clear that the father's abusive brutality extended precisely to enforced incest, while the idea that the papal treasury was able to benefit from the confiscations secured by a manipulated trial is not compatible with the evidence of the legacies left by Beatrice. The papal government under Clement VIII was arguably pursuing in this case – by publicly demonstrating that even nobles could not escape punishment for heinous crimes – an imposition of law and order which previous popes of the later 16th century had found difficult enough, not only within the city of Rome but in the face of bandits and their aristocratic protectors in the Papal States.[22]

In many states of the Italian peninsula, from the Venetian Republic in the north to the Neapolitan kingdom in the south, the 1590s did indeed see an increase in banditry and violent, organized crime, as economic difficulties affected many areas.[23] Among those guilty of the violent disorder characteristic of Rome in this period, as of course of many cities in early modern Europe, was the painter,

Caravaggio. His dramatic realism, achieved by the use of models drawn from the common people of Rome, has also been associated by many with the ethos of Rome specifically in the pontificate of Clement VIII. Most recently the explicit linking of his religious art with the spirituality of the Roman Oratory has been questioned.[24] But it remains clear that among his patrons in Rome were prelates, some of whom, at least, were in contact with the Oratory, where the innovative staging of religious and dramatic music, as an experimental form of instruction and edification, was epitomized in the 1600 Jubilee by Cavalieri's *Representation of the Body and the Soul*. The Roman Oratory was associated, too, with the earliest systematic explorations of the Roman catacombs which provided evidence of Catholic continuity against Protestant criticism; Cardinal Baronius, by means of his ecclesiastical history and restoration of ancient Roman churches, also demonstrated this.[25]

The Rome of Clement VIII was indeed marked by ecclesiastical erudition. At the start of his pontificate an emended edition of the flawed version of the Vulgate prepared by Sixtus V was published. In this way the implicit mandate of the Council of Trent – that the authorized text of the Vulgate should be made as correct as possible – was finally fulfilled by the papacy, though the necessity to amend Sixtus's version did not escape adverse Protestant comment. A new edition of the Roman Missal, issued during this pontificate, would also be a reminder to seminarians in Rome, including Scots as well as English, that the old local rites, such as the Use of Sarum, were no longer authorized. The same ideal of liturgical uniformity was evident in a new edition of the Roman Breviary, and of the *Pontificale* (1595) and *Caeremoniale Episcoporum* (1600). The new edition of the Roman Index, in 1596, also represented a relative, if minor, relaxation compared with previous versions, thanks in part to the influence of Cardinal Baronius.

Indeed, Clement's own family, the Aldobrandini, shared with Neri the association of an adopted Roman identity, marking such originally Florentine followers of the ecclesiastical reform tradition initiated by Savonarola, in opposition to the power of the restored Medici rulers of Florence. Yet it was consistent with the pope's policy towards France to approve the new Catholic marriage of Henri IV to Marie de'Medici, as part of the consolidation of French Catholicism. A Catholic restoration in Scotland or England had certainly not proved possible by 1600 or 1602, nor was it to do so while Clement remained pope or, indeed, after his death. Nevertheless, the expansion of Roman obedience in Christian Europe achieved one great triumph in Clement's pontificate, reflecting his earlier skill while papal representative in Poland. This was the Union of Brest, concluded in 1596, by which large numbers of Eastern-rite Christians within Poland-Lithuania came into communion with Rome. The generous vision shown by the pope in this episode was not demonstrated in the same way for all inhabitants of the city of Rome, however. The existing Jewish ghetto there continued under close restrictions and, compared with some, though certainly not all the popes of the Counter-Reformation, Clement's policy towards Jewish communities was more, rather than less, severe. Indeed, he returned to the exclusion of such communities from papal territory, other than those in Rome itself, Ancona and Avignon.

The last of these cities, however, Clement used as a gateway by which the best standards of Italian Catholic reform might be introduced to French Catholics after the dislocation of the Church in that kingdom during the religious wars, by his appointment of Oratorians to head the dioceses of the papal enclave. But in Rome itself, not only in the Jubilee of 1600, Clement maintained the emphasis on charitable provision for the poor of the city which had been associated with Neri. In the area of Rome where the earlier locations of the Scots College were found, the dominating bulk of the new papal palace, on the ridge of the Quirinal hill, had been developed since the pontificate of Gregory XIII and was customarily the papal residence for the hotter part of the year at least. But though the papacy was to acquire Castel Gandolfo before the end of Clement's pontificate, it had not yet been developed as a summer residence. Similarly at St Peter's, where the dome had already been completed, the surmounting ball and cross were affixed in 1593. But the extended nave to the East had not yet been created, sweeping away the last vestiges of the old basilica.

However, the more basic provisioning of Rome, especially at a time of Jubilee, with the temporary swelling of the population, necessarily tempered Clement's enthusiasm for demonstrating papal authority independent of the power of the Spanish Habsburgs. Even as he defended the Church's jurisdictional rights, the pope had simultaneously to appeal to the Spanish monarch for a grant, preferably cost free, of grain from Sicily, in order to maintain Rome's essential food supply.[26] The 'normal' population of Rome is estimated to have reached about 110,000 by 1600. Grain shortage, relative to population and demand, caused a momentary peak in the price of grain in 1603 (despite the import of grain from the Marches) within the Papal States in 1601–2. Since Rome depended on maritime supply for much of its necessities, Clement VIII ordered the dredging of the Tiber in 1602, though such action was also seen by the papal government as a precaution against the frequent flooding of the river within the confines of the city. The pope also withdrew debased coins from circulation in preparation for the Jubilee of 1600, replacing them with a better issue.

In that year, the pope's own public participation in the appropriate devotions included his visits to the major basilicas and churches, following his return to Rome after his progress to Ferrara in 1598. Clement had also secured peace between Savoy and France by 1601, in pursuit of the stabilization of Northern Italy in particular and Catholic Europe more generally. This contrasted with the failure of a hoped-for Catholic restoration in Sweden by 1599. Papal plans to involve Russians and Persians in the anti-Turkish struggle were equally unsuccessful but, closer to Rome, Clement achieved more with a new organ of government within the Papal States, the *Buon Governo*, and a new tribunal to protect the poor against baronial oppression. Secular taxation within the Papal States continued to rise, but papal finances had to meet the costs of anti-Turkish campaigns and the incorporation of Ferrara, as well as continued work on the interior decoration of St Peter's. So nepotism, typified by the elaboration of the Villa Aldobrandini at Frascati, was not the only burden on papal funds by a long way. Clement attempted to ensure that the native population of the Italian peninsula should not be contaminated by foreign heresy. But non-Italian Catholics, including Scots, could be sure of the pope's pastoral concerns, expressed not only with regard to religiously divided Western Christendom, but evident also in his promotion of foreign missions among non-Christian peoples.

A Quatercentenary

That the first century of the existence of the Scots College in Rome was not without its problems is hardly surprising. Indeed, by the end of that first period a proposition had even emerged that the Scots College should be combined with the English and Irish Colleges to form a single institution in Rome. This project and its failure are discussed again at the conclusion of the present volume. But from the opening chapter, on the years from 1600 to 1707, readers will be able to detect the nature of the difficulties confronting the Scots College from the start. While the tensions between the Society of Jesus and non-Jesuits over the direction of the College and the eventual vocation of its students have traditionally been seen as central to these difficulties, Abbot Dilworth is able to show that this is not merely a tendentious impression created by the influential interpretation of the College's history in the account written by Paul MacPherson. On the contrary, uncertainty and limitation of financial resources were clearly real enough, quite apart from disputes over control and application of these. Moreover, an apparent shortage of potential students, at least for the first fifty years, and still on occasion thereafter, can best be assessed by comparing the situation in other Scots institutions, in Paris, Spain, the Netherlands and Germany, during this same period. The number of secular priests proceeding from the College in Rome to serve in Scotland remained obstinately low for decades, despite a much debated oath intended to bind students to this duty. But Jesuit superiors of the College were alleged to manipulate the matter of the oath, and even the choice of students, in such a way as to encourage their entry into the Society of Jesus itself. However, as Abbot Dilworth demonstrates, other students also became regulars, beyond the undoubted number who became Jesuits, and this outcome reflected the absence of adequate support for secular priests both while in Scotland itself and in potential old age thereafter.

The less than satisfactory situation, in such respects, was not immediately transformed by the creation of the Roman Congregation of the Propaganda, though the protection of the new Congregation arguably allowed the proper interests of the Scots secular clergy to be defended with much greater success by the beginning of the eighteenth century. The associated, if comparative, greater security of Catholic communities in Scotland itself by then was evidently related to another product of Propaganda's interventions, the provision of a Vicar Apostolic in episcopal orders from the mid-1690s, whose authority, remarkably, even the Jesuits in Scotland itself came to acknowledge. But these eventual results were arguably as much a tribute to the ability of a long-lived representative of the secular priests of Scotland, now recognized by Propaganda as an authorized mission, who was resident in Rome and managed the crucial relations with Cardinal Protectors as well as with Propaganda and with Jesuits, both Scots and Italians. All this enabled the priests produced by the Rome College to play a part in the survival of Scots Catholicism to 1707, despite the dangers created by the debacle of the brief reign of James VII and II and the complications later engendered by the intervention of the Stuarts in exile, not least while tension continued between the papacy and Louis XIV of France. At crucial moments, in the first century of the College's existence, papal intervention was, indeed, evidently determinative. The mid-century association of the Barberini with the affairs of the College was followed, at the end of the century, by a moment when the interest of a non-papal family, the Barbarigo, from the Venetian Republic, was helpful. There was, by then, a history of links between Scots clerics and the exemplary continuation of Tridentine episcopal care at Padua associated with Gregorio Barbarigo and his diocesan seminary there.

In the long subsequent history of the College, certain transformations from these earlier conditions inevitably stand out. All the institutions in Rome under Jesuit direction were, of course, profoundly affected by the dissolution of the Society of Jesus ordered by Pope Clement XIV in 1773, including, for example, the Venerable English College. The impact of the French Revolution and then of Napoleonic regimes in Italy was major too, leaving Rome without a papal presence for some years. In the present century, the life of the Scots College was naturally changed by the final move from its historic site in the centre of Rome to a new building on the Via Cassia, opened in 1964. But, in other respects, the twentieth-century history of the College reveals more remarkable continuities of problems and their possible solutions, despite the seemingly very different conditions of modern life. This appears so, even allowing for other developments affecting the College, in Italy and Rome itself and in Scotland: the end of papal temporal government in 1870, interrupting the First Vatican Council; the Concordat of 1929 creating the independent Vatican City State; and the restoration of the Scots hierarchy in 1878. Above all, any seminary, preparing future priests, was bound to be challenged by the changes in the Church itself represented by the Second Vatican Council and the gradual incorporation of the Conciliar decrees' implications. Yet the account of the College in the twentieth century by Monsignor McIntyre shows the extent to which older problems recurred in new guises.

The modern edition of MacPherson's history of the Scots College recalls the fact that in the earliest period the Scots Jesuits never formed a Province or Vice-Province, only a Mission of the Society of Jesus, though it might be added that there are English parallels for this. The 1627 foundation of a Scots College in Spain, originally at Madrid and later at Valladolid, or the 1718 completion of a Scots seminary within the enclosure of the Scottish Benedictine abbey at Ratisbon are reminders that the evolution of the Scots College Rome took place within a wider context of continuing development in the training abroad of Scots priests. Nevertheless, in the period to 1773 during which the College was under Jesuit direction, this must be understood to have involved Italian rather than Scots superiors from 1724. Even after the suppression of the Society of Jesus it was Italian secular priests who took over the direction, until the French invasion of Rome in 1798. At this point Italian direction was removed and the College buildings were commandeered. The hero of the hour proved to be the representative in Rome of the Scots secular clergy, Abbé Paul MacPherson. Having evacuated English and Irish as well as Scots students from Revolutionary Rome, he himself returned to watch over such of the College's property as he had been able to recover, also securing with the help of Cardinal Erskine, a former student, the important ruling that future rectors should be chosen from the Scots secular clergy. In due course he himself became the first such rector, until his retirement to Scotland in 1827. But a fairly swift vacancy in the office saw him resume this position for another period of years, prior to his death in 1846. During his period of rectorship, substantial repairs were necessary on the College buildings. Later in the 19th century, in the 1860s, there was a more complete rebuilding.

Even more fundamental than the question of suitable buildings, though equally related to questions of finance, was the issue of the staffing of the College and the number, as well as capability, of the students. As Monsignor McIntyre demonstrates, the rectors and their assistant staff in the twentieth century had to be found by the agreement of the Scots bishops, not all of them, in fact, in agreement as to whom they could spare from their dioceses for such work. Nor were all the bishops equally convinced of the value of the Scots College in Rome and the education received by its seminarians. The latter was admittedly very largely beyond the immediate control of the College, being regulated by general papal provisions and, more specifically, determined by the curriculum and examinations of the Gregorian University, which changed considerably in the end, but only quite late in the century. With some Scots archbishops, on occasion, the question arose of creating in their own archdiocese a regional seminary as a better central focus for the adequate training of a twentieth-century clergy. Indeed, by the end of 1964 the Scots hierarchy itself for once contained not a single product of the Rome College. Yet the archbishops themselves were not necessarily perfectly at ease with each other at all times, which could put the rector in Rome in a potentially difficult position. The rectors and their staff found on occasion that they were expected to act as more general agents in Rome for the Scots hierarchy, not only at major moments of celebration, as in Holy Years or a canonization, but also in less congenial roles, in negotiations on particular affairs with the Roman Curia or Curial prelates. The 'ancien régime' of the Cardinal Protectors, overseeing as well as, if necessary, protecting the College and its interests, only in mid-century gave way to the single authority of the Congregation of Seminaries, whose prefect Pizzardo was named as the last Protector in 1951.

As in earlier times in the College's history, the number of students, now largely sent by diocesan bishops, could drop to an alarming low point, even when diocesan funding of the Rome College had finally been reorganized in such a way as to encourage bishops to take up places there. But when such a low point was reached, as in 1971, the fact that this might well also reflect a general fluctuation in similar institutions throughout the Church was of little immediate consolation, when it specifically endorsed the sense of continued financial difficulty. Some of the bishops moreover, particularly if coming from a different educational background, were rather dismissive of the intellectual quality of the College students and the priests it produced. The eventual presence of postgraduate as well as ordinary students among those in training at the College might, in one way, have been an answer to such criticism, but in turn gave rectors or their staff new challenges in maintaining the discipline of the student body. The evolution of the plan to move to new buildings, outside the historic city centre, took place against a background of economic developments decidedly beyond the control of the College. The decline, at times, of the value of British in relation to Italian currency represented a further reason for doubting the worth of the College to those bishops who were dubious of its necessity anyway. Yet the move to a new site finally took place despite the earlier threat to the old buildings posed by one of Mussolini's many schemes for new streets in central Rome, and despite the danger to those buildings presented by the Second World War, and the inevitable absence of staff and students from Rome. But post-Conciliar seminary life was also, of course, changing everywhere, making of less obvious use the summer villas of foreign seminaries, as students' return to their native countries during the vacation became newly accepted.

In the long pre-Conciliar decades of the century, however, the daily life of the Scots College, for the major part of the year, was clearly well-regulated; proving, in a longer historical perspective, that the disciplined and, where relevant, quasi-monastic routine of a seminary under secular priests was perfectly possible, and in no way dependent on Jesuit direction. The underlying continuity in the history of the College, despite historical upheavals, was in a way recognized by confirmation in 1929 of its title as 'Pontifical'. On the other hand, the still tenuous nature of the College's existence, for essentially financial reasons, was revealed only six years later, when a momentary proposal to withdraw all the students sent by one archdiocese would have reduced numbers to such a level that the whole College would have closed. But such a moment of crisis could also threaten the continued existence of the Scots College Valladolid, too. It was all the more of an achievement that the Rome College, in fact, reopened quite promptly in 1946, and with a viable number of students, so that the War years could be represented as a 'prolonged vacation'. The changes introduced into seminary life generally by the effects of the Second Vatican Council were, however, obviously not easy to manage for rectors or staff who were very much the products of their own, pre-Conciliar training. The continued importance of funding for the Rome College from the resources of larger, or relatively wealthier, Scots dioceses naturally meant that Rectors had to consider the views of some diocesans with particular attention. In the light of such difficulties, the preservation of the Rome College, across the centuries, and through such fundamental changes as the end of Jesuit direction, is all the more worthy of the historian's interest and, it is hoped, the reader's admiration.

NOTES

1. A. D. Wright, 'Catholic History, North and South, Revisited', *Northern History*, 25 (1989), 120–34.
2. H. Jedin, *Crisis and Closure of the Council of Trent* (London, 1967).
3. J. I. Tellechea Idígoras, *Fray Bartolomé Carranza y el Cardenal Pole. Un navarro en la restauración católica de Inglaterra (1554–1558)* (Pamplona, 1977).
4. A. Fliche and V. Martin (eds), *Histoire de l'Eglise*, XIX, pt. I (Paris, 1955), 324.
5. *Nuntiaturberichte aus Deutschland*, 3. Abteilung, 7. Band, *Nuntiatur Giovanni Dolfins (1573–1574)* (Tübingen, 1990); 8. Band, *(1575–1576)* (Tübingen, 1997).
6. M. E. Williams, *The Venerable English College, Rome* (London, 1979), 4, 21.
7. *Dictionary of National Biography* (63 vols; London, 1885–1900), s.v.
8. L. von Pastor, *History of the Popes* (40 vols, London, 1891–1953), XXIV, 49, 261.
9. J. Freiberg, *The Lateran in 1600. Christian Concord in Counter-Reformation Rome* (Cambridge, 1995).
10. Pastor, *History*, XXIV, 66–7, 269–79.
11. F. de Borja Medina, 'Intrigues of a Scottish Jesuit at the Spanish Court: Unpublished Letters of William Crichton to Claudio Acquaviva', in T. M. McCoog, *The Reckoned Expense. Edmund Campion and the early English Jesuits* (Woodbridge, 1996), 215–45, especially 231.
12. Pastor, *History*, XXIV, 65.
13. Pastor, *History*, XXIV, 61–2.
14. Pastor, *History*, XXIV, 65–6.
15. T. M. McCoog, *The Society of Jesus in Ireland, Scotland, and England 1541–1588. 'Our Way of Proceeding?'* (Leiden, 1996), 219, 264.
16. K. Jaitner (ed.), *Die Hauptinstruktionen Clemens VIII für die Nuntien und Legaten an den europäischen Fürstenhöfen 1592–1605* (2 vols; Tübingen, 1984), I, clxxvii.
17. J. Lestocquoy *et al.* (eds), *Acta Nuntiaturae Gallicae*: Vol. 7: R. Toupin (ed.),

Correspondance du Nonce en France Giovanni Battista Castelli (1581–1583) (Rome–Paris, 1968); Vol. 8: I Cloulas (ed.), *Correspondance du Nonce en France Anselmo Dandino (1578–1581)* (Rome–Paris, 1970). See also F. Rocquain, *La France et Rome pendant les guerres de religion* (Paris, 1924).

18. Pastor, *History*, XXIV, 64.

19. Pastor, *History*, XXIV, 49–57; Borja, 'Intrigues', 225-33; W. B. Patterson, *King James VI and I and the Reunion of Christendom* (Cambridge, 1997).

20. G. Piras, *La Congregazione e il Collegio di Propaganda Fide di J. B. Vives, G. Leonardi e M. de Funes* (Rome, 1976).

21. J. Bossy, *Giordano Bruno and the Embassy Affair* (New Haven and London, 1991).

22. *Dizionario biografico degli Italiani* (Rome, 1960 onwards): see entry under 'Clemente VIII'.

23. A. D. Wright, 'Venetian Law and Order: a Myth?', *Bulletin of the Institute of Historical Research*, 53 (1980), 192–202.

24. C. E. Gilbert, *Caravaggio and his two cardinals* (University Park, Pennsylvania, 1995).

25. L. Bianconi, *Music in the Seventeenth Century* (Cambridge, 1987), 124–25; R. De Maio *et al.* (eds), *Baronio storico e la Controriforma* (Sora, 1982); R. De Maio *et al.* (eds), *Baronio e l'arte* (Sora, 1985).

26. Archivo General de Simancas, Spain: Estado: Sicilia: Legajo 1885, ff. 12, 69, 186, (1592–1603); L. Rice, *The Altars and Altarpieces of New St Peter's. Outfitting the basilica, 1621–1666* (Cambridge, 1997).

CHAPTER 1

Beginnings 1600–1707

Mark Dilworth OSB

The history of the College during its first hundred years forms part of the Scottish Church's slow rise from almost total disorder to a reasonably well organised missionary enterprise.[1] The Reformation Parliament sitting in August 1560 imposed the Protestant Confession of Faith and abolished the Mass and papal authority. Gradually, as Protestantism gained control, ministers took over the network of parishes, while priests ordained before 1560 died out and were not replaced. Organised Catholic practice likewise died out, except in the south-west and the north-east and in isolated pockets where a local magnate stayed Catholic. A residual Catholicism survived in the remote western Highlands and Islands. The only fresh missionary effort, beginning in the early 1580s, came from the Scottish Jesuits, never more than a mere handful in number. Leadership and organisation of the Scottish Church were non-existent. In 1598 Scotland was included in the jurisdiction of the English archpriest, an arrangement that was a dead letter from the start, while the only surviving bishop was the aged James Beaton in Paris, who died in 1603.

On the Continent, however, initiatives were not lacking and the foundation of the College, far from being an isolated event, is to be seen in that context. And, indeed, the College was closely linked with other bodies and institutions of various kinds. This was a period of fervour and rapid expansion for the Society of Jesus (the Jesuits) and not only did Scots enter Jesuit novitiates in various provinces but they also found places in Jesuit-conducted seminaries such as Braunsberg (Prussia), Worms and the German College in Rome.[2] Scots continued to matriculate at various Catholic universities on the Continent. As a result of efforts by Bishop John Lesley and Ninian Winzet, Scots Benedictines by 1595 were in possession of three surviving Schottenklöster in Germany. In Paris, Beaton, acting for Queen Mary, financed Scottish students and in 1580 assisted what was eventually to become the Scots College in Douai. He also helped to rehabilitate an ancient foundation for Scots in Paris, which, combined with his own benefactions, gave birth to the Scots College in Paris.[3]

An institution for Scots in Rome itself was an obvious desirable initiative.[4] Gregory XIII (1572–85) had this in mind but was led by the Scots Jesuit William Crichton – perhaps in 1581 when he briefed Gregory on Scottish affairs – to help the future Douai college instead.[5] In Rome there was a hospice for Scots, sadly in need of restoration, which Alexander Seton (the future earl of Dunfermline) in the 1570s considered might be made into a seminary and, supported by John Lesley, he also petitioned unsuccessfully for Scots to be admitted to the English College.[6] There were renewed efforts in the 1590s, though accounts of these mostly lack any detail. John Lesley petitioned Clement VIII (1592–1605) to establish a Scottish seminary in Rome, as did William Chisholm (Bishop of Vaison 1584–1629), who in 1596 took steps to rehabilitate the hospice. About this time too, Archibald Hamilton and the Jesuit James Tyrie were likewise petitioning pope and cardinals, and it was Tyrie who was deputed by the two bishops to keep up pressure on their behalf when they left Rome.[7] Crichton, however, in 1597 remained of the same mind as before, preferring the Low Countries to Rome.[8]

The First Years (1600–22)[9]

Clement VIII's bull of 5 December 1600 established the College, putting it under the authority of the Cardinal Protector of Scotland, Camillo Borghese, and granting it the privileges of other pontifical colleges, the English, German and Greek.[10] The first students, eleven in number, were admitted in 1602 and studied at the *Collegio Romano*. The first house, not very suitable for its purpose, was lost through a lawsuit in 1604, to be replaced by one donated by Clement, not much better but with ground allowing expansion. The funding of the College, meagre to begin with, was increased slightly each year 1601–3, then received a more valuable addition in 1606 from Borghese, who had succeeded to the papacy as Paul V the year before. The premises and funding of the former hospice had proved almost valueless.

   To begin with, the affairs of the College were well managed by a papal official, Mgr Paolini, appointed by Borghese; he, in turn, put in men, whose names are not recorded, to do the immediate administration. All went well while Paolini was alive and active, but his health declined and he died in 1612. Discontent and disturbances increased, as no successor was appointed and the College had no rule-book, while the Protector who followed Borghese, Cardinal Maffeo Barberini, had more important matters to occupy his attention. The students themselves petitioned Barberini to appoint Jesuits as superiors and, in January 1615, a Scots Jesuit, Patrick Anderson, was made rector.[11]

   There was, however, an even more fundamental weakness, for the purpose of the College was expressed in Clement's bull in only general terms: to educate young Scots in good morals, piety, sound doctrine and Christian virtues, with no mention of priesthood or mission work in Scotland. Although Paolini strongly encouraged this apostolate and obtained a papal grant for journey expenses, lack of any organised authority in the Scottish Church remained an insuperable difficulty. The College register is enlightening.[12] Of the sixty-one students enrolled 1602–15, no information is given on the career of fourteen of them, either as students or later; six died while still students; of fifteen others it is merely recorded that they did not finish the course or left without being ordained, and the information given on two others is without significance; which leaves twenty-four students whose career has some significance. The largest homogeneous group comprises eight who became Jesuits, all of whom (apart from one man who died on his way there) worked on the Scottish Mission. Another nine entered various religious orders, of whom three worked in Scotland, one before becoming an Oratorian, the other two as religious priests. Of the seven men remaining, five became secular priests, all but one of them having connections with France, and Paris in particular, but not known to have worked in Scotland. Finally, two men not known to have been ordained became well-known scholars: George Strachan, the orientalist, and David Colville, linguist and librarian in the Escorial. Others too made their mark. Robert Philip was confessor to Queen Henrietta Maria; George Leslie is known as the famed *Cappuccino Scozzese*; Alexander Baillie was abbot and saviour of the Scots abbey in Ratisbon.[13] An almost contemporary list adds three men not in the register, one of whom was Thomas Duff, the poet-monk at Würzburg.[14]

Although Fr Anderson remained rector only five months and was succeeded by Italian rectors of the nearby Maronite college, he drew up a body of rules which survived the test of time. The regulations for discipline and spiritual duties were much as one would expect.[15] More important were the requirements that only students aged 17–25 and ready to begin philosophy were to be received and that after six months they would take an oath to receive holy orders and return to Scotland if their superiors so wished. The oath at least was surely imposed by higher authority. Although the register from 1616 on records the oath-taking by each student, it seems fairly clear that the record is not complete. The extant register was compiled in or shortly before 1693 from earlier documents, including apparently the autograph oaths, but there is evidence that not all of these had survived.[16] In early 1616, when the students were given three months to decide either to take the oath or leave the College, the first anniversary of John Ogilvie's martyrdom on 10 March is said to have persuaded them all to take the oath. There were fifteen students at the time but only five oaths dated 1616 are extant.[17] It was Anderson who, being rector at the time, received reports of the martyr's death and compiled the so-called Italian Narrative.[18]

Of the twenty-four students recorded in 1616–22, three died in the College in 1617 and nine left prematurely, apparently without taking the oath. Four of these, however, went on to become religious (two Dominicans, a Benedictine, a Jesuit), while one was ordained priest in Belgium, and George Conn, who left for health reasons, was later the papal envoy in London. Of the twelve who did take the oath, two left to become Jesuits. The remaining ten were ordained priest but not all served the Scottish mission, for three became religious (two Oratorians in Paris and a Franciscan) and one man's career is unrecorded. Another, who surely took the oath though it is not extant, died on his way to Scotland. Of the five who did work in Scotland, three later entered religion as, respectively, a Jesuit, a monk of Würzburg and an Oratorian in Paris. As so few became mission priests, the Irish Franciscans in 1618 wanted financial help from College revenues for their

Highand mission.[19] The difficulties of taking up mission work in Scotland are clearly indicated and taking the oath did not solve them.

Consolidation (1623–49)

Important changes took place in 1622–23, providing great stabilising influences on the College. Sharing with the Maronites had not gone well and a Scottish Jesuit was again appointed rector in September 1622: George Elphinstone, who was to remain in office for twenty-three years.[20] The Cardinal Protector, Maffeo Barberini, was elected pope in August 1623 and as Urban VIII reigned for twenty-one years. As successor he appointed his nephew, Cardinal Francesco Barberini, who remained Protector until 1679. Also in 1622 there took place one of the most significant events for the Church in Scotland: the foundation of the Sacred Congregation *De Propaganda Fide* (for the Propagation of the Faith), usually known simply as Propaganda, a word with unfortunate pejorative connotations in modern English. Propaganda's remit was the missionary effort of the Church world-wide, covering both non-Christian countries in the New World and Protestant countries in Europe.

Propaganda's influence on the College was not felt at once, for it had other priorities, in particular the mission to the Gaelic-speaking Highlands and Western Isles. It did, however, consider the role of the Scots Colleges to be its concern for, in February 1624, it decided against the Jesuits taking control of the Paris college and the proposal to move it to Rouen. Individual students in the 1630s sent petitions to Propaganda regarding their future. The Irish Franciscans conducting the mission to the Highlands complained in 1626 that no priest had come from the Scots Colleges to work in the Gaelic-speaking districts and three years later they petitioned Propaganda to oblige the colleges to take in some Highland students.[21]

In November 1625 Urban sanctioned an addition to the oath, made at the request of the English and Greek colleges, binding students to serve the mission for three years before entering a religious order.[22] In 1632 he appointed his nephew, Cardinal Antonio Barberini junior, to be prefect of Propaganda, with his own brother, Cardinal Antonio Barberini senior, as vice-prefect.[23] This was nepotism as a respectable institution, and the four Barberinis and Propaganda wielded great influence on the College despite its rector being a Jesuit. Collections in Barberini archives show interest in the Scottish mission and the College in particular at this time, with lists of all students since 1602, all those ordained priest, and those in the College at a given time.[24]

Various lists show nine students resident in 1623.[25] For the years 1623–49 the register has seventy-one students, of whom two died and thirty-three left during the year they entered or the following year. Of another eighteen who left at a later stage, nine had a career connected with the Church, including two Jesuits, two Benedictines, a Dominican, a canon of Saint Quentin and a professor of philosophy at Padua. The remaining eighteen were ordained priest. The careers of fourteen of these are mentioned: two became Benedictines; two went to France, one of them as chaplain to a Scots regiment; one was later rector of the Scots College, Paris. Nine went to work in Scotland, mostly in the 1640s, two of them later becoming Jesuits.

MacPherson's history adds a few details about George Elphinstone: that he was a man of letters, that matters went on quietly during his time as rector, that he introduced *convictores* (lodgers) into the College. From 1623 the register lists these, never numerous and mostly Scots or Italians, which MacPherson disapproved of though it surely helped the finances.[26] In January 1644 Elphinstone was replaced as rector by William Christie who was already resident as prefect of studies. The Barberini pope's long reign also came to an end when Urban died in July. Christie's term of office was short for he was succeeded by Francis Dempster in December 1646 though he stayed on for some time acting as confessor, but one notable achievement was his doing.

Since the demise of the hospice, Scots in Rome had no church for celebrating feasts or burying their dead. Christie, while in Scotland, had been chaplain to the Huntly family and received a large benefaction from the dowager marchioness who died in France in 1642.[27] This he used to extend the College buildings and build a church. He was helped in this by three other benefactors, all former students of the College. William Thomson, a Franciscan priest and one of the first students in 1602, had been chaplain to Queen Henrietta Maria (wife of Charles I), accompanied her into exile and went on to Rome where he gave Christie the money he had acquired. John Wedderburn, likewise a student in 1602, had been a professor in the university at Padua. Thomas Chalmers, a student from 1630 to 1637, now a priest, had been almoner to Cardinals Richelieu and Mazarin. (The careers of all three, incidentally, show the possibilities open to educated Catholic Scots.) The church structure was in place by 1646 – leaving decoration and furnishing to be completed later – and it was planned to open the church in the Holy Year of 1650.[28] One most interesting feature was the side altar dedicated to St Margaret, for Rome was aware of her growing *cultus* at the Scots College in Douai where the saint's head was exposed for veneration, and popes were granting a plenary indulgence to mark her feast. The Scots College in Rome was later to replace that in Douai in promoting Margaret's status.[29]

An annual list of residents in the College 1643–58, giving inconsistent but detailed information, has survived. The course of studies can be seen as three years of philosophy (termed logic, physics and metaphysics) and four years of theology, with two years of moral theology or 'cases' as an option or alternative. In 1643 there were nineteen residents, including ten students ranging from one in his second year of theology to five studying logic. The remaining nine persons comprised two Scots Jesuits, two lodgers and the servant of one of them, and four College officials or servants: procurator, tailor, janitor-cum-refectorian, cook. In 1644 six students received the tonsure and minor orders and in 1645 ordinations to the priesthood began: three that year, two in 1646 and one each in 1647 and 1648.

Two of the domestic assistants were identified as, or perhaps replaced by, two Jesuit laybrothers: Patrick Crusan, a Scot, and Andrew Cassedi. With so many being ordained and leaving the College, student numbers dropped to five but began to pick up again.[30] The most important factor of all, however, was that all but one of the eight new priests (for one had been ordained earlier in the 1640s) embarked on the Scottish mission and six of them decided to act as a group and not as individuals.

Sister Institutions and Conflicting Interests

Various bodies were dedicated to the promotion of the Roman Catholic Church in Scotland. All were agreed on the end to be achieved though they differed in their ethos and corporate loyalty and in the methods they employed. As has been said, very little remained of the pre-reformation Church, and in particular no diocesan structure and no episcopal authority. Scottish institutions on the Continent had, however, survived and been given a counter-reformation ethos and orientation. These were the three Scots monasteries in Germany and the Scots Colleges in Paris and Rome. Two new Scots Colleges were founded: one eventually settled at Douai and the other was founded in Madrid in 1627.

Of great importance, and certainly more effective in the early seveteenth century, was the help afforded by institutions not themselves Scottish. The seminary in Braunsberg continued to provide places for Scottish students into the 1640s.[31] Of the Scots who entered the Dominicans and various branches of the Franciscans, many worked as priests in Scotland. It was Jesuits, however, who achieved most in mission work in Scotland, even though they were never numerous enough to form a province of their own but entered various Continental provinces as individuals, and even though Scottish Jesuits worked in other countries besides Scotland.

The three Scottish monasteries did not form a constitutional unity. The Ratisbon abbey was subject to no Church authority except the Holy See and was a consistorial abbey, that is, its abbots had to be provided in a consistory (formal meeting) of cardinals. Würzburg was a prince-bishopric where the bishop was both spiritual and temporal ruler with the Scots abbey there subject to him and his officials. The abbey in Erfurt, an enclave subject to the archbishop-elector of Mainz, never developed an autonomous community and eventually became a dependent priory of Ratisbon.[32]

The four Scots Colleges were likewise very disparate in their foundation and constitution. The Douai college was funded, to some extent at least, by revenues collected by the Scots Jesuit, William Crichton, when he was rector in the 1590s and received further endowment from another Scots Jesuit, Hippolytus Curle. It was subject to the superior of the Belgian Jesuit province, though from 1632 its rectors were Scots. Students commonly entered at an early age and did not normally receive the priesthood at Douai but moved on to Jesuit novitiates or other seminaries, including the Scots College in Rome.[33]

The Scots College in Paris differed from the others in important ways. It was not exclusively for Church students and it accepted boys at an early age, even a few under eleven. It was the only one not under Jesuit control for its ecclesiastical superior was the local Carthusian prior who left its administration entirely in the hands of Scottish secular priests. It is not known whether Beaton deliberately chose a non-Jesuit superior or had no choice, since Jesuits had been expelled from Paris at the time of his bequest. The College also had official status in the university. Twenty students up to 1682 went to the Scots College in Rome to complete their Church studies after some time in the Paris College. The two Colleges also began to co-operate to their mutual benefit, with students heading for Rome from Scotland wintering in Paris and priests ordained in Rome spending quite lengthy periods in Paris gaining pastoral experience before taking up work in Scotland. Proposals were later made for Paris to act as a feeder college for Rome.[34]

Douai lay near the North Sea coast, while Paris was not only far easier than Rome to reach from Scotland but was also a centuries-old focal point for Scots outwith Scotland. The special relationship between Scotland and France, dating from the days of the Auld Alliance, continued with Catholic Scots in the seventeenth century, and many Scots priests ordained in Rome enjoyed benefices or served in France. In December 1688 France was the obvious place for the refugee James VII to seek asylum.

A seminary much further afield was founded when the expatriate Scot, William Semple, established the Scots College in Madrid and put it under the authority of the Jesuit provincial of Toledo, with his own nephew, the Jesuit Hugh Semple, as rector. Initially Urban VIII did not favour its foundation and would have preferred its students to come to Rome instead. From the beginning the College suffered disabilities, financial and constitutional. Most of its first students came from Douai, which lay in the Spanish Netherlands, and there was movement in the reverse direction from Madrid to Douai. Semple's foundation also paid funds over to the Douai College. The few priests produced by Madrid became Jesuits and never served in Scotland.[35] Nevertheless, the Madrid College, with its special relation to its sister College at Douai, formed an integral part of the seminary system for Scotland. Douai could term itself College of the Scots of the Society of Jesus; the same was to happen at Madrid and the Jesuit general reminded the Toledo provincial in 1636 that the College was not Jesuit property but only administered by the Society. According to MacPherson, Jesuit rectors in Rome had the same outlook and used the same terminology.[36]

The Scots College in Rome was thus a unit in the Scottish Church in exile with institutions in France, Germany, Italy, Belgium and Spain, and with priests in various religious orders. The College was national and pontifical like other such colleges in Rome, that is, it was established by a pope and for the Scottish nation.

This gave the College a special relationship to the reigning pope and to the Cardinal Protector of Scotland who was its superior. Although its rectors from 1615 on were Jesuits, the process whereby these were appointed is not clear. The choice was surely made by the Jesuit general, either directly or by someone delegated by him, and surely the Protector's approval was always sought.

An important new element was introduced with the establishment of the Congregation of Propaganda Fide in 1622. Propaganda set about its enormous world-wide task with speed and some efficiency, though its effort was spread over many and very diverse lands. There was, however, one serious flaw in Propaganda's organisation, one large gap in the task it confronted, which was that the body most active in carrying out missionary work was not subject to its control but was empowered by the Pope (who empowered Propaganda) and was responsible directly to him. This was the Society of Jesus, the Jesuits. The history of the Scots College in Rome, as indeed of missionary work in Scotland in the seventeenth century, is very largely the story of two powerful and influential bodies, Propaganda and the Jesuits, acting in rivalry if also in common purpose, with the Cardinal Protector somewhere between them.

To understand Catholicism in Scotland in the first half of the seventeenth century, one should visualise a line drawn slantwise roughly from the Clyde to the Moray Firth. West and north of that line, mission work was mostly carried out by Gaelic-speaking Franciscans from Ireland. To the east and south, in Lowland Scotland (though containing areas mostly Gaelic-speaking), mission work was done by individual secular priests, but apparently never for any lengthy period, and by religious priests, Jesuits in particular. These, though never numerous, worked with more continuity and organisation. One must realise the immense prestige and vitality of the Jesuits at this time. MacPherson acknowledges their well-deserved reputation in three fields: learning, teaching and dealing with youth.[37] They also had a remarkable *esprit de corps*, the downside of which was that they tended to regard others as less fitted for necessary apostolates. As a result, students coming to Rome were more likely to be acquainted with Jesuit priests and missionary activity in Scotland, were then educated under Jesuit auspices and were thus more likely to want to be Jesuits themselves. Or, to put it negatively, if they opted directly for mission work in Scotland, they had no organisation or means of support and no resources to fall back on if for any reason they returned to the Continent. Thus mission priests, after a period of work in Scotland, often entered a religious order, in particular the Jesuits.

Scottish Jesuits naturally sought to recruit suitable young men to their ranks and they have been accused of sending such to the College to be educated and exerting influence on them in the College to become Jesuits. Beyond doubt, this sometimes did happen. But, given the state of the Scottish mission at the time and the complex situation of the College, it hardly constitutes wrong-doing. Nor are the relations of the various parties in Rome sufficiently known. The pope, the Jesuit general, the

Jesuit Roman provincial, the Cardinal Protector, the cardinals and officials of Propaganda and the Scots College rector all lived in close proximity to each other. As superior of the College, the Protector had wide powers and had to give his approval, for instance, for a student to be dismissed. Supervision of such matters as finances and accounts was perhaps left to the Jesuit authorities. The unclear situation is shown by visitations made by various parties, for instance by the Jesuit general, and one in 1644 by the Protector, another cardinal and the secretary of Propaganda.[38]

The basic purpose of the College, however, coincided with the aims of Propaganda. The relationship of Propaganda, the Protector and the Jesuit authorities was crucial. MacPherson rather implausibly states that Maffeo Barberini, Protector and then pope, was so disgusted with the Jesuit take-over of the rectorship that he took no further interest in the College, while Francesco Barberini, his successor as Protector, was no use as he was entirely supportive of Jesuits.[39] Tensions were not resolved by the modification of the oath requiring students to work for three years as secular priests in their homeland before they could enter a religious order. Scottish Jesuits insisted that this was harmful for so many students did not want to be secular priests. Their opponents declared the oath was useless and easy to circumvent, for the Protector could dispense and the Jesuit rectors sometimes delayed administering the oath beyond the statutory time. Innocent X ruled in August 1645 that the obligation to serve the Mission was lifelong and not merely for three years; Propaganda gave leave to students to become religious but with the obligation to help the Mission still holding good.[40] In the winter of 1649–50, however, a new factor came into play which radically changed the situation as regards the whole Scottish mission and the College in particular.

Conflict and Development (1650–60)

In the winter of 1649–50, six secular priests, all former students of the College, met in Paris and made two momentous decisions: first, to petition Propaganda to subsidise a number of secular priests as missionaries in Scotland, with one of them appointed as superior and, second, to keep one of them resident in Rome to act on their behalf. The man they chose for Rome was Will Leslie. Leslie, who belonged to a traditionally Catholic family in the north-east, went when aged fourteen to the Scots College in Douai (where his uncle, also called William Leslie, was the Jesuit rector), moved on to Rome and after seven years' study was ordained priest in 1647. He then set out for Paris to gain pastoral experience in preparation for working in Scotland and was still there when the priests met and decided. At that time Carlo Barberini was legate in Paris and about to return to Rome. Leslie returned with him as tutor to his nephew and so, aged almost thirty, had a position in the powerful Barberini network, especially after Carlo was created cardinal in 1653. As he remained in Rome until his death in 1707, Leslie became an 'institution', serving under eight popes and known to all as Don Guglielmo. In October 1661 he was made Propaganda's first permanent archivist. Leslie's coming to Rome as clergy agent was of the greatest significance for the College, for he turned out to be a single-minded man dedicated to the interests of the Scottish secular priests and of Propaganda. The Scots College, administered by Jesuits and of more benefit to them and other religious orders than to the secular clergy, received his constant close and critical attention.[41]

At the time of Will Leslie's arrival, the College was not in a happy state. A new rector, Andrew Leslie, arrived on 4 July 1649 and there was much coming and going in the College in the latter part of the year. Two students left for health reasons, one recent arrival was dismissed as he refused to take the oath, another after three months' stay as a guest went on to a Jesuit novitiate. Two men arrived, one from the Scots College in Madrid, the other a lodger wishing to study theology. The year 1650 saw even more arrivals and departures. The senior student went in April, being (according to the rector) unsuitable and troublesome; the man from Madrid left in September to claim an inheritance. Meanwhile five students had arrived, though two stayed only until June and two departed in February 1651 after creating a disturbance, about which the rector informed everyone in authority. Two more students arrived in November 1650, one of whom lasted only three months before taking French leave. The College had two other guests for a month each, one to be instructed in the faith – an unsuccessful initiative – and the other because it was the Holy Year.[42]

The College register has twenty-eight entrants in the decade 1650–60, twelve of them in the first two years. No fewer than twenty-two left unordained, though ten of these later became religious (five Jesuits and five others), or perhaps actually left in order to become religious. Only four men of the twenty-eight completed their studies in the College and went to work in Scotland as secular priests, hardly a situation to satisfy Will Leslie. It must also have been a disappointment that Robert Watson, who had entered before 1650, was ordained priest after seven years' study but died in the College in August 1652 and was the first to be buried in the new chapel vault. Of the two remaining students, one died and the other studied humanities for seven years with the leave of the Protector, while Propaganda paid for his brother to study humanities as a lodger in the College.

In the spring of 1652 Fr Adam Gordon acted as vice-rector while Andrew Leslie was in Naples on business and in May took over as rector when Leslie set off for Scotland at his own request. It was decided at this time to give the College a resident prefect of studies despite its limited revenues. The rector was always a Scot serving usually a three-year term but Italian Jesuits are found on the staff: Colombi, Rosa, Constantini. Students averaged about eight in number, with a few not yet ready to begin philosophy, but at the end of 1658 only four were in residence together with the teenaged lodger. Only two new students entered in 1659 and none in 1660. One very useful and positive step was, however, taken by

Fr Adam Gordon, a former student of the College, when he purchased a vineyard and house near Marino 'about eleven English miles from Rome'. It provided a place for students to escape from the summer heat of Rome and a supply of acceptable wine.

Propaganda was beginning to have more effective relations with the College. The mission of secular priests was set up in October 1653 with William Ballantine as prefect and four others as associates. Although two years later Propaganda refused to add a newly ordained priest to their number, considering the mission adequately provided for, the next man to be ordained, Alexander Winster, was appointed in 1657 and the man turned down before was added in 1659 as a replacement. This was Alexander Leith, ordained in 1655, who had gone to Scotland with faculties given him by the Protector. Every one of these men was a former student of the College, and Propaganda's reason for refusing or admitting a missionary was apparently merely financial. In December 1655, Propaganda enquired if the College had any student fit for the Highland mission (meaning, presumably, that he was competent in Gaelic) and in June 1657, considering a report on Scotland, agreed that the mission prefect could summon to Scotland the students ordained to the priesthood in all four colleges. The colleges as a collective unit were now within Propaganda's purview.[43]

Many of the so-called Blairs Letters for this decade have been published. They are not easy to read, even in their printed form, but they give useful insight. For the most part, both writers and recipients were Jesuits resident in Paris, Douai and Rome and they wrote frankly to each other. What most concerned them at this time was the oath taken by the students in Rome to serve the mission for three years before entering a religious order. Aspirants wanted to study in Rome and Scots Jesuits would have liked to send them there, but the oath deterred students who did not want to spend three years as secular priests, while their Jesuit mentors had great misgivings about sending them. As Fr Robert Gall, rector in Douai, wrote: 'Wee would endanger them to loose their vocation & become (as the most part of all educated there not Religious) our professed enemyes.' These revealing words were written on 20 November 1649, before Will Leslie was active in Rome as clergy agent, and show that the hostility was not his creation.

It should be added that Jesuits did send to Rome some young men who had no intention of becoming secular priests. Robert Gall urged Andrew Leslie to do all he could to get the oath changed to a promise to serve the mission as a secular or regular. William Christie, former rector in Rome and twice rector at Douai in the 1650s, urged the same and advised Andrew Leslie to delay imposing the oath, as he himself had done while rector in Rome. Some students similarly did their best to avoid having to take the oath. It is difficult to judge whether this tension was more serious than formerly, though letters give indications that the situation was exacerbated in the 1650s. They reveal that the young men accepted at Rome in 1650 were unsuitable, that Andrew Leslie's shortcomings as rector were serious and in the absence of another Jesuit priest he unfortunately 'used the counsel' of

Brother Patrick. Then, when a second priest was appointed, it was sometimes an Italian, with whom it is said the students did not agree.[44]

There was conflict in Paris too. An attempt by Jesuits in 1649 to take over the Scots College was thwarted by secular priests, including Will Leslie who was there at the time. Later there was an extraordinary situation when Fr James MacBreck, appointed in 1654 to the staff of Clermont College in Paris, influenced students at the Scots College to transfer to Rome against their rector's wishes in order to become Jesuits. As procurator of the Scottish Jesuit mission, MacBreck apparently had some role in allotting aspirants' places. Enticing students away from another seminary was reprehensible enough, but he seemed genuinely surprised at its rector's hostile reaction.[45] Perhaps the main factor in the tension was the build-up of the secular mission body, acting cohesively since 1649 and granted official status in 1653. It was on the way to becoming a formidable rival, for it had the backing of Propaganda and a very competent agent in Rome.

Will Leslie countered Jesuit assertions that the oath deterred students by offering to fill the College if the Jesuits handed over administration. Frs MacBreck and Christie now wanted the College to become entirely Jesuit property. When Jesuit authorities did not support this, the plan thereafter (according to MacPherson) was to use College revenues for the benefit of the Society. Will Leslie was in touch with the college in Paris and with the students in Rome poached from it by MacBreck. He was also aware of how few Scots students there were in Rome. Having failed to get the Protector to intervene, he petitioned Propaganda to remedy the paucity of missionaries in Scotland and the failure of the Jesuit-administered colleges to provide them. In eloquent language he lectured the cardinals on their sacred duty and the divine judgement they faced if they neglected it. To their Eminences' credit, they responded by asking him to suggest remedies. Leslie's proposals were threefold: to make the oath binding perpetually instead of for three years, to bind former students to write annually to Propaganda and to oblige rectors of pontifical colleges to inform Propaganda fully about each student on his arrival and departure. Propaganda accepted all these and they were promulgated by Alexander VII on 20 July 1660. His bull forbade rectors, under pain of suspension, to permit any delay in taking the oath.[46] Will Leslie, after ten years as clergy agent in Rome, had played a major role in determining policy not for the Scots only but for all the pontifical colleges.

Slow Progress (1661–84)

To judge from the register, the change in the oath was a turning-point. Beginning in 1661, each student took the new oath or is recorded as leaving before taking it. Students entering the College were fewer in number, only thirty-three in the twenty-four years from 1661 to 1684, of whom seven left before taking the oath, four were dismissed (all of them in 1671) and two left for health reasons: thirteen in all. Of a further six who left, most of them with the permission of the Protector, two entered religion and a third, William Leslie, went to teach theology at Padua and was later bishop of Laibach in Austria. The remaining fourteen were ordained as secular priests, one of them after going to Paris to finish his theology, and all but one of these served the mission. But although it was a great advance to have over a third of the students becoming mission priests, progress in the mission itself was slow, for only two of these were ordained in the 1660s and only two men who had entered the College earlier were ordained in that decade. New arrivals in Scotland barely made up for those dropping out.[47]

The prefect, William Ballantine, died in September 1661 and was succeeded by Alexander Winster (or Dunbar) who was a former student of the College, as indeed were all who were considered for the post. Winster did not enjoy an auspicious start, for the number of serving priests in the 1660s never exceeded half a dozen and, from April 1665, Propaganda was considering his urgent reports on the situation. By preventing the wholesale creaming-off of students by religious orders, the new oath had removed one great obstacle to the growth of a mission conducted by secular priests, but Propaganda now had to face a major reason for the creaming-off which was the lack of provision for secular priests suffering from ill-health or old age or in exile. One proposal debated for several years was to establish a hospice in France for these priests, but Propaganda's funds were limited.

In December 1668 Winster sent a detailed report to Propaganda complaining that all four Scots Colleges were in a defective state and in urgent need of reform. They had always, he said, produced three times as many religious priests as secular, and twice as many religious priests as secular were living at the moment.[48] In 1668 there were six secular priests, eleven Jesuits and five other regulars working in Scotland, while at least eleven secular priests were living in France or Rome.

Propaganda continued to concern itself with the West Highlands and Islands, wanting the colleges to help, and in 1668 Robert Munro, from the diocese of Ross, entered the Scots College in Rome and duly completed his theology. The proposal was also made that mission priests should learn a trade to provide cover for their activities. Propaganda, while not opposed to the idea, did not want this to be done during their formal studies in the colleges. There is frequent mention of the procurator of the mission suggesting, advising or being consulted.[49] This was Will Leslie; whatever his fellow priests had in mind when they made him their agent in 1649–50, he seemingly now had official status in Rome.

Following on the imposition of the new oath, there was not unnaturally some difficulty and some confrontation in Rome. Questions and doubts about it needed to be resolved.[50] MacPherson was sure these were intended to hinder the full working of the oath and in this he may have been right or wrong. Dr W. E. Brown wrote that much of MacPherson's anti-Jesuit stance is not supported by the evidence.[51] Two reservations, however, need to be made about this judgement. The first is that Brown did not take into account the wider evidence from the Scottish mission background, the other colleges and the letters written by Jesuits. The second is that one needs to distinguish, on the one hand, between MacPherson's remarks about (say) the Jesuit rector's intentions and, on the other hand, his summary of some reasoning by Will Leslie followed by an official decision or action. In the latter case it must be presumed that MacPherson is using actual documents.

The first exchanges after 1660 between Leslie and the rector fall into this category. Leslie, as archivist, knew that the information of students required by the papal decree was not being provided for Propaganda by Fr George Bisset (alias Gilbert Talbot) serving a second term as rector (1663–60). Leslie wrote to Bisset (and MacPherson quotes) but in vain, so he brought the matter up at a meeting of Propaganda. The latter's secretary wrote to Bisset demanding full compliance but when this was not effective the cardinal prefect himself brought all guns to bear and, of course, won the day. There was trouble over the *viaticum* or viatic (journey expenses) for newly ordained priests returning to Scotland. A former rector, William Christie, wrote to Bisset: 'What have we to do with the journey of the seculars? That College is only obliged to defray the journey of our own people; let the seculars provide for themselves.' Leslie, therefore, approached the Protector who agreed to a compromise that, at a student's departure for the mission, Leslie would petition the Protector to direct the rector to provide a competent sum.

There is an error in the next incident narrated by MacPherson, for the mission prefect concerned is said to be Ballantine who, in fact, died in 1661. The prefect in question was surely Winster. He arrived in Paris bringing two promising young men whom he wished to send to Rome, since the Scots College in Paris was full. Rather innocently he told Fr James MacBreck, who proved completely unco-operative, and the two young men had to remain in France. But Bisset, alarmed at his own shortage of resident students, took in some quite unsuitable men. Will Leslie's subsequent appeal to Propaganda deploring the taking in of vagabonds and army deserters as clerical students was outspoken and emotional. (One can see why Will Leslie's friends dubbed him 'the Homelist'!) The cardinal prefect responded with a blistering letter to Bisset, ordering the instant dismissal of the unsuitable men and commanding that in future no student was to be admitted without the approval of lawful superiors which was interpreted as meaning the mission prefect. Bisset now gave up many of the academic and spiritual exercises customary in the College. Leslie advised the students to complain to the Jesuit general who ordered Bisset to rectify matters.[52]

Fr John Strachan took over as rector in November 1670 but died after two months in office.[53] MacPherson asserts that his successor, the Italian Fr Marini, ruled so badly that scarcely a student remained. The fact, if not the reason for it, is borne out by the register, for all seven students entering the College since 1664 departed in 1671: two to the mission, one because of ill health and four dismissed – which, of course, may be only an expression of the rector's displeasure. Perhaps the last student had not yet gone when two new entrants in 1671 arrived, in which case the College was never completely emptied of students.

In March 1674 Fr William Aloysius Leslie succeeded Marini as rector. He belonged to the Leslies of Balquhain, a senior branch of the family, and so was a cousin of Will Leslie and about twenty years younger. He too had gone to Douai at an early age and then had graduated in theology at the Jesuit *Collegio Romano*, not the Scots College. Taking over as rector, he found four students and, according to MacPherson, at once began to persuade them that the oath they had taken was unlawful as it prevented a greater good, that of joining a religious order. He thought it could be dispensed at a jubilee which was expected soon, when confessors would have enlarged powers to commute vows. One student, however, John Irvine (Belty), expressed his misgivings to Will Leslie and received a lengthy reply countering the rector's arguments. This quite convinced the students who reproached the rector for misleading them, whereupon Will Leslie wrote another long epistle rebuking them for disrespect to superiors. He then petitioned Propaganda who decreed that no confessor could dispense from the oath. MacPherson's account, one-sided perhaps, is supported by his use of documents.

Not surprisingly relations between the two Leslies were now strained and the consequences, as narrated by MacPherson, were not edifying. An attempt by the rector to get the agent sent to the Scottish mission in accordance with the oath he had taken was unsuccessful. The agent invited the students to visit him frequently, and the rector then hinted that the agent was tainted with Jansenism. Winster at this time wrote to Will Leslie begging him to get the colleges made more efficient in supplying desperately needed priests. The agent laid a memorial before Propaganda condemning the College comprehensively and asking for an apostolic visitation, but because of Propaganda's wish not to offend the Protector – a factor often mentioned by MacPherson – this did not happen.[54] In 1679 Francesco Barberini died, to be succeeded as protector by the English Dominican cardinal, Philip Howard. Great hopes were entertained that he would prove an effective patron and the agent laid before him the needs of the mission and the College and the measures that needed to be taken, but the visitation of the College which he persuaded Howard to conduct was quite ineffective.[55] Then, in November 1683, Fr Andrew Mackie succeeded as rector.

The record of these years may not be inspiring but there were also positive steps and hopeful signs. Of the students entering the College in this period, five were ordained and went to Scotland in the 1670s, another two in the early 1680s and four men were soon to follow them. In 1684 there were 12 Scottish secular priests working on the mission. The development of St Margaret's *cultus* shows that the expatriate Scots Catholics were not lacking in self-confidence. Devotion to her had been centred in the Scots College at Douai, where the saint's head was venerated, but the initiative now passed to the Scots College in Rome. The two Leslies, Will and William Aloysius, joined in petitioning for Margaret's feast to be added to the

Church's universal calendar. Pope Clement X ratified this in December 1673, some months before William Aloysius became rector. The new rector in 1675 obtained a relic of the saint from Douai and he had the decoration of the College chapel, including a picture of St Margaret for her altar, completed with funds from his uncle, Count Walter Leslie. Also in 1675 he published her life in Italian: *Vita di Santa Margherita*. He then had St Margaret officially recognised as patron of the Scots Colleges and a patron of Scotland. As her feast on 10 June was often impeded though falling within the octave of Pentecost or Corpus Christi, he petitioned for another date and it was tranferred to 8 July.[56] These were not his only initiatives at the time. The new wing was completed in 1676, the sodality of Our Lady was established in the College and in 1681 he was apparently planning a continuation of John Leslie's *History of Scotland*.[57]

Two other Scots Catholic institutions experienced an upturn during this period. Robert Barclay, rector of the Scots College Paris (1653–82), improved the finances and built fine new premises and a chapel. The large and commodious college had twelve students in 1669; Winster had brought five the year before. Students went to Rome to complete their Church studies, and priests ordained in Paris went to the mission. The college acted as financial agency for the mission, helped to provided pastoral training for priests going to Scotland and provided refuge for priests exiled from Scotland.[58]

The Scots Benedictine abbey in Ratisbon flourished under a man whose career resembled Will Leslie's. Placid Fleming, elected abbot in 1672 when just thirty, devoted himself single-mindedly to his monastery and the Scottish mission. Already in 1675 he was telling Will Leslie of his plans to educate youngsters and send them to Rome when their humanities were completed.[59] The Scottish mission and its institutions on the Continent were growing in stability and confidence.

Rapid Changes (1685–1707)

A series of notable events transforming Scottish Catholicism began with the accession of James VII and II to the throne in February 1685. James openly declared himself Catholic, his Scottish chancellor became a Catholic, a Catholic centre was opened at Holyrood, every available priest on the Continent was ordered to return to Scotland. When James fled in December 1688, a complete debacle ensued. None of this is even mentioned by MacPherson. In late 1688 there were some forty-five priests operating in Scotland: sixteen seculars (eleven from the College), about twenty Jesuits and eight Benedictines.[60] They were imprisoned or exiled almost to a man and for some years Catholicism had hardly any visible presence. From the mid-1690s, however, it began to rise from the ruins.

The process of giving Scotland a bishop – not an 'ordinary', with full jurisdiction in his diocese, but a Vicar Apostolic in episcopal holy orders, though only with the powers delegated by Rome – had been halted by the Revolution of 1688, but finally, in September 1694, Thomas Nicolson was appointed. Quite apart from his advantages of scholarship and social status, it was a wise choice as he was not a product of the Scots Colleges but had been ordained while teaching theology at Padua and so was not labelled as being in either camp. Having received episcopal consecration secretly, he was unable to return to Scotland and so spoke with the two Scots abbots in Germany. At the time he was engaged in acquiring powers from Propaganda to exercise control over religious priests in Scotland. The abbots voluntarily promised more than Nicolson was asking for. He finally arrived in Scotland in July 1697 and the Jesuit missioners formally submitted to his episcopal authority in 1701.[61]

In the space of two decades the Scottish mission had experienced triumph, disaster and gradual recovery. The affairs of the College seemed hardly affected. The register, for example, shows little change. Recruitment remained at about the same level, thirty-one entrants in the twenty-three years from 1685 to 1707, of whom six left without taking the oath, one died and one was dismissed (eight in all). A further nine left later: three for health reasons and six with the Protector's leave. The remaining fourteen were ordained for the mission, two of them leaving for Scotland before ordination as there was now a bishop who could ordain them there. The success rate as regards producing mission priests was somewhat higher than previously, almost 50 per cent, but perhaps more significant was that not a single student left to become a Jesuit or entered the Jesuits later. The College had ceased to be a source of recruitment for Jesuits or a stage on the way to becoming one.

An extraordinary episode took place about 1691. The rector having died in December 1690, Fr Musanti took over as vice-rector. The students naturally were staunch supporters of the Stuart king exiled for his faith, though James was not *persona grata* in Rome as he had taken refuge with Louis XIV, the sworn enemy of the pope. Musanti, an Italian, followed the papal line, quarrelled heatedly with the students and called in the police to threaten them with imprisonment. The next morning they announced their intention of leaving in a body, whereupon Musanti (in MacPherson's lively account) threw himself on his knees in repentance and thereafter was an ideal rector. The current witticism was that, for Europe to have peace, the pope should turn Catholic and Louis turn Protestant. Extraordinary as it sounds, at the battle of the Boyne in 1690, the pope was on the side of the Protestant William of Orange.

In 1691, a second edition of William Aloysius Leslie's *Life of St Margaret* appeared, dedicated by the teachers and students of the College to the Countess of Melfort, wife of James's, Scottish secretary and now in exile.[62] William Aloysius became rector again in June 1692. Innocent XI, perhaps through Will Leslie's advocacy, ordered a congregation of cardinals to conduct a visitation of all the pontifical colleges. The agent, who had influence with Cardinal Marcantonio Barbarigo, chosen for the Scots College, approached him and was asked to write a full and frank report on the College and its needs. This he did under six heads, suggesting that he himself should be given a supervisory role in three of them and paying particular attention to the finances. William Aloysius, on his side, realising that the visitation would be no mere formality, had work done on the accounts and on the burial vault, since the high altar of the chapel was immediately above it, contrary to liturgical law. The commission in September 1693 approved stringent acts of visitation embodying most of what the agent had hoped for. Moreover, Mgr Sperelli, a Roman prelate of the agent's choice, was appointed by the pope to oversee execution of the acts, assisted by Leslie himself.[63]

Meanwhile two young Aberdeen men were sent from Scotland to the College. Hugh Strachan arrived at Douai in January 1693 and in June entered a Jesuit novitiate. The other, Robert Gordon, arriving at Douai in July, was sent on in September.[64] His destination was the Jesuit novitiate at Bologna, which caused indignation in Rome where places had been allotted them at the mission prefect's request. The rector had also, contrary to the visitation decrees, admitted a young man on his way to the Jesuit novitiate in Naples. The Protector ordered him to be sent away at once without a viatic. Gordon wrote to explain his actions and the agent's lengthy reply persuaded him to enter the College in July 1694 to study for the secular priesthood. It was at least a partial victory for the agent.

In November 1695 Fr James Forbes became rector. Cardinal Howard had died in 1694 and was replaced as Protector by Mgr Caprara, appointed by King James and having only limited authority as he was neither a cardinal nor appointed by the pope. Mgr Sperelli, created a cardinal, ceased to have oversight over execution of the visitation decrees, thereby depriving Will Leslie, as his deputy, of any authority. When the new rector refused to pay journey expenses as decreed, Leslie found himself powerless in the circumstances.

Since Leslie was now in his mid-seventies and not in good health, John Irvine (Cuttlebrae) was sent in 1698 to assist him.[65] The College now went through a very troubled period. In 1701 an Italian, Fr Calcagni, was appointed rector – the same had happened in the Irish College – and proved to be both tyrannical and capricious. Eventually Caprara persuaded the Jesuit general to remove him but the new rector, Fr Naselli, appointed in January 1704, was no improvement. As one student put it, instead of an old tyrant, they now had a young one. Another student, Gregor MacGregor, a man like his father, a turbulent Highland laird, defied Naselli who went to the pope himself for authority to dismiss him but was thwarted in this by Will Leslie.[66] James Gordon, who had replaced Irvine as Leslie's assistant, lobbied the Jacobite court to have Scots rectors appointed once more and achieved partial success when James Forbes was made prefect of studies.

A far greater danger now threatened. Clement XI appointed a congregation of cardinals to adjudicate on a proposed merger of the Scots, English and Irish Colleges. This was, according to MacPherson, the Jesuit general's idea. The reasons given were broadly concerned with the greater efficiency of one larger unit, while the Jacobite court and each of the three nations opposed the merger.

James Gordon petitioned the cardinals against it while Forbes, in a meeting of the Jesuit general congregation, accused the Italian Jesuits of intrigue and asserted that their motive was to appropriate the Scots College chapel and garden. The scheme was eventually dropped.

All this, combined with an unsatisfactory rector, was surely unsettling for the students. In 1705 there were only three and Bishop Nicolson complained that he had received no missioner for five years and seemed unlikely to receive any. The number of secular missioners in Scotland had dropped from twenty-three in 1698 to below twenty.[67] Naselli not only refused to pay the journey expenses from Paris of two youths sent by the bishop but refused to admit more than one of them and instead agreed to accept an unsatisfactory subject from Douai. Though he eventually admitted both men sent by Nicolson, the visitation of 1693 was now clearly ineffective.

In August 1705 James Gordon was nominated coadjutor and successor to Nicolson. On behalf of all Scottish Catholics he petitioned the Jesuit general congregation to restore Scots rectors to the College, and Forbes did the same on behalf of the Scots Jesuits. The queen mother (for her son was still in his teens) supported the petition and the newly elected Jesuit general promised that the present Italian rector would be the last. Now, however, wanting to have more security for the College, the Scots began to press for it to be united with the College of Propaganda, though still retaining separate identity. The Scots clergy, both bishops, both agents – William Stuart had replaced Gordon as Leslie's assistant – and the queen mother were agreed on this, though naturally the Jesuits were opposed to it.[68]

Will Leslie's last days were made happy. Caprara was expected to be made a cardinal; the Jesuits wanted him then to be Cardinal Protector while the mission clergy and the Jacobite court wanted Cardinal Sacripanti. Leslie approached Innocent XI who appointed Sacripanti in September 1706. The new Protector, who was both prefect of Propaganda and a friend of Will Leslie, welcomed the old agent affectionately and at once issued orders: the viatic for each student was to be increased, no student was to be admitted without the bishop's written approval, Leslie was to write off at once for three more students as only five were in residence. Finally, Leslie was to draw up a full report on the mission and the College and the proposal to merge with Propaganda's college. This was the last task accomplished by Will Leslie who died on 23 April 1707 at the age of eighty-six. Conflict between the Protector and Propaganda was surely at an end with the same cardinal being both Protector of Scotland and prefect of Propaganda. To all appearances, everything Will Leslie had worked for during almost six decades had reached a happy conclusion.

Conclusion

Various threads run through the history of the College. One such is its belonging to a group of pontifical colleges, from the foundation bull of 1600 granting the privileges of membership to the merger scheme in 1704. The group was affected by the oath binding for three years and later for life, by the papal regulation about *convictors* in 1675, by the visitation of 1693. A pleasing glimpse is given in 1704 of the Scots and English students inviting each other on their respective feast-days.[69] Another thread is the development of the College from a precarious start to possessing its own vineyard and summer-house, extending its buildings and having a fine chapel which provided a focus for devotion to St Margaret. And this despite the often straitened finances, relieved by occasional benefactions.

The main thread was surely the increasing definition of the College's purpose as provision of secular priests for the Scottish mission. The chief means to achieve this was the oath and one can see the increasing stringency. What is surprising is the ineffectiveness of legislation due to the freedom of action enjoyed by the Jesuit rector and the apparently uncommitted stance of the College's superior, the Protector. There seems to have been no common determination to resolve the issues in one direction. The Protector was given powers by Alexander VII (1655–67) to absolve from the oath after three years.[70]

One obviously crucial issue was who decided which students to accept. Propaganda ordered c.1668 that the mission prefect's approval was needed. Alexander Leslie's proposals in 1681 following his visitation of Scotland recommended the same and it was again an issue in 1693.[71] Yet the Jesuit Fr MacBreck considered he had a role and, in 1705, the rector was still deciding. Another important issue was journey money for students travelling to and from Rome. Even in 1705, after so much dispute and negotiation, the rector still held the purse strings.

The complex authority structure was undoubtedly to blame, with the Jesuit factor isolated from the others for, unlike the Protector and the cardinals of Propaganda, the Jesuit general was neither appointed by the pope nor within the normal papal command structure. Appointing a national or an Italian rector was a Jesuit internal matter, whether it was a policy decision or due to shortage of Scots Jesuits. Up to 1701 no Italian had been appointed except when the Scots rector died in office. After 1685, too, a Catholic king had added to the complexity.

The College, of course, had its internal life and structures, its customs, rules and sanctions, its distinctive student's uniform, its student prefect or *decano*. The library grew and was added to by various benefactors.[72] One abiding issue was the nature of the studies, rather abstruse for future missionaries and complained about by Ballantine in 1661 and Leslie in 1693.[73] Occasional attempts were made to add some practicality during the course, but the studies fitted those inclined for academic work. A firm link was established with St Gregory Barbarigo's celebrated seminary at Padua, where William Leslie (later bishop), John Irvine (Cuttlebrae), John Jameson and Robert Strachan taught after leaving Rome.[74] There too Thomas Nicolson taught and was ordained. It was no coincidence that a Barbarigo cardinal was appointed to conduct the visitation of the College in 1693.

Much work remains to be done on the College in the seventeenth century. For many priests information is scanty, though dispensations from the impediment of heresy supply one detail about background.[75] Even less is known about those not ordained. It is not clear why student numbers were so small, even when conditions in the College were favourable. Perhaps candidates were not numerous enough to fill all four Scots Colleges, despite the dissimilar role of each. But the achievement of the Scots College in Rome, though far from spectacular, should be recognised. Besides being the main supplier of mission priests, it provided at least part of the training for many other priests, secular and regular. Students who made their mark in later life have been mentioned; the calibre of the mission priests too was high enough to maintain and expand Catholicism in Scotland. Both prefects apostolic were alumni of the College. Thomas Nicolson very quickly stamped his authority and some uniformity on the Church, bringing seculars and regulars, Lowlands and Highlands under his leadership and producing statutes for the country that would stand the test of time. The Scots College in Rome had been, perhaps, the greatest single factor in the progress towards this situation.

NOTES

1. The main lines can be followed in A. Bellesheim, *History of the Catholic Church of Scotland* (4 vols; Edinburgh, 1887–90); P. F. Anson, *Underground Catholicism in Scotland 1622–1878* (Montrose, 1970).
2. M. Dilworth, 'Scottish students at the Collegium Germanicum', *IR*, 19 (1968), 15–22; *MacPherson*, 13. See, also, note 31 below.
3. These institutions will be considered more fully below.
4. The most important source is *MacPherson, passim*. More than four-fifths of this source concerns the period up to 1707. Its reliability is assessed in the same volume of the *IR* (3–5, 157) and sources for the College's history are also outlined (157–61). It should be noted, however, that the printed account in Gordon, *The Catholic Church in Scotland* (Glasgow, 1874), 191 ff, is condensed entirely from *MacPherson*.
5. *MacPherson*, 12–13; T. F. Knox (ed.), *The Letters and Memorials of William Cardinal Allen* (1892), xxxvii.
6. D. McRoberts, 'The Scottish National Churches in Rome', *IR*, 1 (1950), 116; Dilworth, 'Collegium Germanicum', 21.
7. *MacPherson*, 9–10, 13–14; McRoberts, 'National Churches', 118; T. McCrie, *Life of Andrew Melville* (Edinburgh, 1899), appendix vi, 483. Chisholm is confused in some of these sources with his uncle and namesake, bishop of Dunblane and then of Vaison, who died in 1593. For Hamilton, a Catholic controversialist, see *DNB* (a new edition with added entries of Scots Catholics is presently in preparation).
8. SCA, SM 1/3/1.

9. References will not normally be given to *MacPherson* as his account is chronological. Other references are additional to MacPherson.

10. Bellesheim, *Catholic Church*, III, 386–7; SCA, CA 3/1. Protectors' portraits are included in *MacPherson* and biographical details given in *ibid.*, 143 ff.

11. SCA, CA 3/8/1 (1).

12. Photostat copy of the original in SCA, CA 3/3, printed in *RSC*, 110 ff. Information on students' progress and later career is often added. References to this source will not be repeated.

13. Strachan: W. J. Anderson in MacPherson, 160–1. Colville: J. Durkan in *IR*, 20 (1969), 49–58, 138–49. Baillie: M. Dilworth, *The Scots in Franconia* (Edinburgh, 1974). Philip(s) and Leslie are in *DNB*.

14. Vatican Library, Barb. Lat. 8629, ff. 26–7; Dilworth, *Franconia*.

15. SCA, CA 3/2/8. Summarised in *MacPherson*, 19–21.

16. The entries 1602–93 are in the same hand. Original oaths in SCA, CA 3/5.

17. W. E. Brown, 'Essay on the history of the Scots College', in *Gray*, 4–5. The editor of this volume was Canon John Gray. See M. Dilworth, 'John Gray: Additions to Bibliography', *IR*, 37 (1986), 48.

18. W. E. Brown, *John Ogilvie* (London, 1925), 228–36.

19. C. Giblin, *Irish Franciscan Mission to Scotland 1619–1646* (Dublin, 1964), viii, 15, 17. See also Thomas Innes' list of early mission priests in *IR*, 7 (1956), 119.

20. SCA, CA 3/8/1 (2). Rectors are listed with dates in Appendix 6; further information on them is in H. Foley (ed.), *Records of the English Province of the Society of Jesus* (1877–83), VII.

21. C. Giblin, 'The Acta of Propaganda Archives and the Scottish Mission, 1623–1670', *IR*, 5 (1954), 39–55; Giblin, *Irish Franciscan Mission*, 90–1, 111–2.

22. SCA, CA 3/2/1 (1), 34–5.

23. Prefects are listed in N. Kowalsky, *Serie dei Cardinali Prefetti e dei Segretari della Sacra Congregazione 'de Propaganda Fide'* (Rome, 1962). Cardinals' dates are in C. Eubel *et al.*, *Hierarchia Catholica Medii et Recentioris Aevi*, IV (Rome, 1935), V (Rome, 1952).

24. Vatican Library, Barb. Lat. 8628–9.

25. Vatican Library, Barb. Lat. 8629, f. 25v. SCA, CA 3/6/1; 3/6/5, f. 5v.

26. *RSC*, 185 ff.

27. J. B. Paul (ed.), *The Scots Peerage* (9 vols; Edinburgh, 1904–14), IV, 544; V, 356. Without suggesting for a moment that there was anything underhand about this benefaction, I mention O. Hufton, 'The widow's mite and other strategies: funding the Catholic Reformation', *TRHS*, (1998), 117–37, giving examples of Jesuits at the time influencing wealthy women to fund projects.

28. McRoberts, 'National Churches', 120–2; *Gray*, 9–10; M. V. Hay, *The Blairs Letters (1603–60)*, (1929), 122–9.

29. M. Dilworth, 'Jesuits and Jacobites: the cultus of St Margaret', *IR*, 47 (1996), 173–4.

30. SCA, CA 3/6/6, ff. 1–7v. Crusan is listed in Foley.

31. Bellesheim, *Catholic Church*, III, 455–7.
32. M. Dilworth, 'The Schottenklöster', in I. B. Cowan and D. E. Easson, *Medieval Religious Houses: Scotland* (London, 1976), 240–4.
33. *RSC*, 1 ff, 96–7; *Calendar of the State Papers of Scotland*, XII, 107; SCA, CA 2/2.
34. M. Dilworth, 'Archbishop James Beaton II: A Career in Scotland and France', *RSCHS*, 23 (1989), 311; B. M. Halloran, *The Scots College Paris 1603–1792* (Edinburgh, 1997), 6–15.
35. M. Taylor, *The Scots College in Spain* (Valladolid, 1970), 18–39; *RSC*, 195 ff, 202–3.
36. Dilworth, 'Jesuits and Jacobites', 174; Taylor, *Spain*, 30; *MacPherson*, 22.
37. *MacPherson*, 22.
38. *Gray*, 7–8; *MacPherson*, 24.
39. *MacPherson*, 18, 23.
40. SCA, CA 3/2/1 (1), 30; Giblin, 'Acta', 53, n. 48.
41. Gordon, *Catholic Church in Scotland*, 575–6; Anson, *Underground Catholicism*, 47–8.
42. SCA, CA 3/6/6, ff. 8v–18v. References to this annual list or diary will not be repeated.
43. Giblin, 'Acta', 56–60. For Prefects and Vicars Apostolic, see J. Darragh, *The Catholic Hierarchy of Scotland* (1986), 2–7.
44. Hay, *Blairs Letters*, 131–54.
45. Hay, *Blairs Letters*, 75–7; Halloran, *Scots College Paris*, 40–5.
46. SCA, CA 3/2/1–5.
47. Annual lists of priests on the mission are in Gordon, *Catholic Church in Scotland*, 627 ff.
48. Bellesheim, *Catholic Church*, IV, 116–21.
49. Giblin, 'Acta', 61–72.
50. SCA, CA 3/2/1 (2); 3/2/4.
51. *Gray*, 33–8.
52. SCA, CA 3/8/2: Oliva to Talbot (Bisset), 10 June 1666.
53. B. M. Halloran, 'John Strachan SJ, Rector of the Scots College, Rome, 1670–1671', *IR*, 48 (1997), 87.
54. Draft visitation decrees endorsed in 1674 are in SCA, CA 3/8/3.
55. Visitation decrees of 1681 are in SCA, CA 3/8/5.
56. Dilworth, 'Jesuits and Jacobites', 174-7; McRoberts, 'National Colleges', 122–3.
57. *Gray*, 10; Dilworth, *Franconia*, 246.
58. Halloran, *Scots College Paris*, 46–52.
59. Dilworth, *Franconia*, 104–5, 181.
60. M. Dilworth, 'The Scottish Mission in 1688–1689', *IR*, 20 (1969), 68–79.
61. W. Doran, 'Bishop Thomas Nicolson: First Vicar Apostolic 1695–1718', *IR*, 39 (1988), 109–32; Dilworth, *Franconia*, 207–9.
62. Dilworth, 'Jesuits and Jacobites', 178–9.
63. There is much documentation in SCA, CA 3/9–10.
64. *RSC*, 62, 122. *Mgr* before Gordon's name (*monsignor* in the index) denotes *Magister*, a graduate.

65. Anson, *Underground Catholicism*, 96.

66. A. Roberts, 'Gregor McGregor (1681–1740) and the Highland Problem in the Scottish Catholic Mission', *IR*, 39 (1988), 84–7.

67. Bellesheim, *Catholic Church*, IV, 151.

68. Material on College affairs 1701–7 is in SCA, CA 3/11–14.

69. *Gray*, 26; SCA, CA 3/8/4; Roberts, 'Gregor McGregor', 85–6.

70. *Gray*, 27. No case is found of this happening.

71. *MacPherson*, 38, 59–60; Bellesheim, *Catholic Church*, IV, 360–1.

72. *MacPherson*, 56; W. J. Anderson in *MacPherson*, 147, 149–50; *Gray*, 10–18. Documentation is scarce and Dr Brown (in *Gray*) made generalisations from documents of particular date.

73. W. J. Anderson, 'Prefect Ballentine's Report, circa 1660', *IR*, 8 (1957), 114; *Gray*, 18–19.

74. *RSC*, 118–20; Gordon, *Catholic Church in Scotland*, 566–7, 617; W. J. Anderson in MacPherson, 150.

75. Vatican Library, Barb. Lat. 8629, ff. 35–7; Giblin, 'Acta', 55n; *Gray*, 14–15.

CHAPTER 2

Development 1707–1820

James F. McMillan

In 1707, at the end of his long and rich life, Will Leslie could die a contented man, having fulfilled his ambition to see the Scots College Rome established as the leading centre for the training and supply of priests for the Scottish Catholic Mission. Throughout the eighteenth century, the faithful served by these priests remained a small and scattered Catholic community which inhabited principally the Highlands and Islands. Lowland Catholicism was concentrated mainly in the north-east, in the Enzie of Banff, in the lands of the Duke of Gordon. Indeed, the geographical divide, exacerbated by still more fundamental differences of culture, meant that there were in effect two distinct Catholic communities in Scotland, Highland and Lowland, each with its own very different pastoral needs – a fact recognised by Propaganda when it sanctioned the creation of a separate Vicariate for the Highlands in 1731.[1] Nevertheless, relations between the Highland and Lowland Vicariates (which provided the organisational basis for the Mission down to 1827) continued to be strained, and at their worst the tensions which emanated from clashes of temperament and culture as well as disagreements over the distribution of the Mission's meagre resources could generate a virtual schism, as happened during the so-called Jansenist controversy of the 1730s and 1740s. Though centred essentially on the affairs of the Scots College Paris, this unedifying spectacle, in which two Scots priests, the 'Pilgrims' Colin Campbell and James Tyrie, went off to Rome to denounce some of their brethren as Jansenist heretics to the cardinals of Propaganda, inevitably involved the Scots establishment in the Eternal City.[2]

If the destiny of the Scots College Rome was affected by the internal dynamics of the Scots Catholic community, it was shaped still more by events in the wider world, both in Britain and on the Continent. At home, Catholic loyalties to the House of Stuart after the Hanoverian succession to the British throne were invoked to justify the maintenance of penal legislation against Catholics in the United Kingdom, and in the aftermath of episodes such as the Jacobite risings of 1715 and 1745 persecution of Scots Catholics in particular could be severe. As late as 1779 there were anti-Catholic riots on the streets of Edinburgh and Glasgow (despite the fact that in the latter city the Catholic population of the city amounted to a handful of souls).[3] Yet by the end of the eighteenth century Scottish Catholics had already begun to emerge from their underground existence and in 1793, in return for their recognition of Hanoverian legitimacy, their situation was further ameliorated by a Catholic Relief Act which confirmed their right to freedom of worship and removed the impediments to Catholic ownership and transmission of property.[4]

In Europe, the immediate contrast between the baroque splendours of Rome and the impoverished Scottish Catholic Mission could not have been more striking, but over the course of the eighteenth century the entire Catholic world was to be convulsed by conflicts which rocked the papacy to its foundations. In the name of secular absolutism, and sometimes also of enlightenment, Catholic princes constantly challenged the authority of eighteenth-century pontiffs who, in any case (with the exception of Benedict XIV) scarcely added to the lustre of their office. One of the most dramatic outcomes of these clashes was the suppression of the Jesuit Order in 1773, an event which had direct repercussions on the Jesuit-directed Scots College Rome.

Still more cataclysmic, however, was the impact of the French Revolutionary and Napoleonic Wars, as a consequence of which two popes, Pius VI and Pius VII, were made prisoners of the French. The peace settlement of 1814–15 restored stability to a Europe which had been shattered by a generation of warfare and revolutionary upheaval, but the new order which emerged at the Restoration, even if it returned the Papal States to Pius VII and confirmed him as a temporal as well as a spiritual ruler, was no longer that of the Ancien Régime. When in 1820 the Abbé MacPherson finally succeeded in reopening the doors of the Scots College Rome to Scottish students, he, more than anyone, would have been conscious of maintaining the links with the past and of continuing the work of Will Leslie, but at the same time, having experienced the effects of war and revolution at first hand, and having witnessed with his own eyes the economic, social and political transformation of Scotland, he was equally aware that his new charges would be sent out to minister to a Mission which increasingly bore few resemblances to that of the underground Church of the eighteenth century.

The Jesuit Era (1708–73)

The College under the Scottish Jesuits (1708–24)

If the early eighteenth century was on the whole a good period for the College, in the view of the Abbé MacPherson this was less on account of the talents of its rectors and more a result of the goodwill and favour displayed by the new Protector, Cardinal Sacripanti, who not only closely audited the College's accounts but also increased its income from investments and pensions to permit it to maintain up to ten students at any given time. In particular, following his visitation of March 1708, the Cardinal stipulated that the College should contribute thirty crowns towards the cost of an individual student's journey from Scotland to Rome. This was certainly a gesture of goodwill, but hardly an example of boundless Roman generosity. As even the frugal MacPherson recognised, the sum was inadequate for its purpose, since it barely covered the expenses of a student's journey down to Rome from Paris, leaving the impoverished Mission to pay the costs of the journey from Scotland to Paris. Nevertheless, under the paternal aegis of Sacripanti, in MacPherson's words 'the students enjoyed peace and happiness; piety and learning prospered'. Similarly, the Mission benefited from the excellent opinion which the Cardinal formed of it from the letters of Bishop Gordon to Propaganda, which 'breathe a flaming zeal, consummate prudence, learning and humility; in fine every virtue that can adorn the episcopal character, and his letters were faithful images of his mind'.[5]

At this time, in the aftermath of the 1708 visitation, the administration of the College had been recovered by the Scottish Jesuits, who, backed by Bishop Gordon and the exiled Stuart Queen at the court of St Germain, though opposed by the superiors of the Scots College Paris, successfully petitioned the General of the Jesuits to replace their Italian brethren. Father Fyfe was named rector and replaced Naselli until 1712. He was succeeded by Father William Clark, who left in 1721 to become rector of the Scots College Madrid and was afterwards confessor to Philip V of Spain. Abbé MacPherson, no great admirer of the Jesuits, was especially critical of the next rector, Father Alexander Ferguson, who, he claimed, had spent so much time abroad that he could barely speak his native language and was devoid of managerial skills. MacPherson's indignation was also aroused by the rector's recourse to the well-known Jesuit practice of trying to inveigle the more talented students to enter the Society rather than to go to the Mission.

But for the vigilance and diligence of Cardinal Sacripanti, Ferguson, 'a turbulent unquiet man', could have done the Mission still more serious damage by the allegations of Jansenism which, on the basis of information received from his colleague, Father Fyfe, Jesuit Procurator in Paris, he made against the superiors of Scots College Paris. Students *en route* between Scotland and Rome, he told the Protector, should not be allowed to stop in Paris for fear of infection. Sacripanti, understandably alarmed, raised the matter with William Stuart, formerly Will Leslie's *amanuensis* and his successor as the Agent of the Scots clergy. Thanks to Stuart's vigorous defence of the Paris superiors, the matter was allowed to drop and no further trouble on this score disturbed the Mission in Sacripanti's lifetime, despite further Jesuit attempts to make mischief.[6] In 1726, when the secular priest and prominent Jacobite James Carnegie went to confer with his King, the exiled James III, now established with his court in Rome, he was the object of jealousy on the part of the Scots Jesuits in Paris, who feared that he was seeking promotion to the rank of Vicar Apostolic. They denounced him as a Jansenist to the Paris nuncio, who naturally informed Rome of the accusations. When Carnegie reached Rome, however, he was greeted by the good Sacripanti, who let him see the letter and remarked: 'Observe the artifices of our Scots Jansenists, and mark the zeal and charity of our Scots Jesuits.'[7] Unfortunately for the Mission, such a level-headed and pragmatic approach to 'Jansenism' was not to prevail for much longer at Propaganda.

The Return of the Italians: Father Gritta and His Successors (1724–47)

Such was the dissatisfaction with Father Ferguson among the Scots clergy back on the Mission that at the end of his first three-year period of office, they petitioned Rome, via Stuart, to have him removed, requesting further that in future the College should no longer be run by Scots Jesuits. James III and his key advisers lent their support and in 1724 the administration was returned to the care of Italian rather than Scots Jesuits, a situation which, if far from ideal, was in MacPherson's view an undoubted improvement, especially under the rectorship of Father Lucas Gritta (1724–1729), who was entirely devoted to his pupils and to the Mission. Gritta even regretted that he himself had not been born a Scot, so that he, too, could have gone to the Mission, about which he constantly informed himself, even learning by heart the letters sent to Rome by the Vicars Apostolic and shown to him by Agent Stuart. MacPherson has left us an affecting portrait of the much loved rector, based on the personal testimony of the likes of Abbé Grant and Mr William Cruickshank, which reveals him as a man who lived only for those whom he called his 'young apostles' and whom he himself tended day and night should they chance to fall sick. Also:

> When the students received holy orders Father Gritta never omitted to attend, was always observed to keep his eyes fixed on them during the whole function, and frequently tears of joy in abundance dropped down his cheeks. That day he served them at table on his knees and washed their feet; the same he did on their departure for the Mission.[8]

Despite attempts on the part of the Scottish Jesuits to unseat him, Gritta was confirmed in office by Cardinal Falconieri, the new Protector who succeeded Sacripanti on the latter's death in 1727.

The Gritta rectorship lasted only another two years, however. In 1729 he was moved by order of the Jesuit General to make way for a Father Francis Martini, who was in turn succeeded by Father John Morici (died 1738) and Father Livius Urbani, who remained in post until 1747. These were altogether much less happy years, which MacPherson passes over in virtual silence on the grounds that little of interest happened. Here he was being economical with the truth, since the rectorships of Martini, Morici, and Urbani coincided with the Jansenist crisis which engulfed the Mission in the years between 1732 and 1746 and which inevitably involved the College and its alumni.

The Pilgrims and the Disputes Over Jansenism

This is not the place to rehearse at length the story of the Scottish Mission and the Jansenist controversy, but some details need to be recalled. The affair began in 1732 when some of the clergy in Bishop Hugh Macdonald's newly created Highland Vicariate renewed the accusations of Jansenist heresy against the superiors of the Scots College Paris and called for an obligatory subscription of the bull *Unigenitus*, promulgated by Pope Clement XI in 1713 to condemn heretical propositions said to be contained in the widely read devotional work *Réflexions morales* written by the French theologian Paquier Quesnel (Thomas Innes, the historian, antiquary and spiritual director at the Scots College Paris was one of its many admirers). The ringleader of the anti-jansenist Highland clergy was Colin Campbell, a convert who was a close relative of the Duke of Argyll and himself a graduate of the Paris house.

Campbell's principal motivation seems to have been thwarted ambition at his failure to become Vicar Apostolic of the Highland District (a failure doubtless exacerbated by the knowledge that the successful candidate was a Macdonald). Colin was abetted by his brother James, who had returned to Scotland from Paris without taking holy orders and who, with the consent of Bishops Gordon and Macdonald, was dispatched to Rome as the bearer of three letters which had been drawn up at Clashinore, a hamlet in the braes of Glenlivet in close proximity to the hidden seminary of Scalan, following a turbulent meeting of the bishops and a number of clerics. One letter, dated 6 June 1733, was signed by the two bishops and addressed to the pope.[9] Another, of the same date and with the same signatories, was addressed to the Cardinal Protector (Falconieri).[10] Both of these letters (though Bishop Gordon would later protest that they had been written under duress) suggested that the Scots College Paris had a case to answer in the matter of Jansenism and that reform was needed. A third letter, also written on 6 June at Glenlivet and addressed to the Cardinal Protector, was drawn up by seven missionary priests, three from the Highland district and four from the Lowland district. These clergymen complained of the errors of doctrine which were taught at Paris and called for the removal of Thomas Innes and his nephew George Innes, the then Prefect of Studies.[11] On his arrival in Rome, James Campbell was not allowed to present the letters in person to Propaganda, and decided to return to Scotland, but not before he had deposited the Clashinore letters with Aeneas Gillis, a student at the Scots College Rome and later a priest who served in the Highland Vicariate.

The failure of James's mission increased the sense of grievance among the Highland missionaries, who were convinced that they did not receive a fair share of the mission's funds. Though the greater part of the Catholic population resided in the Highlands, most of the money seemed to be spent on the missionaries of the Lowlands.[12] Bishop Hugh was pressed by his clergy to go in person to Rome to seek redress of their grievances. Having first agreed, then retracted, the bishop consented that in his place two delegates should be sent. These were the 'Pilgrims', Colin Campbell and John Tyrie (the latter, sadly, a product of the Scots College Rome), who, setting out from the Highlands in August 1735, eventually reached Rome in February 1736. According to Bishop Macdonald, the commission of the Pilgrims was strictly limited to the matter of finance: in no way were they mandated to make representations to the Roman authorities concerning matters of doctrine. The bishop was right, however, in his suspicion that his unruly priests would refuse to restrict themselves to the issue of resources, since their real aim was to gain control of the Paris College after it had been 'reformed' and the Inneses removed.

In pursuit of their goal, the Pilgrims did not hesitate to threaten Bishop Gordon and even Bishop Hugh with charges of Jansenism: Gordon because he had dared to consecrate Alexander Smith, a graduate of Paris and by definition, therefore, a Jansenist as his coadjutor bishop (rather than Colin Campbell); Macdonald for assisting at the ceremony. On their way out to Rome, Campbell and Tyrie stopped over for a time at the Scots Benedictine abbey of Wurzburg, where they received support and encouragement from the firebrand Father Gregory Killian McGregor, a monk with a grudge against both Bishop Gordon and the Scots College Paris, from which he had absconded as a student back in 1706. He had already been involved in spreading rumours about the Jansenist orientation of the Paris College's superiors in 1731–32, while his fellow Benedictine at Wurzburg, Robert Gallus Leith, likewise made common cause with the Pilgrims and even elected to accompany them down to Rome.[13]

On their arrival in Rome, the Pilgrims bombarded Propaganda with their accusations against the Paris College, but rapidly lost credibility when it was seen that many of their wilder charges were demonstrably false. By themselves, they would have made little impression on the cardinals of Propaganda. This, however, is where the Scots College Rome enters the story. It was the great good fortune of Campbell to obtain possession of the kind of evidence which Rome could not afford to ignore, namely copies of the Clashinore letters signed by the bishops back in 1733. The originals had remained in the possession of the Roman student Aeneas Gillis, who refused Bishop Gordon's demands for their return on the grounds that he would part with them only on the orders of his own bishop. Bishop Macdonald did, in fact, write to him but before his letter arrived Gillis had been made to hand the letters over to Cardinal Rivera, the new Protector who had succeeded Falconieri on the latter's death in 1734. Rivera was disturbed to discover that the letters had been unsealed, and ordered Gillis to seal them again. But the damage had been done. In the meantime, Gillis had allowed copies to be made by Colin Campbell, and since in these letters the Scottish bishops themselves had expressed misgivings about the direction of the Paris College, Rome was bound to investigate.[14] Consequently, a special congress of Propaganda decided by a decree of 10 September 1736 that all Scots priests should be obliged to sign a formulary expressing their adherence to the constitution *Unigenitus* and rejecting the use of proscribed catechisms. The decree also ordered a further investigation into the affairs of the Scots College Paris to be carried out by the nuncio at Paris, Monsignor Lercari.[15]

Lercari's report, dated 4 March 1737, ensured that the Jansenist affair would rumble on. Though riddled with errors of fact, having been put together on the basis of hearsay and calumny on the part of the enemies of the College rather than as the result of an even-handed independent inquiry, the Lercari report presented the Paris College in the most unfavourable light possible, damning it as a hotbed of heresy.[16] Meantime the Pilgrims, lingering on in Rome rather than returning to their mission stations, multiplied their accusations against the Paris superiors and their friends, ultimately to the irritation and disgust of the Roman authorities. They left only on 9 October 1738, having somehow managed to acquire a papal benefice through the intervention of Sir Thomas Durham, much to the ire of Rivera who was absent from Rome at that juncture.[17] Campbell returned to Scotland where he carried on his vendetta against Bishop Gordon and the Paris College right up to his death on the field of Culloden, while Tyrie dallied in Paris, pursuing his intrigues with the help of two *émigré* Scots clerics, Abbé Melfort, William Drummond, son of the Earl Melfort, and Abbé Sempil. Denunciations and anti-Jansenist letters, therefore, continued to reach Rome from Scotland as well as from Paris, among them complaints from two former students of the Scots College Rome, William Reid and Charles Cruickshanks, now working as secular priests on the Mission.[18] As a result, Rome carried out yet another special investigation of the Scottish situation on 10–24 April 1741.[19]

By 1742, the Cardinal Protector was heartily sick of the very name of the Scots College Paris and he therefore instructed the Agent Peter Grant (successor to Mr Stuart, who was murdered in 1737?) to ensure that no student travelling out from Scotland to Rome should stop over in the Paris house. George Innes, now Principal at Paris, was prepared to obey the order, fearing that defiance of Rivera would only lead to financial sanctions against the Mission. Bishop Gordon and Bishop Smith, on the other hand, refused to bow to the Cardinal Protector's order, and sent two students out to Rome via Paris in the usual way. The two boys, Alexander Macdonald and John Macdonald, arrived penniless at the College, and George Innes was obliged to shelter them. Otherwise, as he wrote to Peter Grant, they might have perished and he would have been blamed for their deaths. He hoped that Grant could make the Protector understand that he had acted out of charity and in no way intended flagrantly to disregard his orders. Rivera, however, remained mightily displeased.

It was 1749 before any more students went out to Rome from Scotland, yet Rivera was still adamant that they should not travel by way of the Scots College Paris. The boys, William Guthrie and John Geddes, therefore made the trip by sea, sailing round Spain and through the straits of Gibraltar – a hazardous journey which produced great anxiety for their safety and convinced Bishop Smith that it should not be attempted in the future. Thus in 1750 he sent the youths, Roderick Macdonald and John Macdonell, by the traditional Paris route, where they were well looked after at the Scots College. Rome accepted the *fait accompli* but until his death in 1754 Rivera retained his suspicions of the Paris College.[20] The new Protector, Cardinal Spinelli, Prefect of Propaganda and a close friend of the exiled

James III, was much more sympathetic to the Scottish Mission generally and keen to augment the number of students in the Scots College Rome in particular. Under his Protectorate, the College began to flourish once more as it had done in the days of Sacripanti and Father Gritta.[21]

A Golden Age: The Rectorship of Fr Alticozzi (1747–66)

Jansenism was by no means the only problem which had troubled the Scots College Rome in the years following the removal of Father Gritta. His successors, especially Livius Urbani, 'a bad economist' in the phrase of Abbé MacPherson, contrived to get the College into considerable debt. It was the next rector, Father Laurence Alticozzi, who not only saved the establishment from ruin but raised its fortunes to new heights. An able administrator and fund-raiser, Alticozzi worked speedily to clear off the College's debts and then sought to increase its revenues, mainly by obtaining charitable gifts and benefactions. So successful was he, indeed, that he was able to embark on new building projects, including the enlargement and refurbishment of the summer house at Marino used by the students for their autumn break. Much of the money seems to have come from King James, passed by way of Spinelli, the objective being to increase the numbers of students in the College to twelve (there were only five at Alticozzi's accession).

When the future Bishop Hay arrived as a student in the College in 1751, there were nine students, two of them, John Geddes and John Macdonald, destined, like Hay, to become Vicars Apostolic on the Scottish Mission. Another contemporary was Mr Charles Erskine (entered 1748), later an eminent prelate and cardinal at the Roman Court. In mid-century, the latter flourished under the pontificate of the enlightened Pope Benedict XIV (1740–58). The city itself was an exciting place to be. Among its inhabitants were exiles like King James III and his Polish wife and queen, Maria Clementina Sobieski, who lived at the Palazzo Savorelli. Their younger son, Henry, had recently (1747) been made a cardinal. Important visitors included Alphonsus Liguori, up from Naples to negotiate the setting up of his new congregation of the Holy Redeemer. Paul of the Cross was organizing the first Passionist missions in the Papal States. The Roman College, where the students studied, boasted celebrated scholars such as the classicist Lagomarsini and the philosopher Boscovich, who taught John Geddes mathematics.

In Bishop Hay's time, the students' day at the College began at 5.30 a.m. By the second bell at six, having dressed and tidied their rooms, they were summoned to morning prayers and meditation in the College Church, which was followed half-an-hour later by Mass, then breakfast, and a short period of preparation for the Schools, where lessons began at 8. Scots students attended the lectures given by Jesuit professors in the Roman College, reached after a ten-minute walk by way either of the Trevi fountains or the Monte Cavallo, across the Corso. Younger pupils went to the Lower Schools of humanities, grammar or rhetoric; the elder went to philosophy and moral and dogmatic theology, later moving on to another School to attend lectures in canon law or scripture. At the Roman College, classes ended at 10.30 a.m. and the boys returned to College to continue with their private studies.

Fifteen minutes before dinner (the mid-day meal), they gathered in the domestic chapel to recite the Litany of the Saints and to make an examination of conscience. In fine weather, they would dine outside in the garden and enjoy a period of recreation until 2 p.m. at which time, in the summer months, a short siesta was allowed. They then made their way back to the afternoon Schools at an hour which varied with the time of sunset, returning not later than half-an-hour after sunset. In the cool of a Roman evening, they would wend their way back by divers routes in order to see the Classical or Christian sights of the city, arriving in time for the *Ave Maria*. They then had time for further private study until they gathered again in the chapel for the rosary, which was followed by supper. After a brief pause in church at the end of the meal, they met together with the Superiors, either outside in summer or round a warm stove in winter, to chat and while away a pleasant half hour. Their day ended with night prayers and preparation of the meditation for the following day.

The academic year in Rome began with the Feast of All Saints. Classes, which consisted of lectures and of weekly and monthly oral examinations, lasted through to Holy Week, with only the odd break for feast days. They resumed after Easter, though with the arrival of the hot weather the afternoon classes in the Upper Schools were terminated. The final examinations, or *concorsi*, took place through August and early September and resulted in the awarding of prizes to the best students. There then followed a six-week vacation, or *villegiatura*, in the country, which usually ended with a retreat lasting eight days directed by a Jesuit Father.

The Scots College owned a country house in Marino, about twelve miles distant from Rome, for this purpose. It afforded spectacular views over the whole Roman *campagna*, with the Sabine Hills on one side and the Mediterranean on the other, with the city and the River Tiber winding its way towards the sea in the middle. It was an idyllic spot, calculated to leave an indelible impression on the minds of the students who stayed there, leaving happy memories of student days in the minds of missionary priests who carried out their labours in very different climes and under very different conditions. Until his dying day, the Roman-educated missionary:

> . . . can never forget the sensation of repose and prayer which he experienced when studying with his companions in the Scotch Vineyard on a Saturday evening, or the Vigil of some high Festival, and listening to the clear-toned bells of the Basilica of Marino, as they ring the *Ave Maria*, and then their welcome to the morrow's festival; with the clustering vines and the silvery olive trees at his feet, and the soft outline of the hill on which Marino stands, seen against the blue sky, broken only by the dark and rugged forms of the houses and ramparts of the mediaeval town, or the towers of the Villa Colonna, under the Hill.[22]

The Alticozzi–Spinelli period was undoubtedly one of the happiest times in the College's history. The College, like the Ancien Régime itself, was in full flower and no one had any inkling of the disasters that lay in store after the outbreak of the French Revolution. Nevertheless, the golden age had begun to ebb away well before 1789. The first blow was the death of Spinelli in 1763. His successor as Protector, Cardinal John Francis Albani, was a man of an altogether different stamp, 'the most useless' Protector in the entire history of the College, in the severe, but only too well-founded, judgement of MacPherson.[23] Nevertheless, while Alticozzi remained in post, the College continued to thrive, though the ever-critical MacPherson claimed that things could have been even better had the Jesuits not maintained two of their own priests as well as a lay brother in the College. One of these, at least, in MacPherson's view, was supernumerary, since he did no teaching and was therefore allowed 'to eat the bread of idleness', the more so since in general the College tended to house only seven students at any given time.[24]

Be that as it may, the real damage to the College was still to come. Alticozzi's rectorship came to an abrupt end in 1766, following a diplomatic rumpus which involved the rectors of all the British houses in the city. In defiance of the example set by the pope himself, the superiors chose to welcome Bonnie Prince Charlie with all the honours due to a king following the death of his father. At the pope's orders, all the rectors, Alticozzi included, were removed from office and banished. Not even an Alticozzi, however, could have saved the College from the forces of opposition which were being assembled against the Jesuit Order and which resulted in their destruction less than a decade after his dismissal.

Towards the Suppression of the Jesuits (1766–73)

The new rector, Father John Corsedoni, was to be the last Italian Jesuit to hold the post. MacPherson, who entered the College as a thirteen-year-old boy in 1770, remembered him with affection, and attested to his good nature and general competence, diminished only by misplaced confidence in the loyalty of some of his servants. Despite having to cope with a reduction in the College's revenues following the confiscation of Jesuit property in the Kingdom of Naples in 1767 and through incurring the costs of expensive lawsuits against the Jesuits in Rome, he was able to maintain seven students in the College throughout his time as rector. The lawsuits were a harbinger of the disaster to come. In 1773, the Jesuit Order itself was suppressed by order of Pope Clement XIV. How the news reached the Scots College is best told in the words of MacPherson himself, who was an eye witness:

> On the 16th August, just as the students had ended supper, Monsignore Passionei, nephew to the famous cardinal of that name, entered the College accompanied by a notary-public. A party of soldiers waited his orders without doors, and a number of

sbirri or constables skulked near the College to give assistance in case of need. The same precaution was used with all the houses where Jesuits resided. The prelate, who on that occasion wore no distinctive dress, called for the rector who happened to be at hand. Honest Corsedoni, knowing neither him nor the notary, much less their commission, supposed that they wished to refresh themselves privately with a glass of wine; for it was a standing custom in the College not only to retail wine in small quantities to such as carried it away in flasks, but also to such as chose to drink it in the house, particularly if they were persons of decent appearance. In this supposition the good man showed them into a private room and said he would immediately send them the butler. Passionei, telling him that he had mistaken their errand, gave the concerted sign to the soldiers, whom the rector seeing rushing in, easily imagined what they were about, as for many months the suppression, or at any rate some great reformation of the Order was dreaded. The prelate gave orders to the soldiers to allow none to go out or come in without his express licence. The other superiors and students being called the Brief of Suppression was read, the superiors deprived of their authority, and the powers of the Cardinal Protector suspended.[25]

Thus ended the Jesuit era in the history of the Scots College Rome. Eighteenth-century historians of the Mission such as MacPherson and John Thomson were highly critical of their administration, but the fact remains that under their rule the College had become the main source of secular priests on the Scottish Mission, exactly as Will Leslie had intended. Priests serving in the Highland Vicariate in particular were largely *alumni* of Rome: twenty-two out of twenty-nine Highland priests who went to the Mission between 1712 and 1765 were products of the Scots College Rome. In 1764, seven out of the twelve priests serving on the Lowland Vicariate had been trained in Rome, as had the coadjutor bishop of the Lowlands and both the Vicar Apostolic and his coadjutor in the Highlands.[26] The full extent of the Jesuit achievement, however, would be appreciated only with hindsight, once it could be compared with the unfortunate era which followed their suppression. In the next twenty-five years, the College would send back only three missionary priests to Scotland.

From The Suppression Of The Jesuits To The Revolutionary Era (1773–98)

Mismanagement and Student Unrest (1773–1782)

The commission which regulated Jesuit affairs in the aftermath of the suppression decided that the Scots College Rome should be ruled by Italian superiors drawn from the secular clergy. The first rector, Don Vincenzo Massa, was an excellent choice, much loved by the students. Unfortunately, his time as rector was all too brief, since through manoeuvres on the part of Henry Cardinal York, the son of James III, Massa's former bishop in the diocese of Frascati, he was removed from office. Over the next quarter of a century, the affairs of the College deteriorated calamitously, as successive rectors failed to instil discipline and students became increasingly discontented.

The period 1773–77 was one of particularly intense student unrest, as we know from an unpublished manuscript memoir compiled for Bishop Hay in 1781 by Paul MacPherson, one of the ringleaders of student protest.[27] Massa's successor, Laurence Antonini, was a decent enough man but a poor administrator, requiring the help of the competent but devious Genoese clergyman Antony Rodini to manage the finances. Disputes between the two superiors created factionalism and indiscipline among the student body. Antonini's social and intellectual pretensions made him look ridiculous in the eyes of the students 'who are ever sharp in observing superiors' foibles'. He also dealt out unjust and arbitrary punishments, which received the sanction of Bishop Passionei. In consequence, such was the degree of student discontent in the College that, with the assistance of Cardinal Marifoschi, who was named Cardinal Protector of Scotland by the ecclesiastical commission set up to regulate Jesuit affairs, they drew up a petition to be presented to Pope Clement XIV, which led to the administration of a strong papal rebuke to Passionei.

But, unfortunately for the students, shortly thereafter their friend Marifoschi himself incurred the displeasure of the pope and was obliged to resign the Protectorship. Before doing so, however, and in line with the desires of the students, he wrote to the Vicars Apostolic in Scotland to advise them that it would be best to seek a rector for the College from among the Scottish rather than the Roman clergy. Cardinal Caraffa di Trajetto, the newly named Protector, was initially of the same mind, though he did not press the matter. But, committing a blunder which they would long live to regret, the Scottish bishops replied to Rome that, on account of the dearth of missionaries, not a single man could be spared from the Mission to take charge of the Scots College Rome. With a degree of complacency which attests to their general satisfaction with foreigners in general and with the Jesuits in particular, they argued that there was no reason why the College should not be as well off under Italian secular priests as it had been under Italian Jesuits.[28]

In this regard, the bishops were singularly ill-served by their Agent, Abbé Grant. Accustomed for decades to hob-nobbing with members of the British aristocracy visiting Rome on their grand tour, the Abbé not only neglected the affairs of the Scottish Mission but completely misrepresented the situation in the College to the Vicars Apostolic, motivated no doubt in large part by his desire to frustrate Marifoschi's plan of making him *interim* rector of the College. Though he was well aware that the calibre of many of the contemporary Italian clergy left much to be desired, since they sought chiefly sinecures and pensions and were devoid of the zeal characteristic of the bulk of the missionaries in Scotland, Grant made light of the difficulties experienced by the students and refused to communicate their grievances to either the Roman authorities or the Scottish Vicars Apostolic.[29]

Thus the disorders under Antonini continued, as the rector indulged the bad behaviour of some of the most indisciplined students. His two favourites, Alexander Sloane and Sandy Macdonald, he took out with him around town, visiting coffee houses and private families, and he also allowed them to read inappropriate books (novels and plays rather than books of devotion). Thus encouraged, the two boys 'even went so far as to carry on amours and intrigues which I (MacPherson) blush to mention'. If discipline and piety suffered, so too did study and learning, as the notoriously anti-Jesuit Caraffa, 'generally known to be a very weak man in his intellectual parts', refused to allow College students to attend any schools run by ex-Jesuits. He insisted rather that the boys attend the schools of Propaganda, where there were problems with both classes and timetabling. MacPherson headed a group of students who once more protested formally against this 'confusion and anarchy' and, after a visitation of the College conducted by Caraffa and Passionei, they secured the removal of Antonini.[30]

His replacement, however, was not the hoped-for Scot but another Italian, Alexander Marzi, who rapidly proved even less capable of maintaining discipline, causing scandal by his friendships with women and his constant entertaining of friends at the College. Yet another student protest was drawn up and presented to the new pope, Pius VI (1775–1799), but at first without any result. Only two years later, in 1777, when the eyes of Abbé Grant were finally opened to the true nature of the Marzi regime, did he finally bestir himself on the students' behalf, assisting them with the presentation of another memorial for the pope which led directly to the rector's dismissal by Caraffa and his replacement with one Ignazio Ceci, despite the student pleas for a Scot to be sent.

Ceci succeeded in restoring a degree of discipline by getting rid of two of the most disruptive students. Unfortunately, once he lost the services of his able, if unscrupulous, bursar, Rodini, he suffered from his own financial incompetence and was constantly cheated by the servants in his employment. In his desperation to raise cash, he began to sell off valuable books and pictures belonging to the College at the Piazza Navona flea-market, receiving in return paltry sums which were only a fraction of their true worth.[31] The situation at the College was now truly piteous, but worse was to come. The next rector, Francesco Marchioni, appointed by Albani in 1780, regarded the College largely as an agreeable sinecure after his experiences in the rough and lawless parish of Ostia.[32]

By 1781, so bad had the situation become that, back in Scotland, the bishops finally realised the enormity of their error in allowing the College to be taken over by Italian secular priests. Every year they received demands for new students, all of whom rapidly renounced their vocations and returned to Scotland with horror stories about conditions in the College. The only remedy, it seemed, was the appointment of 'national superiors', and Bishop Hay set out for Rome in person to arrange the matter. In August 1781 he left Edinburgh and, journeying by way of Germany, he reached Rome in early October, installing himself at the Scots College. Delicate negotiations were held with Cardinal Antonelli, Prefect of

Propaganda, and the Cardinal Protector, who since 1780 was once again Albani (Caraffa having been promoted Legate at Ferrara). Hay even raised the matter with Pope Pius VI, by whom he was cordially received, but the pontiff astutely referred the whole affair back to Propaganda.[33]

There things did not go as Hay could have wished. The bishop's proposal, expounded in a memorial, was that a Scot should become rector of the College and that the post of Agent should be combined with that of the rectorship in one person. Despite attempts at secrecy (for Hay was in Rome on other missionary business besides that of the College) word of his project inevitably leaked out and produced strong reactions among the Italian superiors of the English and Irish Colleges as well as of the Scots College. At the special meeting of Propaganda on 28 January 1782, none of the Cardinal Protectors was prepared to speak in favour of the reform, and discretion was left with individual Protectors. Hay was bitterly disappointed, as he admitted in a letter to Bishop Geddes. His sole consolation was that he thought Albani still to be a supporter, but all he obtained was a verbal promise to put in a Scottish rector when the times were more propitious. In the meantime, as a transitional arrangement, the bishop was empowered to send out a secular priest from Scotland who would serve as assistant to the aging and ailing Abbé Grant and who would be allowed to have board and lodging in the Scots College.[34]

In retrospect, it is clear that Hay put too much trust in Albani's promises. He would have done better not to leave Rome until the business had been concluded to his satisfaction. Instead, he returned home, hopeful that his negotiations would enable a Scot to take over the management of the College within a relatively short space of time. He was to be cruelly disappointed. Some twenty years would elapse before a Scottish superior was finally appointed.

John Thomson and the Quest for National Superiors (1782–92)

Bishop Hay's choice for the post of assistant to Abbé Grant and eventual rector of the Scots College was Mr John Thomson, a native of Aberdeenshire and a convert who entered the Scots College Rome in 1759 at the age of seventeen. Ordained in 1767, he taught at the little seminary of Scalan and then served in a number of mission stations before being made Procurator of the Mission in 1779. According to Abbé MacPherson, who had been his pupil at Scalan, Thomson was:

> . . . an honest upright man, had talents and was addicted to study. He had however some natural foibles that made him appear rather in an unfavourable light to such as were not well acquainted with him. His manners were unpolished, his address was awkward, and his utterance embarrassed. He likewise was thought by some hasty in his resolutions and a little too quick in his resentment. These failings rendered him rather unacceptable to his fellow missionaries, and to the generality of Catholics.[35]

MacPherson's view that Thomson was not the right man to be sent to Rome to conduct the delicate business in hand has been widely accepted.[36] That may or may not be the case, but what is certainly true is that the failure of his mission to obtain national superiors had far more profound causes than the Agent's alleged personality defects.

News of Thomson's appointment to Rome undoubtedly aroused consternation among a number of the Scots clergy, who protested not only about his selection but also about the lack of consultation over his appointment on the part of Bishop Hay. Some missioners even carried their objections to the despicable lengths of writing an anonymous letter of complaint to the Cardinal Protector, attacking Hay's arbitrary decison-making and highlighting Thomson's uncouth manners and appearance, which would be sure to project an unflattering image of the Scottish Catholic clergy among the sophisticated Romans.[37] The letter was seized on by Albani as an excuse to renege on his agreement with Bishop Hay and to appease the Italians who had browbeaten him into lending his voice at Propaganda against the creation of national superiors, which would put them out of a job.

Thus the unfortunate Mr Thomson, oblivious of all the machinations against him both at home and abroad, arrived in Rome only to discover that, by order of Albani, he was barred even from entering the College, let alone from playing any role in its administration. Thanks, however, to intervention on the part of Bishop Hay's old schoolfellow, Monsignor Erskine, to whom Thomson had a letter of introduction, Albani's order was overturned by the pope himself, which at least secured Thomson bed and board at the College. But, as if to confirm the anonymous denunciation of his lack of diplomatic skills, Thomson soon made an inveterate enemy of Albani by upbraiding him for his breach of promise and neglect of the College, and by telling him to his face that he would be more accurately described as the Persecutor rather than as the Protector of the Mission.[38] Thereafter, Mr Thomson was banned from the Cardinal's presence, which did nothing to facilitate his mission.

From the beginning, therefore, Mr Thomson's situation was hardly enviable. As he wrote to Bishop Hay: 'I am here all alone a stranger without almost a friend to open my mind to, and all about me are jealous of me.'[39] To Bishop Geddes he opened his heart even more frankly. Having heard something of the objections to his appointment raised back in Scotland, he said that any one of his brethren who wanted his job was welcome to it.[40] In a subsequent letter, he adumbrated on the deficiencies of the rector's character and lifestyle:

> He has not a book in his room but his Breviary. He says Mass in the morning, goes out to take the air or to pay a visit, comes home and dines, takes his nap, goes out to a shop on the course [Via del Corso] where there is a rendezvous of his friends such as the rector of the Irish College and there stays every night till two or three hours after twenty-four [7 to 8 p.m.].[41]

Thomson's opinion of Marchioni did not improve with time. In a letter of November 1786, he complained of the rector's dictatorial style and of his ill treatment of the students:

> The victuals are very deficient in quantity and quality from what they were in former days and I have been thinking often of taking a portion to myself from an eating house. For as few [students] as have been here since I came they had so few shirts that they could scarce get one to change in the heats of summer. Both the shirts and sheets are such rags that you never saw a beggar worse and they are so coarse cloth and so rough that a ploughman never wore coarser for which reason the good rector gives the shirts and the sheets to the servants to wear for some weeks and months before he gives them to the boys.[42]

Throughout his ten years in Rome, Thomson continued to live at loggerheads with Marchioni, who resented his presence in the College and encouraged the students to treat him with disrespect. As MacPherson sorrowfully relates, 'their brawls were extremely prejudicial to the discipline of the house by dividing the students to parties', and the College 'was now in as bad a condition as it had been in the worst of times'.[43] At least half a dozen students abandoned their vocations.

Outraged by his own treatment and by the state of financial penury to which he was reduced on his arrival in Rome, Thomson initially encouraged Bishop Hay to remonstrate forcefully with Albani and Antonelli.[44] The bishop's response was to threaten to send no more students from Scotland – which pleased Marchioni, who was left with more revenues for himself, but which offended Albani, who retaliated by stopping payment of James III's legacies to the Scottish seminaries.[45] But, as Mr Thomson's own material situation improved, he began to offer wiser counsels to the Scottish Vicars Apostolic. Abbé Grant died on 1 September 1784, and Thomson succeeded immediately to his post and pensions (the latter obtained through the benevolent intervention of Henry Cardinal York). A degree of financial comfort seems to have made for clearer thinking, since by June 1785 he was advising Bishop Hay to make his peace with Albani, and to rescind his decision not to send boys. Propaganda was totally against the granting of national superiors, and for the time being nothing could be done.[46] As Thomson explained to Bishop Geddes: 'Padrons are so ambitious of power and so jealous of their jurisdiction that they cannot suffer anyone, much less a stranger, to meddle with it.'[47] At the end of 1786, Thomson again pleaded with Bishop Hay to send out students and to stop writing to the pope and to the Cardinal Duke 'complaining of maladministration and wanting alterations here in Shop . . . I beg of you in writing to him (Albani) don't exasperate him more, rather expostulate with him in a friendly manner'.[48]

Thomson, it would appear, had absorbed something of the ways of *romanità* over his time in Rome, and though he was unsuccessful in the matter of securing national superiors, he proved himself a worthy Agent, expeditious in the dispatch of financial and other business. He also occupied himself profitably in compiling his manuscript history of the Mission which, with all its imperfections, is an invaluable record.[49] His sudden death in 1792 at Naples, where he had repaired in the hope of improving his health, was much regretted by Bishop Hay, who wrote to Bishop Geddes lamenting the loss of 'our valuable friend, whose candour, uprightness, and zeal for the common good of our little Body I have always admired'.[50] John Thomson may have failed in his bid to become the first Scottish rector of the Scots College Rome since 1724, but he has an honoured and important place in the annals of Scottish Catholic history.

The Mission of Abbé MacPherson (1793–98)

Thomson's replacement as Agent was a man of a very different character. In a long and distinguished career, Paul MacPherson (1756–1846) became a legendary figure, one of the most remarkable priests ever to have served on the Scottish mission.[51] A native of Glenlivet, he began his studies for the priesthood at Scalan and continued at the Scots College Rome between 1770 and 1777. Having transferred to Valladolid for health reasons, he was ordained in 1779 and then returned to Scotland, serving mainly at Stobhall before becoming Procurator at Edinburgh in 1791. Rome retained a special place in his heart, however, and when Bishop Hay asked him to return as Agent he accepted with alacrity, telling the bishop it was the greatest happiness he could look for on this side of the grave.[52]

A born diplomat, MacPherson quickly established good relations with the Protector, Albani, whose secretary was one of his former tutors. Having discovered that he had arrived in Rome without Bishop Hay's letter of recommendation to Albani, he coolly forged a new one and managed to get himself installed in College, despite the rector's initial objections.[53] Soon he had taken over responsibility for the maintenance of discipline, since, as he reported back to Bishop Hay, the rector was interested only in his title and in the College revenues, but 'does not appear desirous of the charge'.[54] Albani gave MacPherson to understand that he was prepared to contemplate a Scots rector at some point in the future, but not at present. MacPherson, like Thomson, had therefore to tell Hay that it was pointless to try to oust the rector, given the weight of opinion against national superiors among the cardinals of Propaganda. In a very frank letter to his friend and mentor Bishop Geddes, MacPherson deplored Thomson's lack of *savoir-faire*, but at the same time he was forced to admit that mistakes had been made in Scotland by trying to pressurise Albani and by sending out boys whose suitability for the priesthood was highly questionable.[55] MacPherson even found a good word to say about Marchioni, who was a 'tolerable good kind of a Body. He is far from having all but he has a good many of the qualifications required in his office'.[56]

In the absence of a Scots rector, MacPherson thought that the best that could be hoped for was to secure the appointment of some Italian ex-Jesuit 'without intrigue or ambition'.[57] Yet he never lost sight of his ultimate goal of obtaining national superiors. Hence, at a time when the threat from Revolutionary France simultaneously encouraged the development of closer ties between Britain and the Holy See and afforded British Catholics an opportunity to demonstrate their loyalty to the British State, MacPherson saw an opportunity to work in conjunction with the English and Irish Agents to push their cause through the offices of Sir John Coxe Hippisley MP, the representative of the British government in Italy between 1792 and 1796 and a prominent English spokesman for Catholic emancipation. Once again, however, the *démarche* met with resistance at Propaganda, and notably from Albani, whom MacPherson dismissed, with more than an echo of Thomson, as 'the miserable tool of designing and corrupted creatures about him.'[58] The Hippisley initiative nevertheless prompted the Scottish Vicars Apostolic to petition the pope yet again in favour of national superiors and, in January 1796, MacPherson was entertaining some hopes of success.[59] By April, however, these hopes had been dashed and, left with only two students in the College, MacPherson, like Thomson, found himself writing to Bishop Hay to request that more students be sent out in order to make the best of a bad situation.[60]

Scarcely had he done so when the College faced dangers of a new sort. As the French Revolutionary army pushed further into Italy, rumours swept Rome that the Eternal City itself was to be invaded. While the nobles and the cardinals panicked and prepared to flee, MacPherson calmly made arrangements for the boys to escape to the safety of Spain.[61] Here he was fortunate enough to secure the assistance of both Mr Graves, the British emissary stationed at Naples, and Alexander Sloane, his assistant, once MacPherson's disruptive fellow student in the College but now a thriving merchant in Italy and 'a real good Christian' much disposed to help his *alma mater*.[62] MacPherson himself planned 'to remain in Town to see what further could be done'.[63] The danger passed, only to resurface in 1797 with the fluctuating fortunes of war. Again MacPherson made preparations with Sloane to evacuate the boys but resolved to stay on himself until he was physically turned out of the College. A second time the danger passed after the pope sued for peace on the humiliating terms of the Treaty of Tolentino, but disaster had merely been postponed rather than averted.[64]

The respite was in fact very short. In the meantime, the economic situation of Rome had continued to deteriorate. Prices soared. New taxes were imposed on ecclesiastical property, including the College. Propaganda was badly affected by the confiscation of its French funds. In the midst of this depressing picture, the one ray of light was that, largely through the diplomacy of Sir John Coxe Hippisley, supported by Cardinal York and Monsignor Erskine, there seemed to be a real possibility of an English superior being appointed at the English College. Unfortunately, the English Catholics were unable to agree among themselves who should become the first native rector.[65] In any case, in February 1798, the whole question of national superiors was rendered superfluous by the occupation of Rome by French troops under General Berthier. A Roman Republic was proclaimed and the tree of liberty planted on the Capitol. The pope himself was taken prisoner. Propaganda was suppressed and its funds appropriated by the French. On 23 February the Scots College likewise was taken over by the French invader.[66]

MacPherson had no alternative but to leave with the boys. His final party numbered twenty-two, since he also had to take charge of English and Irish students abandoned by their superiors. Given travel expenses and safe passage by the French authorities, MacPherson and his extraordinary band travelled through the France of the Directory, and reached London in June 1798, where he was much feted as a celebrity and presented to the Prince of Wales as well as to government ministers.[67] A few months later he was back in his native north-east, settled as priest at Huntly.

The Road To Recovery (1798–1820)

For the next two years, in MacPherson's absence, the interests of the College were looked after as best he could by Mr Sloane. The French were forced to withdraw from Rome in October 1799 but ecclesiastical property remained sequestered in the hands of those who had purchased it from the French. In the summer of 1800, mandated by Bishop Hay, MacPherson returned to attempt to recover the Scots College. He found both it and the vineyards in a deplorable state. No repairs had been carried out and the rooms were occupied by squatters. Undaunted, MacPherson set to work and, with the aid of a substantial interest-free loan from the ever benevolent Alexander Sloane, began to provide the College with some income from its vineyards and from rents. He had no financial help from Scotland or from the Holy See, and at one point he thought his plight so desperate that he might be forced to sell off the College. The financial position was rendered even more precarious when Mr Sloane died suddenly in January 1803 and his heirs demanded immediate repayment of the loan. Bishop Hay was deaf to all appeals for help, and but for the generosity of two of MacPherson's friends on the Mission, Mr Farquharson and Mr Maxwell, who paid off the loan with their own money, the College would surely have been lost.[68]

Fearing to see the College revert to the care of Marchioni and Albani, who had returned to Rome in the hope of regaining control of it, MacPherson lobbied to have Cardinal Erskine, a fellow Scot and College alumnus, appointed Protector. Largely through the latter's influence, a papal decree of 1801 finally recognised the right of the British Colleges to appoint national superiors, though they were supposed to be banned from the administration of temporal affairs – a ruling to which MacPherson took justified exception.[69] MacPherson thus became the first rector of the College from the ranks of the Scottish secular clergy but he remained a rector without students since the uncertainties of the political situation during the Napoleonic wars made it impossible for the bishops to send out boys from Scotland.

Inevitably the College once again became a victim of the titanic quarrel between Napoleon and Pius VII. In 1809, in response to French aggression, the pope excommunicated the French emperor, who retaliated by annexing the Papal States and making a prisoner of the pope. Cardinal Erskine, who was deported into exile with the pope, advised MacPherson to sell everything and escape. MacPherson, however, stayed on long enough to lease the College and its vineyard to two Italian laymen and further delayed his departure after the official deportation of all British clergymen in order to keep an eye on its affairs. On one occasion, he prevented the seizure of the villa and vineyards at Marino by a direct appeal to General Radet, the French military governor. It was during this time and in the midst of danger to life and limb that MacPherson applied himself profitably to his historical research, working on his continuation of Thomson's history of the Mission and on his own history of the Scots College. But even MacPherson could not defy the French for ever, and in June 1811 he received his orders of expulsion. By the end of the year, he was back at his mission station in Huntly.[70]

He was not long away. In the spring of 1812 he received a letter from Bishop Poynter, Vicar Apostolic of the London District, beseeching him to act as Agent for the English as well as the Scottish bishops in the negotiations with the Roman authorities regarding the removal of remaining penal legislation against the British Catholics – no easy task while the pope was a prisoner at Savona on the Italian Riviera, and the outcome of the struggles with Napoleonic France was still uncertain. In addition, MacPherson had a further commission entrusted to him by Sir John Coxe Hippisley, which was effectively to make him a secret agent in the service of the British government. A plan had been conceived in London to liberate the pope by means of the British Navy and MacPherson was to make personal contact with the pope and to tell him about the attempt. Unfortunately, news of the plot leaked out to the French, and Napoleon had Pius removed to the greater security of Fontainebleau. MacPherson finally arrived back in Rome in November 1812, and succeeded in obtaining assurances that the British Colleges in the city would not be sold.[71]

Much of the Abbé's time between his return and the defeat of Napoleon was occupied with the business of the terms on which Rome might be persuaded to accept the British government's proposals for Catholic emancipation (the most divisive issue being the question of whether the government should have any veto over ecclesiastical appointments). This required a brief visit to Britain in 1814. On his return to Rome, MacPherson became seriously ill, and even thought himself on the point of death, as he related to his friend Bishop Cameron. He also suffered the pains of exile, deprived of news of his friends at home. But the final defeat of

Napoleon at Waterloo (1815) gave him new heart and, having resigned his commission as English Agent, he devoted himself entirely to the College, regaining possession of its vineyards and working to restore its financial viability.[72]

MacPherson's conviction that the College still had an indispensable role to play in the supply of future priests for the Scottish mission was not shared by the Scottish Vicars Apostolic, who could now boast a splendid new native seminary at Aquhorties.[73] Even appeals to his old and dear friend Bishop Cameron fell on deaf ears.[74] Undaunted, MacPherson set about building up the College's income, recovering pensions and monies it had enjoyed from Propaganda in the eighteenth century. He then deployed the money in refurbishing the College buildings.[75] By 1818 his demand for boys to be sent had become more insistent, and he also wrote home to ask for a priest who would be his helper and successor.[76] When the bishops still demurred, MacPherson informed them that their refusal would be taken as an affront at the Roman court.[77] Despite a succession of illnesses, including severe sunstroke sustained in June 1819 while supervising work at the vineyard, MacPherson kept up the pressure on the Scottish bishops.[78] His efforts finally paid off when, later the same year, Mr James Macdonald arrived from Scotland to be his assistant. He found the College in spartan circumstances: the Abbé had managed to evict the tenants, but the rooms had been stripped of their furniture. There was 'not a chair, bed, stool, book or anything else'.[79] The Abbé's ill health had not permitted this situation to be remedied.

Nevertheless, to MacPherson's eternal glory, his work was crowned with the success which it merited. In 1820, five students (three from the Highland College of Lismore and two from Aquhorties) were sent to Rome and the Scots College reopened its gates to permit the students to matriculate on 28 June.[80] There can be no prouder date in the College's history, and the Abbé MacPherson was truly its second founder.

NOTES

1. For an introduction, see J. F. McMillan, 'Mission Accomplished? The Catholic Underground', in T. M. Devine and J. R. Young (eds), *Eighteenth-Century Scotland: New Perspectives* (East Linton, 1999), 90–105. For more detail, see P. F. Anson, *Underground Catholicism in Scotland 1622–1878* (Montrose, 1970) and C. Johnson, *Developments in the Roman Catholic Church in Scotland 1789–1829* (Edinburgh, 1983).

2. On Jansenism, see the series of articles by J. F. McMillan, 'Scottish Catholics and the Jansenist Controversy: the Case Reopened', *IR*, 33 (1982), 23–33; 'Thomas Innes and the Bull *Unigenitus*', *IR*, 33 (1982), 23–30; 'Jansenism and Anti-Jansenism in Eighteenth-Century Scotland: the *Unigenitus* Quarrels on the Scottish Catholic Mission, 1732–1746', *IR*, 39 (1988), 12–45; 'The Root of All Evil? Money and the Scottish Catholic Mission in the Eighteenth Century', *Studies in Church History*, 24

(1987), 267–82; 'Scottish Vicars Apostolic and the Imposition of Anti-Jansenist Formularies in the Eighteenth Century', in B. Vogler (ed.), *L'Institution et les pouvoirs dans les églises de l'antiquité à nos jours'*, (Louvain, 1987), 407–414. See also B. M. Halloran, *The Scots College Paris 1603–1792* (Edinburgh, 1979), chapter 7.

3. On the riots, see A. Bellesheim, *History of the Catholic Church of Scotland* (4 vols; Edinburgh, 1887–90), IV, 236–7.

4. Johnson, *Developments*, 29–32.

5. *MacPherson*, 120. This supplies the essential narrative. Page references will only be cited for quotations and for certain specific and important points.

6. *MacPherson*, 122.

7. J. F. S. Gordon, *The Catholic Church in Scotland* (Glasgow, 1869), 533.

8. *MacPherson*, 123.

9. APF CP86, ff. 269 (recto et verso), 274: Bishops Gordon and MacDonald to the Pope, 6 June 1733. The importance of the 'Clashinore letters' is emphasised by Halloran, *Scots College Paris*, 110–114, where the full texts are given in translation. Dr Halloran also makes a strong case in arguing that the 'Clashinore letters' were, in fact, drafted at Scalan. See also John Watts, *Scalan: The Forbidden College 1716–1799* (East Linton, 1999), 73–75.

10. APF CP86, f. 270: Bishops Gordon and MacDonald to Cardinal Falconieri, 6 June 1733.

11. APF CP86, ff. 271–2 (recto et verso): Colin Campbell, John Tyrie and five other missionary priests to Cardinal Falconieri, 6 June 1733.

12. McMillan, 'The Root of All Evil?', *passim*.

13. A. Roberts, 'Gregor McGregor (1681–1740) and the Highland Problem in the Scottish Catholic Mission', *IR*, 39 (1988), 81–108.

14. Halloran, *Scots College Paris*, 118–19.

15. McMillan, 'Jansenism and Anti-Jansenism', 17.

16. Lercari's report is reproduced in translation in Bellesheim, *Catholic Church of Scotland*, IV, 408–13.

17. Halloran, *Scots College Paris*, 135

18. APF SR Scozia, vol 2, ff. 369 ff: letters of William Reid, 10 July and 18 September 1740; letter of Charles Cruickshank, 7 July 1740.

19. APP CP 87 (1737–41).

20. Halloran, *Scots College Paris*, 138.

21. *MacPherson*, 126.

22. The preceding paragraphs are based on Gordon, *Catholic Church in Scotland*, 26–7 (quotation at 27).

23. *MacPherson*, 129.

24. *MacPherson*, 128.

25. *MacPherson*, 130.

26. Johnson, *Developments*, 50

27. SCA CA 3/16/3: *A Short Account of the Scots College at Rome from 1773 to 1777*. This

memoir, though in John Thomson's hand, is obviously a copy of an original prepared by Abbé Paul MacPherson who draws directly on his first-hand observations as a student.

28. *MacPherson*, 132.

29. SCA 3/16/4: 'A Short Account of the State of the Scotch College at Rome since the Dissolution of the Jesuits in 1773 confronted with Mr Peter Grant's letters concerning it during that period'. This manuscript is again in Thomson's hand and was clearly written *c.*1781 as a briefing paper for Bishop Hay before his departure for Rome. It contrasts the true situation (as described by Paul MacPherson) with the more favourable gloss put on events by Grant.

30. SCA CA 3/16/3.

31. *Ibid.*

32. *MacPherson*, 137.

33. Gordon, Catholic Church in Scotland, 21–31.

34. *MacPherson*, 138–9.

35. *MacPherson*, 139.

36. See Johnson, Developments, 51.

37. The author of the letter seems to have been Dr Alexander Geddes, whom Thomson visited in London on his way out to Rome. See Gordon, *Catholic Church in Scotland*, 220.

38. *MacPherson*, 142.

39. SCA BL, John Thomson to Bishop Hay, 23 November 1782.

40. SCA BL, John Thomson to Bishop Geddes, 8 January 1793.

41. SCA BL, John Thomson to Bishop Geddes, 25 January 1783.

42. For example, SCA BL, John Thomson to Bishop Geddes, 11 November 1786.

43. *MacPherson*, 142.

44. SCA BL, John Thomson to Bishop Hay, 21 February 1783; John Thomson to Bishop Hay, 23 April 1783.

45. *MacPherson*, 142.

46. SCA BL, John Thomson to Bishop Hay, 29 June 1785; John Thomson to Bishop Hay, 8 April 1786; John Thomson to Bishop Geddes, 8 April 1786.

47. SCA BL, John Thomson to Bishop Geddes, 12 August 1786.

48. SCA BL, John Thomson to Bishop Hay, 9 December 1786.

49. John Thomson, *Some Account of the State of Religion and of the Mission in Scotland since the Reformation, Compiled from Letters and Other Original Monuments*, 2 vols, manuscript in SCA.

50. Gordon, *Catholic Church in Scotland*, 336.

51. See D. McRoberts, *Abbé Paul MacPherson 1756–1846* (Glasgow, 1946).

52. Quoted in Gordon, *Catholic Church in Scotland*, 342.

53. SCA BL, Paul MacPherson to Bishop Hay, 26 October 1793.

54. SCA BL, Paul MacPherson to Bishop Hay, 16 November 1793.

55. SCA BL, Paul MacPherson to Bishop Geddes, 7 December 1793.

56. SCA BL, Paul MacPherson to Bishop Geddes, 1 March 1794.

57. SCA BL, Paul MacPherson to Bishop Geddes, 1 March 1794.

58. SCA BL, Paul MacPherson to Bishop Hay, 7 March 1795. On the Hippisley initiative, see Johnson, *Developments*, 102–3.

59. SCA BL, Paul MacPherson to Bishop Geddes, 2 January 1796.

60. SCA BL, Paul MacPherson to Bishop Hay, 9 April 1796.

61. SCA BL, Paul MacPherson to Bishop Hay, 25 June 1796.

62. SCA BL, Paul MacPherson to Bishop Hay, 18 June 1796.

63. SCA BL, Paul MacPherson to Bishop Hay, 2 July 1796.

64. SCA BL, Paul MacPherson to Bishop Hay, 11 February 1797.

65. Johnson, *Developments*, 105–6.

66. SCA BL, Paul MacPherson to Bishop Hay, 24 February 1798.

67. McRoberts, *Abbé Paul MacPherson*, 9.

68. Johnson, *Developments*, 187–9.

69. SCA BL, Paul MacPherson to Mr Sloane, 1 June 1801.

70. McRoberts, *Abbé Paul McPherson*, 10.

71. McRoberts, *Abbé Paul McPherson*, 11–12; Johnson, *Developments*, 190.

72. McRoberts, *Abbé Paul MacPherson*, 13–14.

73. On the opening of Aquhorties, see Johnson, *Developments*, 195 ff.

74. See, for example, SCA BL, Letters of Paul MacPherson to Bishop Cameron, 25 August 1815; 19 November 1815; 15 March 1816; 22 June 1816.

75. SCA BL, Paul MacPherson to Bishop Paterson, 29 April 1817.

76. SCA Preshome Letters, Paul MacPherson to Bishop Paterson, 23 May 1818.

77. SCA BL, Paul MacPherson to Bishop Cameron, 13 March 1819.

78. SCA BL, Paul MacPherson to Bishop Cameron, 3 July 1819.

79. SCA BL, James MacDonald to Bishop Cameron, quoted in Johnson, *Developments*, 191.

80. *RSC*, I, 46. The boys were, from the Highlands, Donald MacDonald, Christopher MacRae and Alexander Chisolm; from the Lowlands, Alexander Grant and William Stuart.

CHAPTER 3

Tribulations 1820–1922

Raymond McCluskey

Saviour Of The College (1820–46)

When, in 1820, the Scots College Rome opened its doors to accept students after the long hiatus of the Napoleonic period, the rector, Paul MacPherson, was sixty-four years of age. His had already been a long and full life and his biography would have been marvellous indeed had he died shortly thereafter. Instead, he was to live for another twenty-six years, growing older but not necessarily wiser. Remarkably, no portrait of the man survives: it is other sources, therefore, which must conjure up a picture of his strong and resilient personality. His obituarist noted his 'zeal, capacity and prudence', a 'sincerity of purpose', manners which were 'highly polished', and his holy death 'in apostolic poverty.'[1] A century later, David McRoberts portrayed MacPherson as 'no ordinary man . . . endowed with courage and intellectual gifts of a very high order.'[2] This was high praise from the most careful of scholars. Yet surely it is right to be wary of a reputation which has wavered so little over so many decades. The dazzling glow of MacPherson's achievement in 'nursing' the Scots College through the critical Napoleonic era and its triumphant re-opening in 1820 is, perhaps, too readily projected onto the ensuing period until the Abbé's death in 1846. MacPherson was not without his faults. The clue, unpursued by future historians, is already there in the obituary: 'he may, in the opinion of a few, have, on occasions, erred in judgement.'[3] It is unsurprising, then, that closer examination of College correspondence makes for a more nuanced presentation of the Abbé: MacPherson the consummate diplomat on behalf of the Scottish Mission but an irascible and unbending rector.

New Beginnings

The College Register records that five young men entered the Scots College in 1820: Donald MacDonald (20), Christopher MacRae (17), Alexander Chisolm (16), Alexander Grant (16; not the future rector), and William Stewart (16).[4] They were destined to have varying careers. MacDonald, ordained in 1826, became a priest of the Western District, dying in 1872; MacRae died tragically in 1822; Chisolm was expelled in 1821; Grant, ordained in 1827, died of fever in his mission of Portsoy in 1833; Stewart, ordained in 1827, also served in the Western District for several years before disappearing from the records in 1843 (though he certainly died in New York in 1849).[5] Long-serving priest, premature death, expulsion, death from fever, emigration to a new life in the United States:

extraordinary though it may seem, that first intake of the reborn College can stand as an exemplar of the multifarious destinies awaiting nineteenth-century students.

The new students' rector had already developed signs of infirmity by 1820. An increasingly incapacitating tremor in one of MacPherson's hands (perhaps the early stages of Parkinson's disease) resulted in an inability to say Mass and, at his request, the Rev James MacDonald was summoned from Traquair to assist him in 1819.[6] MacDonald knew Rome, having been a student at the Propaganda College (ordained 1796). In February 1821, Bishop Ranald MacDonald of the Highland District wrote to MacPherson, expressing the hope that the latter's 'old complaint' was better, especially 'at your time of life'. He hoped to see the Abbé in Scotland before too long.[7] The indications are that James MacDonald was meant to be left in charge of the College.[8]

Not for the last time, however, would MacPherson survive a potential successor. James MacDonald's health was deteriorating fast by August 1821 when Bishop MacDonald asked to be kindly remembered to him.[9] Eight months later, with tuberculosis now diagnosed, the rector of the English College, Robert Gradwell, wrote to MacPherson (who had only just reached Edinburgh at the beginning of what one can only presume was intended to be a prolonged stay) to urge the necessity of sending 'some other Scotch priest to Rome without delay'. The English vice-rector, Richard Gillow, was staying at the Scots College to look after its affairs in the interim but this could not continue indefinitely.[10] MacPherson set out at once for Rome. By the time he reached the Eternal City, however, James MacDonald had long since expired on 1 May.

Only two years after the re-opening of the College, despite an aborted attempt to return to Scotland, the Abbé MacPherson was back in harness. This bare fact – the unhesitating and generous response to crisis when the hapless death of an 'heir presumptive' enforced retreat from a well-earned 'retirement' – would play its part in forging the MacPherson legend of later years. Yet there is a wider context which must not be ignored. Rumours were rife in the Rome of 1822 that the Society of Jesus, restored by Pius VII in 1814, was ready to take on once more the government of colleges formerly under its authority. Gradwell's note of urgency, therefore, was an astute piece of advice which appealed to MacPherson's vanity as saviour of the College. The trials and tribulations of the previous two decades were to be avoided at all costs.

Bishop Alexander Paterson, coadjutor bishop of the Lowland District, evidently agreed with this interpretation of the situation in Rome. Resident in Paris in pursuit of recompense for the loss of the Scots College in that city, his letter heavy with proclamations of modesty and deprecations of his poor style, he did not wish to be outshone by MacPherson in matters of ecclesiastical one-upmanship. He would see to it that the Jesuits were kept well at bay; perhaps, too, he wanted to curb MacPherson's proprietorial relationship with the College. In 1822, without consulting anyone, Paterson sent a John MacDonald from the seminary of St Sulpice, in Paris, to Rome, proclaiming him to be 'a treasure' and suggesting that his ordination to the priesthood be brought forward. However, he prefaced his remarks with a reference to the Jesuit threat:

> I understand that John MacDonald has letters of introduction from the Jesuits here [Paris] to the Jesuits in Rome. I am sure I am not prejudiced against the Jesuits; on the contrary, I am partial to them; but the Jesuits have an *esprit de corps* and I would not wish it to take possession of our young friend.[11]

Did Paterson intend John MacDonald (like his deceased namesake before him) eventually to take over the reins of the College from MacPherson? The Abbé was not getting any younger. What would happen should he die? This was to become a constant theme in correspondence over the next two decades. In John MacDonald's case, the jury must remain forever out as he was dismissed within weeks by MacPherson from the College and, to Bishop Paterson's consternation, was replaced by an Italian assistant. The rector had found MacDonald extreme in his scruples and pious observances yet, for the first time in unequivocal terms, it was MacPherson's style of government which was questioned by the bishop: 'the tone of [your] authority and command might do more harm than good: perhaps you proposed measures before you had a long enough trial of the disposition of the young man'.[12] What makes this remark particularly telling, and not simply the throwaway barb of an embittered superior, is the fact that at this juncture MacPherson still warranted Paterson's admiration as an Agent of the Scottish Mission.[13] But in this particular bishop's mind, a dichotomy between the Agent and the rector was beginning to emerge. Outright distrust between the two men would surface later.

Bishop Paterson's disposition towards the Abbé MacPherson is indicative of a further context which deserves mention: the lack of unity in the polity of the Scottish bishops. In 1824, Paterson was still officially coadjutor to the aged Bishop Alexander Cameron, Vicar Apostolic of the Lowland District, resident in Edinburgh. With the Vicar Apostolic's best days behind him and evidence of ever-worsening bouts of depressive inaction, his coadjutor sought to present himself in contrast as *the* dynamic force in the Scottish Church, getting things done in Paris. As far as Paterson was concerned, MacPherson was the Vicar Apostolic's man. Two years later, he would work towards imposing his own man, Angus MacDonald.

In its turn, Paterson's relationship with the Vicar Apostolic of the Highland District, Bishop Ranald MacDonald, was equally problematic. Based in his seminary of Lismore and endowed with a crusty, 'seen-it-all-before' attitude to life, the Highland bishop was just as ready as Paterson to take unilateral action. Having learned in a letter from one of the students of the Scots College Rome that the Jesuits were about to be returned to the government of the *Collegio Romano*, Bishop MacDonald became alarmed at the prospect of Jesuit tentacles spreading further. What if they were to claim back all the institutions they had once administered? The Scots College itself might be at risk. In March 1824, MacDonald wrote to the Abbé MacPherson informing him that he was sending out twenty-eight-year-old Neil MacDonald as assistant.[14] 'Muckle' Neil, as he was popularly known, lasted no more than a few months into the next year. Shortage of manpower on the Scottish Mission may have prompted this early recall but, alternatively, MacDonald never seems to have settled in his new role. He was aloof in his dealings with students, probably tired of seminary life. Years later, former students still recalled how he came down to breakfast reading a book.[15]

With 'Muckle' Neil gone, however, the perceived aggrandisement of the Jesuits continued to be uppermost in the minds of the Scottish prelates. Indeed, in the letter from Bishop MacDonald to MacPherson already alluded to above, the straight-talking bishop declared that he thought the new pope, Leo XII, was too close to the Jesuits and it would be better were he already in heaven! Sometimes such fears reached what can only be described as the realms of fantasy – even in formal documents prepared for Propaganda Fide. The *Mission Report* of 1825 to that Congregation, signed by Bishops MacDonald and Paterson (Cameron was too ill), contained a plea for the transfer of the Scots College students to the classes of Propaganda's own College in the Piazza di Spagna. The grounds were twofold: firstly, the bishops claimed to have been informed that the British government would pass the most restrictive legislation ever against Catholics if students continued to be taught by Jesuits; secondly, that Propaganda College was physically closer and had been attended by Scots College students after the suppression of the Jesuits in 1773.[16] Such a petition seems especially extraordinary with the hindsight that Catholic Emancipation was only four years distant and one must seriously question the bishops' analysis of the situation. Money, as ever, was at the heart of matters – a concern to preserve control over the College yet, at the same time, wishing Propaganda to feel compelled to offer greater financial assistance to boys who would be, at least in part, their own.

Paul MacPherson was not impressed by such episcopal dealings with Propaganda. He distanced himself with protestations that they continually refused to act on his advice as Agent. In early 1826, he reminded the bishops' procurator in Edinburgh, the Rev William Reid, that College investments were now worth a quarter of their value before the French Revolution. In the past couple of years, he had at last begun to receive interest on those investments and spent it on the College. His justification of this expenditure is telling: 'The College forms a part of the Mission and the opening of it must have been desired by all. This could never be done till we got clear of debt.'[17] The bishops had been for ever slow in their timing of petitions to Propaganda for grants for the College and, indeed, their credibility with the Congregation was at an all time low. Thus did MacPherson succinctly sum up what would become a (if not *the*) predominant paradigm of the College's material existence: the persistent need to justify that existence in the context of a mission Church with limited economic resources.

While MacPherson might find occasion to criticise bishops, others took the opportunity to criticise him. A leader of student dissension himself in the 1770s, the Abbé's style of rectorship now saw the tables turned on him. John Paterson of Badenoch, all of 15 years of age, addressed a letter to Bishop Cameron in 1825 in which he catalogued complaints about MacPherson. However, the letter had fallen into the hands of Bishop Paterson (young John's uncle) who, impatient at Cameron's clinging to life and behind the old man's back, had contrived for himself the granting of full powers by Rome. From Aberdeen, therefore, it was as the new superior of the Lowland District that he informed MacPherson of the incident, proclaiming that the youngster had probably been put up to the rebellion by an older student, Walter Lovie of Edinburgh. Young Paterson was a 'cat's paw'. Lovie, however, had already been removed to a Parisian seminary.[18]

Nevertheless, the complaints would not go away. On 16 February 1826, Bishop Ranald MacDonald penned the following words to MacPherson:

> Enclosed you will receive a joint letter from Bishop Paterson and me to the boys with the best advice he and I could give them. To you, my dear Sir, he has no doubt said all that is necessary and I sincerely hope we will hear no more complaints from any or all of them. I am far from encouraging complaints from students of their superior, tho' when so many join in them, it is rather alarming, considering the need we have of a speedy supply of good missionaries. Bishop Paterson writes me that he informed you that we would be willing to send you any person you would mention out of either District, whom you thought would be agreeable to you and fit to succeed you, whatever time God pleases to call you to himself. I repeat the same offer.[19]

Surely, one would have thought, MacPherson was getting the message. But a man who identifies so closely with an institution that he claims a sort of ownership through the writing of its history is not going to be removed so easily. Thus it was with Paul MacPherson: when a successor finally materialised in 1826, there was nothing cut-and-dried about the hand-over.

Angus MacDonald (1826–1833)

The public record recounts that the Abbé MacPherson was insistent in his pleading for a replacement so that he might 'return home to spend the evening of his life among his "ain folk"'.[20] Angus (sometimes Aeneas) MacDonald's obituary would state only that he was sent from the island of Barra in the Hebrides to Rome as MacPherson's successor.[21] The truth of the matter is much more complex, however, and there are elements of hugger-mugger in the transfer of rectorial power, which often, indeed, seems more apparent than real. MacPherson's ghost refused to leave the College (even when in the flesh he was back in Scotland) and it haunted Angus MacDonald almost from the beginning of his administration. One writes 'almost' for, at least initially in the transitional period of 1826, MacDonald claimed to get on well with the Abbé.[22] Yet MacPherson seems either not to have been privy to the full picture of what was going on or simply to have refused to accept the situation.

It was in May of 1826 that the Scottish bishops petitioned the Cardinal Protector, Pacca, to accept Angus as MacPherson's successor. Already there was some doctoring of MacDonald's past: the petition claimed that the Barra priest had been a student at the Scots College when, in fact, he had for a short time been at Propaganda College before completing his studies at Douai.[23] It was at this latter seminary that MacDonald had made the acquaintance of another student who would be in a position to promote him in later life – namely Alexander Paterson.[24] It cannot be mere coincidence that so soon after Paterson at last seized the reins of power from Bishop Cameron, he saw to the appointment of his old friend to the rectorship in Rome.

However, MacDonald was a priest of the Highland District, Paterson was Vicar Apostolic of the Lowland District and it was only with the co-operation of Bishop Ranald MacDonald that Paterson's man could be sent out.[25] To inspire the confidence of both these very different men – and the backing of Bishop Cameron who independently sent a further petition to Cardinal Pacca[26] – suggests a man of some integrity or guile or both. Ordained in 1791, aged thirty-two, Angus MacDonald had taught in the Highland seminaries of Samalaman (1791–1802) and Lismore (1802–4), before taking up his pastoral responsibilities in the mission of Barra.[27] There he had earned the nickname 'The Commodore', leading a fleet of boats from the island to Glasgow each year to sell kelp at market. He is described as cutting an archaic figure in his green, swallow-tailed coat with metal buttons, though in Rome he may have reverted to the customary cassock.

Clearly, unlike his namesakes James and 'Muckle' Neil, Angus MacDonald was not a young man when he arrived in Rome on 28 June 1826.[28] Why send a sixty-seven-year-old (MacDonald) to replace a seventy-year-old (MacPherson)? What of the argument that a younger man was required lest a rector should die and the College fall once more into Italian hands?[29] In fact, at least initially, the rectorship was a front for MacDonald to promote in Rome Bishop Paterson's scheme for a new threefold division of Scotland into Northern, Eastern and Western Districts, which scheme became reality in 1827. MacPherson was no friend of the proposals and became an obstacle to progress. The Abbé himself must have been suspicious of the true reasons for MacDonald's arrival in Rome for he seems never to have *formally* presented his resignation in writing (though he may have intimated it) to Propaganda or the Scottish bishops before his departure for Scotland on 1 May 1827. He had, in fact, every intention of returning to the Eternal City in 1828, 'to finish his days in Rome' as he put it.[30] It is entirely reasonable to believe that MacPherson looked on the impending sojourn in Scotland as a sabbatical rather than a retirement.

Angus MacDonald was left to stew over his appointment as rector to eight resident students. 'How far the Scotch Vicars considered the good of the Mission in appointing me superior of their Roman College time will tell', he wrote, claiming at the same time that he had not sought the appointment, 'but my powers were made out before I knew anything upon the subject'.[31] The bishops remained concerned about the precise extent of those powers and went to extraordinary lengths to strengthen the new rector's legitimacy. A further petition to Cardinal Pacca from Bishops Paterson and Ranald MacDonald was sent in September 1826.[32] Even more noteworthy is the 1826 document entitled *Nomination and Power of Attorney by the Right Reverend Doctors Paterson and MacDonald in favour of the Revd Angus MacDonald*, signed by the two bishops, James Kyle (a future bishop) and James McHardy, the Sheriff Clerk Depute of Lanarkshire, in which the bishops claimed that the Abbé had earnestly entreated them to name and appoint a successor as rector and Agent.[33] The overall impression is of bishops who 'protest too much'. MacPherson was not to be retired off through wishful thinking.

Nevertheless, Angus MacDonald was very quickly writing home as the man-in-charge and the students reputedly warmed to him. 'I am glad you are satisfied with the boys', wrote Ranald MacDonald in August 1828, 'and I have reason to think that they are amazingly attached to you.'[34] In the same year, the rector drafted an appeal on behalf of the College to be shown to prospective patrons in Britain. What is striking about this text is that it appealed beyond a narrowly Catholic audience but aimed, instead, to strike a common patriotic chord in *all* Scots. In essence, it emerged out of the contemporary experience in Scotland of some Catholic boys (including two future bishops, James Kyle and John Strain) receiving some, if not all, of their education in Protestant schools.[35] After detailing the College's difficulties of recent decades, Angus MacDonald was at his most eloquent:

> As the present age is so happily disposed to diffuse knowledge and promote the education of youth, without distinction of persuasion, it is confidently hoped that British Subjects will take interest in a ruined, but once flourishing national Establishment, and consider it an act of patriotism to show their liberality in restoring it in some measure to its ancient dignity.[36]

A False Alarm (1830)

Unlike MacPherson before him, MacDonald took (eventually) to his rectorial role like a hand to a glove. It is not hard to understand, therefore, the indignation which emerges from a remarkable correspondence in 1830. The cumulative effect of these letters on the Scots College was to be seismic. One of the most important is that sent from Glasgow to Angus MacDonald in February 1830 concerning the Abbé's proposed return to Rome (his first since leaving in 1827). MacPherson prefaced his remarks by claiming that his funds had run out (he had been too spendthrift, he says, on the new chapel in Glenlivet) before stating that he must

now throw himself on MacDonald's charity. He was, therefore, making his way to
Rome. Almost immediately, however, he contradicted himself, writing that, in
fact, his finances were 'not entirely done away with' and he would be 'as little
burden' to the Scots College. Yet again, he changed tack – he would have to
depend on the College 'for a good deal'. Then to the crux of the matter: he
understood that MacDonald was 'much alarmed' for fear that he was intent on
reclaiming the rectorship. This was a folly dreamt up by others. He ended with a
most illuminating disclaimer:

> Before I undertook the charge of governing youth, I had pride enough to believe I was
> sufficiently qualified for the task. Very short time elapsed when I was made perfectly
> sensible I was greatly deficient and thereafter never ceased requesting the bishops to
> relieve me from a burden to which I was not equal and hailed your arrival with sincere
> pleasure.[37]

Bishop Paterson in Aberdeen, however, confided a quite different version of
events to MacDonald. He was annoyed with MacPherson's usual stubborn
response to his own will in building the chapel at Glenlivet in a position quite
different from what Paterson had wanted (though, since 1827 and the new
threefold division of districts, Glenlivet was no longer Paterson's responsibility).
He would be keeping a close eye on the Abbé's movements and keep MacDonald
informed: 'It is almost impossible that he (MacPherson) would think of taking up
again the charge of rector. But it's best to be prepared for the worse that can
happen'. The bishop proceeded to comfort MacDonald with the thought that the
bishops had no plans to replace him. The rumour that the Rev John Gordon of
Greenock was to be sent to Rome as rector was nothing but a mischievous ploy:

> I have not your last letter here but I think you say something of what we mentioned to
> Cardinal Pacca about recalling you and sending a younger missionary in case Mr
> MacPherson regained the rectorship, contrary to what he had declared both in writing
> and by word of mouth. The truth is we never dreamed of recalling you and sending
> another; but we thought that such a threat would enduce the Cardinal immediately to
> install you as rector. [If] Mr MacPherson took it into his head to resume the rectorship,
> you of course would refuse to act under him, as you could show from our letter and from
> his own also, that it was not as an assistant to him, but as his successor that we had sent
> you. I think he would pause before he took upon him the whole and sole management;
> and neither I nor Bishop MacDonald, you may be certain, would ever consent to send
> him an assistant.[38]

James Kyle, Vicar Apostolic of the Northern District, was more sympathetic to
the Abbé but added his own support for Angus MacDonald:

> I am well aware of the discontent that prevailed in the College during the later years of
> his (MacPherson') administration. Much of that was unquestioningly owing to the
> character of some of the subjects which he had to govern. But, from the enquiries that I
> have made, and I have extended them as far as I could by examining every one who was

in the house whether friendly or otherwise to Mr MacPherson, I am satisfied that so much of this discontent resulted from the rigidity and inequality of his temper, and his not taking the best mode of directing or correcting young people, that I would be extremely sorry to see him again at the head of the house, even though that was not by displacing so active and indefatigable an Agent as you are.[39]

The saga rumbled on. In April, MacPherson directed another letter to Angus MacDonald reporting a most curious development. With the heaviest of irony, the Abbé told the increasingly besieged rector that 'friendship and candour demand' that he transcribe part of a letter he had received from an Italian friend (a Signor Argenti). The friend had informed an Abbé Sala who, in turn, had let the Cardinal Protector, Pacca, know of MacPherson's imminent return to Rome. The Cardinal Protector was described as being overjoyed at the prospect of the Abbé's return for, at last, the Scots College would be back in prudent hands. 'Don Enea' (Angus MacDonald) was a fine person from other points of view but not suited to the office, and the Protector had been constrained to appoint Monsignor Luzzi to superintend him. Pacca had never wished to recognise MacDonald as rector but only as vice-rector and wished the Vicars Apostolic to withdraw him from Rome.[40]

It is the boldness with which MacPherson quoted the entire letter in Italian, not sparing MacDonald the least complimentary comments, which is most revealing of the character of the man. Years of experience in ecclesiastical diplomacy meant that he knew exactly what he was doing. In the same letter he asserted that only the express command of the Cardinal could induce him to take on the rectorship again. However, a contemporaneous letter to MacDonald from Bishop Paterson remarked that MacPherson had written to the latter indicating that if he were to be persuaded to take on the rectorship again by the Protector, then he would be determined to have an assistant equal to the job – an Italian if necessary.[41] Paterson's advice was that MacPherson was duping the Protector, and MacDonald should be just as bold in his turn, informing the Protector of the contents of the Abbé's letter. He also recommended that the students produce a petition in the rector's support.

The said petition was, indeed, produced and sent to Cardinal Thomas Weld, an Englishman, who was resident in Rome, had only recently received his red hat, and was clearly considered an appropriate independent advocate on the students' behalf. The testimonial was a sustained assault on the abilities of MacPherson as rector. It included the statement that:

Before we left Scotland, it was definitely made plain to us that Rev Mr MacDonald would be rector: relying on the good reputation he had gained in our country, we happily agreed to lead our lives under his rule. And we have not repented of that determination. For from the time of his coming here complete harmony was to be found where before there had always been the rumble of discontent . . . And so we humbly beg of you, Eminent Lord, to prevent such a rector (MacDonald) being taken away from us and our

being made subject again to Mr MacPherson . . . We are firmly persuaded that it would
be impossible for us to remain under the jurisdiction of one who cares nothing for the
welfare of us or our College without greatly endangering our peace, our health, and our
vocation – we have unanimously decided rather than accept this to return straight away
to our country and put ourselves in the hands of our Vicars Apostolic.[42]

The petition ended with an attestation that it had been submitted *without* the
knowledge of the rector, though one must reserve judgement on this. What is
certain is that Cardinal Weld acknowledged the petition and commented that 'he
saw no mutinous spirit in its dictation' which may only have been the soporific
effect of the document's tortuous Latin.[43] It was signed by eight students: Stephen
Keenan (already ordained), Charles McKenzie, John Strain (future archbishop),
Alexander Gillis, George Griffin, Alexander Grant (future rector), Alexander
MacKillop (future father of Blessed Mary MacKillop), and John Fraser. Not all had
signed with total commitment to the cause. Alexander Grant wanted it made clear
that his assent to the petition was 'modified' (as he put it): in the event, it was not.

The whole episode does not reflect well on MacPherson. Yet it must be said that
when the Abbé arrived in Rome in summer 1830, he seems to have been content to
be a resident and did not push his case. However, this cosy picture – given the
general atmosphere of intrigue – is one which will require further examination by
future scholars. He was back in Scotland by 1832. This time he may well have
resigned himself at last to thoughts of ending his days in his native land.
Circumstances were to dictate otherwise.

The Second Coming (1834–46)

After struggling with illness for some months, a final bout of fever carried Angus
MacDonald off to his Maker on 3 January 1833.[44] There was no one on the spot to
replace him and, on the orders of Gregory XVI, the Scots College students were
transferred to Propaganda College on 10 January. Some Scots on special bursaries
traditionally attended this College but it had a reputation for harsh discipline and
famously spartan accommodation. Alexander Grant, one of the students removed
to Propaganda, considered the transfer ill-managed and not tailored to individual
needs, despite the excellence of the professors, though this may have been sour
grapes at having to repeat material with which he was already familiar.[45]

However, as described above, transfer of Scots College students to the classes of
Propaganda had already been mooted as a possibility in 1825 and the subject had
continued to raise its head from time to time. Angus MacDonald in 1826 had
extolled the fact that education at Propaganda was *practical* (useful for those who
would have to work in mission territory) in comparison with the rarefied learning
offered by the *Collegio Romano*.[46] Nevertheless, MacDonald accepted the
continued attendance of students at the Jesuit institute. In this he had the support of
Pacca, the Cardinal Protector. In an undated document, most probably from late

1828 or early 1829, Pacca wrote a long letter to the pope, offering his resignation should the Scots students' classes be transferred to Propaganda (as had been suggested to him by Cardinal Cappellari, Propaganda's Prefect and, later, Pope Gregory XVI). Amongst other arguments Pacca declared that it was important for the future peace of the Church that students destined for the secular priesthood be exposed to the teaching of regulars – the Jesuits of the *Collegio Romano* in this instance.[47]

When, in 1832, Bishop Andrew Scott of the Western District seemed to favour, for economic reasons, the transfer of students not merely to the Propaganda classes but to the College of Propaganda itself, he did not consider it a definitive move:

> There is no doubt but national vanity and feelings would induce us to preserve a national College, but the good of religion in Scotland must take place of every other consideration. But we earnestly request that in case of such a transfer, they would be pleased to keep the funds separate, in case that by pious legacies or from other sources the funds of the Scotch College should ever be able to maintain a sufficient number of students, we might again re-establish it. We also hope that in the case of such a transfer, as we must have an Agent in Rome, they would allow our Agent the use of our little College in the meantime for his residence and allow him a sufficient salary.[48]

Shortly afterwards, Bishop Scott informed MacDonald that Propaganda would have none of any of this, probably in response to negative advice from Cardinal Pacca.[49] The emergency of 1833, however, brought on by MacDonald's death, forced matters and twelve Scots College students were duly transferred to the missionary College in the Piazza di Spagna.

Paul MacPherson's role at this juncture was not obvious. There appears to have been no great alarm amongst the bishops regarding the transfer of the students but the lack of an Agent in Rome to represent Scottish interests was certainly considered damaging to the Mission. They had, for example, difficulty preventing the Rev John Murdoch being appointed coadjutor bishop in Kingston, Canada, rather than in the Western District. Particularly pressing was the need to have someone on the spot in Rome to deal with the matter of the late Cardinal Duke of York's legacy which was reputed to contain promises of monies for the Scottish Mission. When, late in 1833, the bishops petitioned Propaganda for permission to send out a new Scots Agent, the Congregation replied that this was not necessary as they could use the rector of the Irish College. Bishop Scott's hackles were raised. His scarcely concealed anger is evident in the letter he immediately drafted to MacPherson in Glenlivet:

> They (Propaganda) must be very ignorant of Scotch affairs and of the present political state of this country when they recommend to us an Irish Agent. That can never be consented to, happen what will. How they take it on them to say that we are acquainted with the Rev Paul Cullen, rector of the Irish College, I cannot tell. I never heard of the man before, nor do I suppose that any of my colleagues know anything more about him than I do.

Scott saw MacPherson's return to Rome as Agent as the only way forward for the Scottish Mission. He appreciated, however, the need for tact in dealing with Propaganda:

> I mentioned to (the other bishops) that your return to Rome could be placed on another footing than our sending out an Agent in direct opposition to the wishes of Propaganda; that it could be made appear to them as if it was a voluntary wish on your part to end your days there.[50]

Duly persuaded, MacPherson set out early in 1834 for Rome, taking up residence at 33 Via del Tritone while repairs were made to the College. He was now an ill man of seventy-eight, the shaking in his hands almost constant; consequently, Daniel Gallagher accompanied him from Scotland as an aide and amanuensis. Gallagher, twenty-two years of age, Irish-born and previously a schoolteacher in Glasgow, was determined to become a priest of the Scottish Mission himself, entering Propaganda College in June 1834. When the Scots College re-opened on 18 April 1835, Gallagher was amongst the seven students who returned from Propaganda, while another five fresh faces joined them the following month.[51] The Scots also resumed classes under the Jesuit professors at the *Collegio Romano* for the 1835–36 session.

In sum, these final years of MacPherson's nominal rectorship (1835–46) saw thirty students (including Daniel Gallagher) join the College community. Twenty-two would be ordained to the priesthood, some going on to wield authority and influence themselves as bishops and rectors: John MacDonald (1836), Vicar Apostolic of the Northern District (1869–78) and first bishop of the restored see of Aberdeen (1878–89); William Smith (1836), second Archbishop of St Andrews and Edinburgh (1885–92); John Gray (1838), Vicar Apostolic of the Western District (1865–69); John McLachlan (1840), first modern Bishop of Galloway (1878–93); Peter Grant (1841), rector of Blairs College (1864–90).[52] However, if truth be told, the Abbé himself took less and less to do with the everyday running of the College in Rome. His first vice-rector, John Cowie (1835–41), was not a Rome *alumnus* and seems to have struggled with language difficulties before being allowed, eventually, to return to Scotland on the pretext of misunder-standings with his elderly superior.[53] Nevertheless, six years seems an inordinate amount of time for someone as unhappy as Cowie claimed to be to remain at his post and one must seriously consider whether Cowie deliberately exaggerated his differences with the Abbé in order to engineer a return to Scotland in the furtherance of his own career.

Cowie's replacement was to be made of different stuff. Cardinal Protector Franzoni let it be known that, after the Cowie experience, the Abbé's assistant must be one 'of those clergymen who studied in Rome', and even made the timeworn threat to appoint an Italian.[54] MacPherson wanted his former travelling companion, Daniel Gallagher, but the now Glasgow-based priest dismissed the

idea on health grounds when approached by Bishop Scott.[55] The bishops then
turned to Alexander Grant, former student of the College, currently teaching at
Blairs. As an old man, Grant told an interrogator that MacPherson had let the
bishops know that if Gallagher was to be sent out, he was not to be given right of
succession whereas he, Grant, was to be given such a right. In any case, Grant had
firm supporters in Bishops Scott and Carruthers. Bishop Kyle of the Northern
District had reservations, asserting that 'Dr Grant would make Jesuits of all the
students'.[56]

Certainly, Alexander Grant did have a predisposition towards the Jesuits,
having fond memories of his former teachers at the *Collegio Romano* (who may
well have fawned over the prodigy which was the young Grant) and always
preserving a sense of grievance that he had been displaced as a student to
Propaganda College in 1833. Within weeks of Grant's arrival in Rome as
MacPherson's assistant in 1841, Bishop Kyle thought he had concrete evidence of
the new vice-rector's closeness to the Society. The bishop received a request from
the Protector, Cardinal Fransoni, asking that Angus MacDonald, a Scots student
whose talents had been noted, be released from his oath to return to the Scots
Mission and, instead, be allowed to join the Jesuits.[57] Kyle immediately suspected
Grant of encouraging such subversion and indicated as much to Bishop Scott.[58] In
the event, Propaganda refused MacDonald dispensation from his oath but Bishop
Kyle had seen enough to convince him of the Jesuits' continuing policy of
befriending clever Roman students and persuading them to join the Society. In an
1842 letter to Paul MacPherson, Kyle summed up his frustration:

> I can never understand the doctrine that is taught in the Roman College (*Collegio
> Romano*) regarding the Mission oath. It is well for us that Propaganda has not the same
> lax principles on the subject, otherwise we might at once shut our Roman College [Scots
> College], or be obliged to people it with dunces. There is room to fear, after what is past,
> that the Scotch bishops may, in their selection of subjects for you, look upon it as a point
> of charity not to expose the Jesuits to the temptation of violating the tenth
> commandment.[59]

Despite Bishop Kyle's misgivings about his pro-Jesuit sentiments, Alexander
Grant became rector of the College in all but name from the outset. He took on
responsibility for administration, academic and pastoral needs, and correspondence with Propaganda and the Scottish bishops. MacPherson retained the title of
rector but his principal occupation was that of occasionally tending to the
vineyards attached to the College's villa property at Marino. When he *was* in
Rome, he kept up his reputation for sartorial elegance, wearing the best cloth coats
and silk stockings, always dining in the finest silk soutanes, taking the air in the
carriages of noble Roman acquaintants. (Grant later recalled being annoyed by
the Abbé's 'foppery'.[60]) Nevertheless, his official obituarist was careful to provide
an affecting portrait of a man of faith to the end, diligently observing his religious

duties, attending daily Mass, confessing and receiving the Eucharist at least once each week. When he died, on 24 November 1846, aged ninety-one, sixty-eight years a priest, the life of one of the most extraordinary Scotsmen of his generation (indeed, of *any* generation) came to an end. Astonishingly, that life still awaits a full-scale scholarly biography.

Gain and Loss (1846–78)

The rectorship of Alexander Grant is exactly contemporaneous with the pontificate of 'Pio Nono', Pius IX. As the new superior of the Scots College contemplated his future in 1846, he could not have imagined the trials and tribulations which Rome, capital of the Papal States, would face over the coming decades, nor the startling summoning of the Council of the Vatican, nor the far-reaching potential of an already developing ultramontanism in the universal Church (and Scotland in particular).[61] Yet his career as rector – and those of students in his charge – would coincide with all these profound developments. At the same time, though far from his native Aberdeen (where he had been born in 1810), he preserved a keen, if polemical, interest in ecclesiastical affairs in Britain. Indeed, he provided a 'bridge' between British and Italian cultures. It was through Grant's essays in the pages of the *Annali delle Scienze Religiose* (edited by Cardinal De Luca, vice-president of the Accademia Ecclesiastica) that an Italian audience was made familiar with the events of the Disruption within the Established Church of Scotland, on matters affecting Anglicanism, and on the Tractarian Movement of Keble and Pusey.[62] Such writing as this gained for him the honorary degree of Doctor of Divinity (Theology) from Gregory XVI in 1844. On the other hand, when English-speaking visitors came to Rome (and there were increasing numbers in this period), Grant was at his ease in the role of local guide, his exceptional knowledge of Roman antiquities illuminating such sites of Christian heritage as the recently excavated and re-opened catacombs.

Studies at The Collegio Romano

The core of Grant's philosophy as rector was the need for a disciplined approach to study. In this, he was aided by the rules of the College which emphasised, in an echo of the Council of Trent, the need for well-prepared preachers of the Gospel.[63] He was much too severe at first, frequently scolding the students and lecturing them on their failings once a week. After representation from the community, lead by their decano (head student), the constant reprimands ceased. This, at least, is how Grant liked to remember himself in old age: respectful of rubric, but human enough to respond to reasonable entreaty.[64] Yet there can be no doubt that Grant was conscious of the reputation of the Scots amongst the students of the *Collegio Romano*. Performing well mattered; national pride was at stake. In Scotland shortly before Paul MacPherson died in 1846, Grant received a letter signed by two senior students, John Ritchie and William Mackay; Ritchie did the actual drafting.[65] The missive waxed eloquent about Scottish achievement in recent examinations:

> To begin with, about the premiations and *concorsi*. We have succeeded not amiss; we might have done better, but considering all, I think we have no reason to complain. Black took the 2nd medal in Perrone's, Carmont tossed for the first in Passaglia's school, and I got the 2nd in Moral. Rory took the 2nd in Ferrini's school, and the first in the other two schools. McKerrell took the second in Chemistry and Joseph Black and Dalbeattie (John Caven) tossed for the Greek Medal. Such is our success in 1846, and if you considered the state of health when the *concorsi* were made, I think you will agree with P[adre] Piancrani and the other Jesuits who say we have done exceedingly well.[66]

The sentiment that 'we have done exceedingly well' was no mere cliché – both Ritchie and Mackay knew only too well the pressures felt by young Scots who found themselves pursuing studies at the *Collegio Romano*. In the absence of student diaries for this period, one can only surmise that the acclimatisation period was testing in the extreme, even for those whose command of Latin (the language of instruction) was good. But, for those who stayed the course, attendance of classes at the *Collegio* and involvement in its traditions became an integral part of the very fabric of life. Ritchie and Mackay's letter to Grant – the earnestness with which they conveyed their successes – provides a tantalising glimpse of that fact.

It is important to remember that until the 1870s, the *Collegio Romano* offered both a secondary education (*Scholae inferiores*) as well as the more advanced courses in Philosophy and Theology (*Scholae superiores*) which would lead to ordination to the priesthood. This provision of Lower Schools was by no means unique as the system was to be found elsewhere in Europe, including Glasgow University. In accordance with their previous educational attainment (especially in Latin), boys – often as young as twelve or thirteen – were placed in Lower, Middle, or Upper Grammar, Humanity or (the highest level) Rhetoric.[67] They would study Latin and Greek authors as well as, at the various levels, Geography, Italian, Ancient History, and the History of Literature. Transferring to the Upper Schools, study of Philosophy was begun, including Mathematics, Physics, Chemistry, and Advanced Greek. It took three years to complete the course.[68] Moving on, finally, to Theology, the emphasis was on Dogmatic Theology, plus Moral Theology, Rites (liturgy and its rubrics), and Sacred Eloquence (preaching). There were also courses in Scripture, Ecclesiastical History, Hebrew, and Controversy (apologetics). In both Philosophy and Theology, priority was given to weekly, sometimes monthly, disputation sessions; twice-weekly 'academies' to discuss and test knowledge of particular points were optional. Towards the end of each academic year, usually running between November and early September, *concorsi* – competitive written examinations – produced the prizewinners who were rewarded at public 'premiations' or prizegivings. Only those seeking their final degree or doctorate in Philosophy or Theology were required to defend theses publicly. Such, in the broadest terms, was the *Collegio Romano* experience.

A Roman Education: A Scottish Perspective

Being able to peer, as it were, through a window of the mid-19th century *Collegio Romano* to see the activities which took place behind its walls is a more difficult task. Clearly, as evidenced by Ritchie and McKay's letter, the Scots were taught by some of the 'leading lights' of contemporary Jesuit scholarship, including Giovanni Perrone (1794–1876) and Carlo Passaglia (1812–87); indeed, Perrone was the author of the foremost textbook of dogmatic theology.[69] Along with others, such as the Austrian Johannes Baptist Franzelin (1816–86), what these professors offered their students was the unique opportunity to be exposed to minds which were not necessarily the most original but were certainly amongst the most influential in forming the theological culture of their age.[70] They were also, however, human characters whose grand status did not protect them from nicknames or caricatures. One of them, Antonio Ballerini (1805–81), professor of moral theology, featured in a somewhat satirical description of a *Collegio* 'academy' (designed to help students get a firmer grasp of material) by an anonymous Scot, written in 1860:

> One of the students appointed the Saturday before goes up to the cathedra and having made a low bow to the assembled audience he reads a moral dissertation, not original, but all word for word from St Alphonsus [Liguori] with here and there a citation from St Thomas [Aquinas]. 'Old Ball' [Ballerini], who we are pretty sure knows by heart every line of St Alphonsus, seems the whole time quite innocent.[71] Every now and then he looks gravely with arched eyebrow at the repeater, or turns his eyes up to the roof of the class-room, apparently bent upon determining the sense of some proposition as if it were quite new to him, although without doubt its sense has been fixed in his mind for the last forty years. At other times he nods with an approving smile towards the delighted student whose mind is immediately filled with the pleasant idea of being certain to have at least one medal at the next premiations . . . The repetitions being finished another student is called who is expected to animadvert on the dissertation, but he frequently sits down after having endeavoured to express his agreement with everything that has been said. Others . . . either attempt to quibble about a word or present us with the important information that they have nothing to say about the matter. After this comes the solution of the case and the animadversions on it. There we generally have something more interesting, and the talking on one side or the other takes a little more the appearance of a debate; but after all we do not learn much that is new, and if we would spend the same time in the study of St Alphonsus or of our *cartellos* [notebooks] at home it would have been spent much more profitably.[72]

A characteristic Scottish whimsy, familiar even to modern readers, runs through this passage. It suggests that some Scots were able to stand back from the educational 'package' on offer at the *Collegio Romano* and send up its weaknesses. Indeed, the same source finds another student complaining about the practice in the Lower Schools of using Jesuit scholastics for teaching – young men broadening their experience between studies in philosophy and theology – a clear

1. Pope Clement VIII (1592–1605), founder of the Scots College Rome.

2. Portrait of an eighteenth-century student.

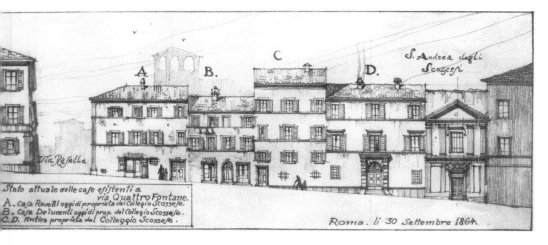

Frontage of the Scots College and neighbouring properties in 1864, prior to demolition and re-building.

The Scots College in the Via delle Quattro Fontane in the early twentieth century.

5. The library of the 'old' College in the Quattro Fontane.

6. Portrait of a nineteenth–century student: John Ritchie (Scots College, 1874–81).

7. Left to right: Alexander Grant (rector), Archbishop Charles Eyre (Western District), Jam Campbell (vice-rector), Bishop John Strain (Eastern District), John McLachlan (future Bishop Galloway), in 1877 or early 1878.

8. Group photograph of 1906, marking the award of an honorary doctorate in Laws to the recto Robert Fraser, by the University of Aberdeen. Donald Mackintosh (vice-rector) is sitting c Fraser's right.

9. Group photograph after the consecration of Donald Mackintosh (rector, 1913–22) as Archbishop of Glasgow in the church of the Oblates of St Frances, Via Tor de Specchi, Rome (21 May 1922).

10. Rev Stephen Thornton, RN, DSO (Scots College, 1891–97).

11. Mgr William R. Clapperton (rector 1922–60).

12. The Scots College villa and vineyards at Marino before 1929.

13. Reconstruction of the villa at Marino (1929–30).

14. The Scots College community in 1938.

5. Scots College musicians (1930s).

16. An audience with Pope Pius XII (28 April 1951), belatedly marking the 350th anniversary of the foundation of the College.

7. Rocco Cornacchia tailoring soutanes (1962).

18. College servants at an entrance to the 'old' College (1962).

19. The Protector, Cardinal Guiseppe Pizzardo, lays the foundation stone of the 'new' College (June 1962).

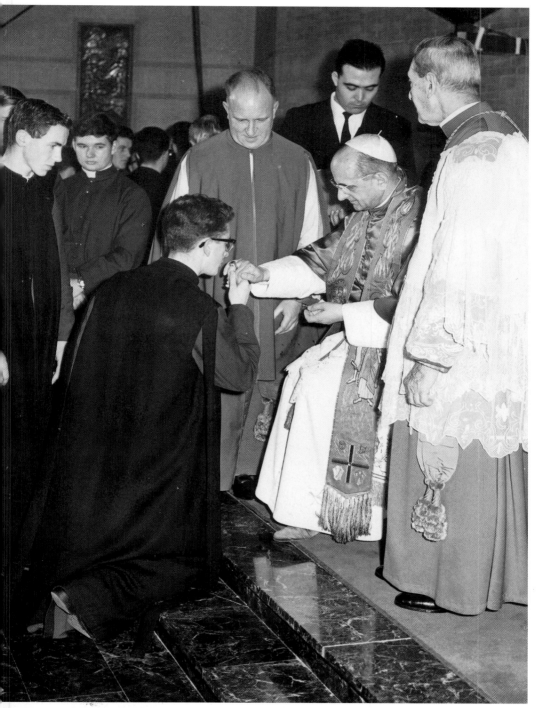

. Students kiss the ring of Pope Paul VI in the chapel of the new College which the pope had
rmally opened (16 November 1964). (By kind permission of Fotografia Felice.)

21. Photograph taken outside the main entrance of the new Scots College with the entire Scotti Catholic hierarchy (present for the final session of the Second Vatican Council, 1965). Thom Winning (spiritual director) is third from the left in the second row beside the rector, Mgr Phil Flanagan. The vice-rector (on the rector's other side) is Hugh McEwan. Lorenzo Martinelli, wh gave long service to the College, is at the window.

22. 'Auld Lang Syne'. Farewell to Pope John Paul II after his visit to the College on 3 June 1984. The rector is James Clancy. (By kind permission of Fotografia Felice.)

case of education benefiting the teacher rather than the pupil. Nonetheless, despite such displays of wit and criticism, it must be said that the Scots remained generally in awe of their teachers. Some were even reflective enough to recognise what education in Rome meant in terms of shaping their sense of identity – as Scots, Britons, and Romans.[73] Nor, when the challenge of the new Thomism began to take a firmer hold in the ecclesiastical schools of the 1870s and 1880s, were Scots unaware of the issues at stake and the repercussions for individual professors as familiar intellectual landscapes were transformed and new breeds of scholars emerged, forged in the full heat of ultramontanism.[74]

Restoration of the College Church

The College which Alexander Grant inherited in 1846, however, was responsible for much more than its students' theological development. Equally, if not more, important in the life of the community was the inculcation of a devotional life based on habitual prayer and constant exposure to liturgies – Masses, the rosary, vespers, exposition of the Blessed Sacrament. The venue for High Mass and important ceremonies was the College Church of Sant' Andrea degli Scozzesi, built next door to the College in the 1640s. Fortuitously, a watercolour of 1833 by the Roman artist Achille Pinelli provides an impression (though inaccurate in some of its detail) of the church's frontage, complete with two Scots students in the foreground, dressed in purple soutane, red cincture, black soprano (overcoat) and wide-brimmed Roman hat.[75]

During the College's years of closure at the beginning of the 19th century, Sant' Andrea degli Scozzesi had become home to a Roman confraternity which whitewashed the walls and refused to leave when the Scots returned in 1820. Grant made it one of his first tasks as rector to dislodge them. Together with Bishop James Gillis, he petitioned the new pope, Pius IX, himself a former member of the confraternity, to have it removed from the church. The pope agreed but still the confraternity's leaders showed no sign of departing. Eventually, in an act which says much about his determination in situations where he was set on a particular outcome, Grant served notice to the confraternity that the church was to be renovated, that work would commence within three days, and that the security of any property of the confraternity still in the College as work began could not be guaranteed. This had the desired effect and, in September 1847, the confraternity collected its possessions and removed them elsewhere. With the students departed for their break at the Marino villa, work began immediately on restoration of the church's interior. Grant commissioned Signor Mantovani, well-known for his work on the Vatican Loggie, to take charge of the restoration, and this distinguished craftsman proceeded to cover the walls with marbled panels and arabesque decoration. When the students returned in November, however, the work was still incomplete and one can imagine the frenzied rush to have everything ready for the church's re-opening on St Andrew's Day, 30 November

1847.[76] In fact, workmen were still hard at it on the eve of the feast and the paint was barely dry as John Henry Newman, famed convert and future cardinal, sang the High Mass of dedication.[77] The interior of Sant' Andrea degli Scozzesi remained largely unaltered until the closure of the old Scots College over a century later.

A Restructured College

Some four years before the refurbishment of Sant' Andrea degli Scozzesi, however, a meeting took place in Rome which was to have significant ramifications for the buildings of the College proper. Miss Frances Elizabeth Plummer was a scion of a short-lived dynasty of merchants in Jamaica whose business collapsed with the abolition of slavery. Nevertheless, sufficient capital was found to educate the young Frances in Abbeville, France; she arrived in Rome for the first time in 1843. It was then that, not yet a Catholic, she first met Alexander Grant who discussed matters of philosophy and religious controversy with her (an intriguing image). Their paths crossed again in London in 1846 by which time she was seriously considering conversion (Grant appears to have helped her out financially). The following year she returned to Rome and was received into the Catholic Church, making her first confession to Grant. She must have been impressed with the new-look Sant' Andrea degli Scozzesi for it is recorded that it was in 1847 that she made her decision to be buried there.[78] Perhaps the attraction of the Scots College for Frances Plummer was that it allowed a person of her 'reduced' circumstances to acquire the status of benefactress in an age when the patronage of religious institutions remained a principal outlet for gentrified lay munificence. She had an eager eye to posterity. To what extent she could claim to have been a co-architect in the plans which began to evolve in Alexander Grant's mind regarding the restructuring of the College building, it is difficult to establish. What is incontestable is that she presented the College with a sizeable donation in 1854 as a contribution towards purchasing some houses adjacent to it.[79]

The decision to enlarge the College was an act of singular courage on Grant's part – some might have described it as foolhardy. Between 1848 and 1850, Pope Pius IX had to flee the city during the period that a short-lived Roman Republic was created. Writing to Grant from Glasgow, Bishop John Murdoch, Vicar Apostolic of the Western District, noted that troubles were not confined to Rome, and feared that 'all will end in a European War'.[80] Such cataclysmic fears proved unfounded, but there were still fears for the future in the Rome of the 1850s – particularly felt by national colleges – which needed to be allayed by the vigorous reimposition of Pius IX's temporal rule. That hope soon evaporated when all the Papal States, with the exception of Rome itself, fell to the armies of the Italian *risorgimento* in 1860 and the pope's control of his erstwhile capital depended on the soldiers provided by the French emperor, Napoleon III. Without stretching the point too far, the rebuilding of the Scots College in the 1860s must be reinterpreted in the light of this distinctive historical context. It was no mere building project. It was born of the same spirit which had moved Andrew Scott, the future bishop, to build St Andrew's (later the cathedral) on the banks of the River Clyde, Glasgow, in 1815–16. It manifested an enormous faith in providence – something which no historian's datafile can quantify. Above all, it betrayed considerable self-confidence – and confidence in a continental future for Scots at the heart of a Europe in turmoil. Scots would take their chances with the peoples of other nations. Indeed, it is far from a simple coincidence that plans for a refurbished Scots College were gathering pace as a North American College was being founded in 1859. The Scots were bathing in those same waters of resilient bravado which were flowing through Rome as surely as the Tiber.

There was always, however, the sober matter of the economics of any planned extension to focus the mind of the rector. In 1858, Grant made a tour of the missions in Scotland, achieving offerings and subscriptions of around £2000. What really made the difference between cosmetic facelift and substantial rebuilding was the windfall which came the College's way in 1861 when Grant was informed that Pius IX had ordered that monies to be paid in compensation for the loss of the Scottish monastery of Ratisbon in Bavaria should be used for the Scots College project. It was a substantial sum – £10,000 – and it transformed the possibilities.[81] Now a complete rebuilding was the goal and, in March 1864, the demolition of the old Scots College buildings began, along with the neighbouring Casa De Lucenti and the Casa Ravelli. In the meantime, the College community moved to 159 Via delle Quattro Fontane, renting two stories and a garden behind.[82] The foundation stone of the new building was laid on St Margaret's Day 1864, but already problems were beginning to emerge with respect to the extraordinary depths which had to be dug before finding solid ground. Such a costly procedure had not entered into any of Grant's fiscal calculations and it became a principal cause of the parlous state of the College's finances on the completion of the building in 1869. The debt incurred seriously inhibited the recruitment of students to the College in the immediate future (there were only three in 1876): in effect, there was a new building which the Mission could not afford to populate.

The architect traditionally credited with the restoration of the College was one of the most famous in Rome, Luigi Poletti, responsible for the restoration of the Basilica of St Paul's-outside-the-walls on the Ostian Way. The extent of his actual involvement in the design must be seriously queried, however. A future rector, William Clapperton, once remarked that Poletti had sketched the façade and then told an apprentice to get on with some rooms at the back.[83] Indubitably, the building could never be acclaimed an architectural wonder. An anonymous nineteenth-century judgement was that it was an example of the great weakness of contemporary architecture, with no real integration of external features and internal functions.[84]

As with the opening of the restored Sant' Andrea degli Scozzesi twenty-two years before, the new Scots College was solemnly inaugurated on St Andrew's Day (1869). High Mass was sung in the morning and was followed by a 'grand dinner'. The eighteen-year-old Thomas Crumly, recently arrived from Govan to begin his College career, informed his parents that the opening was attended by Archbishops Manning of Westminster and Spalding of Baltimore, two bishops from Nova Scotia, Bishops John Strain of the Eastern District and John McDonald of the Northern District, 'several other Scotch and English bishops', and various rectors of colleges, as well as a multitude of 'respectable English gentlemen'. The Irish Cardinal Cullen and the Third Marquis of Bute should have been present but were delayed.[85] Here was a hint of the cosmopolitan world which Roman students found at their doorstep, the universality of nineteenth-century Catholicism made flesh. It was also an indicator of how vital elite patrons had become in the Scottish Church, especially converts like Bute. Rome introduced students to a social network which, when ordained and back in Scotland, might be called on in times of necessity and in building schools and churches.

First Vatican Council and an Audience with Pius IX

Archbishops Manning and Spalding, of course, did not make the journey to Rome solely on account of the opening of the new Scots College. They were in Rome to attend the Vatican Council which had been convened by Pius IX and was duly opened on Wednesday, 8 December, just over a week later. One of the Scots students, Angus Macfarlane, ordained priest in 1868, acted as a stenographer during the sessions and, no doubt, witnessed the solemn definition of papal infallibility in 1870.[86] These were now heady days, with the withdrawal of the protective lines of French troops from Rome, the adjournment of the Council, and the surrender of papal Rome to the Italian nationalists in September. Reflecting on these events, one begins to appreciate how ultramontanism for the young Scots, in common with other ecclesiastical students in Rome, was less of a cerebral philosophy and more of an emotional reaction. The image of Pius IX as persecuted martyr, or 'prisoner of the Vatican', was all the more powerful when viewed at close range. On 4 January 1871, a few months after the Italian troops had entered the city, the Scots had an audience with the pope. Thomas Crumly's account of the meeting vividly evokes the sentimental bond that was felt with 'the poor old man, amidst all his sorrows and afflictions'.[87] A purse of 200 francs was presented to Pius, along with a written address assuring the pope of loyalty 'in this hour of your anguish'.[88] These feelings did not disappear on return to Scotland; in most cases, they lasted a lifetime, influencing the outlook of the Catholic community at every level.

Supporter of the Jesuits

The occupation of Rome in 1870 evoked dark forebodings in the rectors of the national colleges. The fear of expropriation of property was very real. Only four days after the entry of the Italian troops, Alexander Grant joined the rectors of the Irish and English Colleges in drafting a letter of thanks to the British acting diplomatic agent, Harry Clarke Jervoise. This gentleman had acted as an intermediary in obtaining assurances of protection for their Colleges in Rome and their villa properties at Marino, Tivoli and Monte Porzio.[89] The *Collegio Romano*, however, was not so fortunate. With anti-clerical mobs taking to the piazzas of Rome, urging 'Death to the Priests', and the Italian authorities determined to make gestures which would encapsulate the transition of the city from clerical-ridden enclave to capital city of a 'modern' nation, it fast became clear that the future security of the *Collegio Romano* could not be guaranteed. Various proposals were touted, including turning the buildings into barracks or a great new *liceo* (which it eventually became) or even a Senate House. Such uncertainty inevitably brought chaos to students' courses. Grant, as the senior rector of a national college in Rome, chaired several meetings of his fellow superiors and, on their behalf, drafted testimonials supporting the beleaguered Jesuit professors.[90] Intriguingly, the Scots rector tried to get the British government to negotiate with the Italians on the grounds that the Jesuits of the *Collegio Romano* were providing education for British citizens (amongst others) and, therefore, their institution should be treated as if it had diplomatic status and its properties inviolable. Gladstone's administration was for none of it and, in a most revealing response, declared the British Colleges to be *Italian* rather than British institutions.[91]

Despite these initiatives, the suppression of the *Collegio Romano* came to pass in 1873. One of Thomas Crumly's letters relates how, in the immediate aftermath, the Jesuits continued their classes elsewhere, theology in the German College, philosophy in the Scots College.[92] This was partly a recognition of the loyal support of the Scots throughout the crisis but, more pragmatically, the College was a substantially new building with space available. After the intake of four boys, including Crumly, in 1869, events and economics meant that there were no new students until four arrived in 1874, and a further eight in 1877.[93] The Scots, however, did more than host lectures. The College became the temporary home of the Jesuit rector, Fr Valerio Cardella SJ, and an assistant, Fr Philippo Monaci SJ. Grant had written to Cardella from the Scots villa at Marino on 22 October 1873:

> The Vice-rector [James Campbell] informs me that you would not be unhappy to stay with us in the College in these misfortunate times. I wish to answer straightaway that I should be very pleased indeed to have you as guest. We shall be in Rome on the evening of Friday 24th of this month and your chambers shall be immediately prepared for you. You will be free to take up residence whenever you wish.[94]

Cardella's warm-hearted reply, lauding Grant's generous offer and asking, not for chambers, but for one room for himself and another for his books, must surely not be dismissed as no more than conventional courtesy.[95] Cardella was in a geniune fix and under great stress. He would not have accepted the Scots' offer if he had not esteemed Grant highly. It says much about the stature of the Scots College, as Grant's period of office drew to a close, that the rector of the *Collegio Romano* in a time of trial did *not* consider it an unworthy address. What was to happen over the next twenty years must not be allowed to dull that perception.

Nadir and Revival (1878–1922)

Death came for Alexander Grant on 26 March 1878. He lingered in his final illness long enough to be informed that the new pope, Leo XIII, a *Collegio Romano* classmate of long ago, had restored the Catholic hierarchy in Scotland. He was the first member of the Scots community to be buried in the College's vault in the *Campo Santo* (the municipal cemetery), rather than in Sant' Andrea degli Scozzesi, due to a law which had recently come into force discontinuing church interments.

James Campbell (1878–97)

In his latter years, Grant had spent more and more of his time away from Rome, ruling by correspondence from Civitavecchia where he enjoyed the sea air, and to where John Richie remembered being taken as a newly-arrived student in 1874.[96] The man responsible for acting on Grant's instructions (which left little room for independent initiative) was his vice-rector, James Campbell. Grant had wanted assistance from the outset of his rectorship but appeals to the bishops in Scotland had resulted only in permission to employ a senior student.[97] Subsequently, William Paterson remained in the College after ordination for one academic year only, 1848–49.[98] Campbell (like Grant, an Aberdonian, born in 1841) arrived as assistant in 1866 and seems to have found Grant's unrelenting insistence on a hierarchy of remits unbearable almost from the beginning. Clearly, Campbell was expecting to be treated differently. He had been a student under Grant since 1858, taking the degree of Doctor of Philosophy, and, after ordination in 1865, had spent two months in Scotland before returning in his new capacity to Rome.[99] Yet nothing seems to have changed in the relationship between the two men. In a *memorandum* from Grant to his assistant – highly critical of Campbell taking the rector's chair in the refectory when he was absent – the rector stated categorically that:

> The rector is the sole superior of the College. He alone is responsible for its good government and he alone is answerable to the higher authorities for whatever may go amiss. The vice-rector is the simple executor of the wishes of the rector in the government of the College, so far as the rector may choose to use him as such.[100]

One can only speculate on the augmentative impact of Grant's treatment for twelve years of Campbell, a man whose naturally choleric nature was not helped by recurrent ill-health.[101] One predicament in which Campbell found himself, however – certainly *not* of Grant's making – must have left its mark on the future rector. On 26 October 1868, while staying at the Scots' summer villa in Marino, Campbell was kidnapped by armed brigands who proceeded to play mind-games with him, threatening physical violence and death. His ordeal lasted at least forty-eight hours before the arrival of police and soldiers scared off his captors and won him his freedom.[102] Insufficient weight has been given to this event in assessments of Campbell: contemporaries, including his *Scottish Catholic Directory* obituarist, recounted it with all the melodrama of a Victorian penny-novel. It made excellent copy. Nowadays, Campbell would immediately have been given leave for a lengthy spell of stress counselling.

When Campbell finally succeeded to the rectorship and (one must not forget) Roman agency of the Scottish Church in 1878, he was determined to be his own man. A person of some psychological complexity, therefore, was launched on an unchartered course which was destined to end in 1897 with his resignation, the College poised on the edge of a financial precipice, and no small amount of bitterness and recrimination. As if this catalogue of disaster were not sufficient legacy to posterity, Campbell was called on to deal with the notorious case of Frederick Rolfe – 'Baron Corvo'; Rolfe lampooned him in a thinly-veiled caricature in his brilliant novel of 1904, *Hadrian VII*.[103] Hindsight can be a stern judge and, of all the nineteenth-century rectors, Campbell has suffered most.

But does Campbell deserve his lamentable reputation? The weight of Rolfe's *Hadrian VII* as evidence must be firmly counter-balanced. It is a work of *literature*, not history, and, indeed, the description of the much put-upon ecclesiastical student, unable to follow his true vocation, became something of a *leitmotiv* in other works by the same author.[104] Rolfe had arrived at the College on 7 December 1889, sent on trial by Archbishop James Smith of St Andrews and Edinburgh, having already been expelled from the English seminary at Oscott.[105] By 3 May 1890, he was expelled again, this time by the Scots – literally carried out by students, still lying on his mattress, proclaiming injustice, and left on the Quattro Fontane. Undignified and painful, no doubt. The details of the case have been argued elsewhere, by Alexander MacWilliam and Brocard Sewell amongst others, but there is little to persuade one otherwise than that Rolfe, arriving unannounced and a latecomer (the academic term had already begun), simply did not possess the character to be acceptable as a candidate for priesthood. Campbell, like rectors before and since, faced with the problem of students sent 'on trial' by bishops, had to make a decision. Perhaps, ultimately, the system failed Rolfe – a seminary system so regimented as to be unable to accommodate such an idiosyncratic aesthete (who had taken to wearing a soutane in the streets of Edinburgh *before* setting out for Rome). But this 'system' was a product of the age

– no ecclesiastical college in late 19th-century Rome could have coped with Rolfe. In sum, Campbell's reputation as rector should not stand or fall on the testimony of Rolfe alone. Unlike the proverbial mountain, it would be wrong to make *Hadrian VII* the final word on Campbell's rectorship simply because it is *there*.

In fact, the verdict of contemporaries on the gaunt Campbell was a mixed one – perhaps the appropriate response to his enigmatic demeanour. Another former student, Duncan MacVarish, (expelled from the College on 8 July 1890 – only weeks after Rolfe – for flouting the rules), also unleashed a broadside at his former rector, in a novel written under the pseudonym John Crane.[106] As with Rolfe, the reader was meant to be both entertained and impressed by the intellectual fireworks of MacVarish's creative mind – a self-affirming riposte to the community of supposed dullards which had rejected him. In truth, MacVarish is a less than satisfactory witness. For a more temperate memory of the Campbell era, one turns to Adrian Fortescue, student at the College from 1891 to 1894.[107] Systematic and rational, Fortescue was not one for flights of fancy. (His book of 1917 on liturgical rubrics would become *the* guide for their proper implementation until the 1960s.[108]) In 1913, he wrote to Campbell's successor after a visit to Rome:

> I have not been in Rome since I came down from the Scots College, nineteen years ago. Since then I had a long period at Austrian and German universities; so that the days when I wore a purple cassock and red belt seem very remote to me. They were not altogether happy days, less so (if I may venture to say this) than if I had had the good fortune to be a student at a later period, under more favourable conditions. But those early years of one's life, when one was first considering the question of being a priest, are naturally full of memories. It was a great and really pleasant emotion to see again the old chapel and garden and corridors and what was once my room. Perhaps I may venture to say this too, that since the other day, when I saw again the old places and the uniform I once wore, I have already a much kindlier impression of my college at Rome and am much more inclined, not only to remember with gratitude my German years, but also to count myself with pride a student of the Scots College.[109]

Fortescue's sense of fairness pervades his writing. The allusion to unhappy times under Campbell is unmistakable but there is no vitriol; his visit to the College summoned feelings of nostalgia, not nausea. This is not surprising. The fact is that the Campbell era produced some of the most enthusiastic *alumni* of the College. Indeed, the Scots College Society, begun in 1904 to preserve links with the College and keep alive a sense of Roman identity amongst priests working in Scottish missions, was founded by a former student of the Campbell years, Gerald Stack.[110] Many early members of the Society were unlikely to remember Campbell with great affection but, nevertheless, there are some recorded opinions which suggest that, having had the good sense to get the measure of the man, one kept a respectful distance and found a *modus vivendi*. John Ritchie summed his rector up as 'a generous little man and the soul of honour', adding in another essay that 'beneath [his] infirmity lay a brave and generous heart which was essentially kind'.[111] Many years later, Fr Denis Sheil put on record that his years at the College (1884–89), were 'very, very happy, my fellow-students always most kind and considerate, and the rector, Mgr Campbell, most understanding'.[112]

Of course, these brief references do not tell the whole story about Campbell – any more than Rolfe's or MacVarish's more extended efforts. But they *do* alert historians to the need for further research. Campbell is a figure who defies pigeon-holing. When the Australian Josephite sister, Mother Mary MacKillop, was in dispute with her local bishop in 1884–85 over the imposition of an oath of silence on her nuns, it was James Campbell who became her champion in Rome, making representations to the Curia, and even exposing the duplicity of her ordinary in claiming to have papal approval for a Visitation of her order when, in fact, he had no such thing.[113] Campbell clearly knew ecclesiastical high-handedness when he saw it. Admittedly, these were early days in the Campbell rectorship, a period when there was still sufficient flexibility in his character to allow for such unselfish action. But the MacKillop episode might also be interpreted as an advance warning of the obsessiveness which was to develop in his later years when so much of his energy was spent on the foundation and spiritual direction of a community of nuns, the Poor Servants of the Mother of God, in the Via San Sebastiano, Rome.[114] This initiative was to end in scandal with the departure and apostasy of the abbess – another nail in the coffin of Campbell's reputation.

Only one student of the Campbell epoch, John Meany, has left behind a diary detailed enough to throw light on the experience.[115] Campbell makes little impact, except in passing, as Meany makes remarks about his friends, professors, and outings. It is not untypical for him to record (as in his entry for 13 February 1886) the imminent arrival of a billiard table or the taking of a community photograph by a Frenchman. This is not just tittle-tattle. Even such brief entries allow one a more three-dimensional impression of College life in the period – reminding one that behind the stiff, starched poses of early photographs of the community lay real flesh-and-blood characters. Indeed, the students who inhabit Meany's pages are far from being automatons. But Meany provides other useful correctives – especially to those who would characterise the biblical scholarship of the late nineteenth century as uniformly static. An entry for 17 November 1886 refers to a lecture delivered by one of the most famous Jesuit scholars of the day. Rudolf Cornely SJ had refused to call the Gospels 'historical books. They are dogmatic and, in proving their various theses, historical materials are used.' Twenty years later, under Pius X, that remark would have been considered both suspect and dangerous. Plainly, the much narrower approach to Catholic biblical studies, enforced in the first decades of the twentieth century, cannot be automatically attributed to this earlier period.

Meany left in 1887 and did not witness the steady decline of his rector. In 1890 Campbell was informed that he had heart problems. He had been rector for twelve years; despite the growing infirmity, however, he would remain in post for another seven, retiring in May 1897. In the final analysis, Campbell, like Grant before him, probably suffered from being in the job far too long. He got pastorally stale and financially reckless. Bursaries were used to pay off debts but the debts kept mounting.[116] He lost interest. Yet even in retirement he was not completely forgotten by his former students, a number of whom sent him a gift of money and hopes for a speedy recovery in September 1901.[117] He died at Fiesole, near Florence, cared for by English nursing sisters, on 17 February 1902, and was buried in the town's cemetery.

Robert Fraser (1897–1913)

James Campbell's death was duly recorded in the rector's log by his successor, Robert Fraser.[118] 'He (Campbell) meant well,' wrote Fraser, 'but foolishly neglected his College.' He added that the Protector, Cardinal Ledochowski, refused the rector 'permission to have a *Public* Requiem for him in the College Church to mark his disapproval of the financial ruin he had brought on the College.' Fraser was more than displeased with his inheritance in 1897; he was angry. It was the anger of the troubleshooter, sent in to clean up another man's mess. A former student under both Grant and Campbell (between 1877 and 1883; he gained the doctorate in Sacred Theology), he had spent half of his priestly career at Blairs College under the exemplary Aeneas Chisholm who, in Fraser's eyes, provided a model of what the ecclesiastical superior could aspire to in terms of upright character and administrative know-how.[119] In his turn, Fraser brought to Rome a capacity for hard work and a head for business. Little wonder Campbell's last years are thrown into harsh relief by comparison.

In fact, Cardinal Ledochowski, impressed by what he had heard of this earnest Blairs professor, had originally wanted Fraser to join the College community as Campbell's vice-rector in early 1897. Fraser replied in the negative, quoting the unfortunate experiences of Campbell's previous vice-rectors, Alexander Stuart (1885–87) and William Rooney (1887–91).[120] He claimed that these two priests had 'found their efforts rendered useless'.[121] Within a matter of weeks, however, Campbell had resigned and Fraser was now ordered to come to Rome as rector.[122] He wasted no time in taking measures to deal with the catastrophic state of the College's finances, immediately negotiating a large interest-free loan from Propaganda Fide to cover sums borrowed by Campbell.

Benefactors

From the outset, however, Fraser was not alone in his efforts – he was fortunate in his patrons. Fate had lead John Gray – a convert and late vocation of thirty-three – to the College in 1898, only months after Fraser's own arrival.[123] Gray came with an established literary reputation, having been part of the circle of Oscar Wilde in his early years. Now he had turned his back on those times, in seeking the priesthood at the College of his father's compatriots (Gray himself was English), but he continued to share with his fellows his sensitive understanding of poetry, the fine arts, and music. They were passions which would never leave him and in the ornate Catholicism of his day he readily found much that was attractive and satisfying. What Gray also gave the College, however, was the patronage of his friend, another convert, André Raffalovich, son of a Parisian banker, minor poet, and beneficiary of a private income. Gray must have been taken into Fraser's confidence almost immediately for the rector's log for 1898 records an investment of £400 by Raffalovich on the College's behalf. It was the first of sundry substantial gifts.

The same entry in the log for 1898 makes mention of another benefactor, Monsignor James Lennon. This time, Fraser himself was the contact. A priest of the Liverpool archdiocese who inherited considerable wealth from a deceased brother, Lennon had become a familiar figure at Blairs College on trips north to see Scottish friends. It was he who provided the money, some £7000, to build Blairs' beautiful new church, begun in 1899. Lennon's donation of the previous year to the Scots College was on a similar scale: £6000, to be 'invested for the benefit of the College in all time coming'. He was also responsible for the electric lighting installed throughout the building for the first time.[124] Nor was such magnanimity directed only towards the property in Rome itself. The villa at Marino caused Fraser further headaches. In 1899 he recorded that 'it was in a bad state of disrepair, very confined, and the chapel which did well enough for a small community was stifling in summer with 20 persons'. Improvements were made all the more imperative after an earthquake on 19 July 1899 caused considerable structural damage. Once more, Raffalovich (£347) and Lennon (£100) provided the lion's share of the funding for a new chapel (inaugurated on 16 April 1900) and a re-ordering of the villa's interior.

Tercentenary (1900)

Gradually, Fraser began to re-establish a sense of order and decorum in the life of the College. Pius X recognised this officially in the personally signed papal blessing awarded him on the Silver Jubilee of his priesthood in 1907.[125] However, the rector was perceptive enough to realise that the successful relaunching of an institution into an auspicious future required more than attention to bricks and mortar or the account books. The College had to be reborn as an ideal in the mind of its students, past and present. Like MacPherson before him, Fraser knew that there had to be a story – a historical narrative – which reinforced institutional pride.[126] The tercentenary of the College in 1900 gifted him a valid opportunity to rework the historic identity of the community. An extended essay of 1899, drafted in anticipation of the up-coming celebrations, begins with the poignant image of a footsore St Ninian arriving in Rome, traverses the three centuries of the College's history with polished prose, and ends with a flourish:

The student whose privilege it is to be trained in Rome has priceless advantages it were vain to seek elsewhere . . . (Rome's) monuments, its ruins, its streets, its public places speak to him of the storied past; and thus his surroundings, his studies, his recreations, all combine to adorn his mind with that wider knowledge and culture which academic studies alone are inadequate to provide. Little wonder, then, that he leaves it with regret, and in after years fondly cherishes the memory of his student's life with its manifold charms and advantages.[127]

In appealing to the antiquity of Rome and presenting the *experience* of being in Rome as a superior education in itself, Fraser created a stirring advert for his College. However, his programme of reform required that students truly identify with his dream. He needed something populist and appealing which would capture the mood of retrenchment in the tercentenary generation. John Gray provided the answer. To music written by Canon Augustine MacDermott (in the style of Sir Arthur Sullivan), Gray composed the words of *The College Song*. Nothing from this period more eloquently embodies the quest for a symbiosis of Roman and Scots identities:

From the land of purple heather,
From the dear and distant North,
Scotland casts our lot together;
Bonnie Scotland sends us forth
To the City by the Tiber,
To the shade of Peter's dome,
To bear the bright tradition back
Of everlasting Rome.

The final stanza ends with a personification of the College, who hopes that her *alumni* will:

. . . keep her colours flying
In the best of bonnie lands:
The men she taught to cherish
All she knows or ever knew;
The hope that cannot perish
Romans all and Scotsmen true.

The song received its first public airing at the tercentenary celebrations on the evening of 5 December 1900.[128] Fraser noted in his log that they sought to 'thank God for the blessings of the past and to implore his blessing of the future of the College'. One wonders if, in looking at that past, Fraser took cognisance of the fact that, since Paul MacPherson re-opened the College in 1820, out of just over 200 students whose names were entered in the register, 162 had been ordained for the Scottish mission. Despite the many tribulations, did these statistics not give grounds for a more assured passage into the new century? Indeed, it must have been in a spirit of great optimism that the rector began the new academic session of 1900–01: it opened with twenty-nine students, 'by far the largest number the College ever had on its register'. Had God not already begun to bestow his blessings?

Academic Standards

In his essay of 1899, Fraser had made much of the peerless education available from the Jesuit professors at the Gregorian University (the name *Collegio Romano* fell into disuse after the confiscation of the original buildings in the 1870s) but he was equally eager to portray study conditions in the Scots College itself as conducive to the promotion of cultured and reflective thought. The students had the benefit of a large and varied library, added to over the years, by courtesy of various benefactors. There was also a reading-room, run and maintained by the students themselves. Besides several newspapers and magazines, there were over 200 volumes of 'standard English authors' (Walter Scott came under this heading), biography, travel, history and science. This reading-room was meant to be 'a diversion as well as a means of education', its principal aim being 'to keep the students well posted in the questions of the day' and to help them 'to acquire that all-round education which is now so necessary for the priesthood of the Church'.

It would be easy to be dismissive of Fraser's high ideals – but matters must be seen from his perspective. One of the College's students, George Bennett (1892–1901), had set a standard which drew gasps of admiration from his companions: three doctorates, in philosophy, theology and canon law.[129] Success breeds success. How many more Bennetts might there be in the future as Fraser's vision of what the College had been, and could be, took hold? Was not a community attracting a more diverse social range of students – including the convert Church of Scotland clergymen, John M. M. Charleson (1901–05) and Henry Grey Graham (1903–07) – to expect ever greater academic achievement?[130]

It must, therefore, have come as a crushing blow to learn, in 1906, that the Scottish bishops were beginning to have doubts about the worth of Roman doctorates in comparison with their British equivalents. (Ironically, this was the same year in which Fraser famously received an honorary Doctorate of Laws from the University of Aberdeen.) Bishop Angus Macfarlane of Dunkeld wrote to Fraser in uncompromising terms:

As you are aware, this degree (Doctor of Philosophy) is never given by the universities in this country except *honoris causa*, and then only to men of age and standing and of exceptional ability. . . This being the custom of the country, it causes no little surprise to find young men issuing from the College with the full title of DD . . . Under these circumstances, the bishops would be glad if you would take steps that would ensure that no students of theirs should be put forward for the examination for the doctorship unless they give evidence of exceptional talents and presevering application, and show such stability of character and solidity of judgement as will hold out a sure promise of their turning out later on distinguished ornaments of the clerical body of the country.[131]

Fraser realised that this directive could not be implemented to the letter. It showed no appreciation of his efforts to confront his students with the challenge of meeting standards which competed with the best in Rome. Indeed, the whole spirit of the letter ran counter to the creation of a confident new generation of Roman-trained Scots. Fraser responded, probably wisely, in a strictly matter-of-fact fashion, simply informing the bishop that he had two students due to take the examination and that both were 'of ability, of sound judgement, and excellent moral character'. They would bring 'no discredit on themselves or their degree'. The sugar-pill he kept for last. After a formal inspection of the College in late 1906, Fr Essor, the Dominican Secretary of the Congregation of the Index, had declared that:

> . . . he found everything most satisfactory, that he was more edified than he could say by the excellent spirit which animated the superior and the students, by the admirable discipline which he found in the College, and by the praiseworthy relations which subsist between superiors and students . . . Father Essor after a minute examination of the books of administration was good enough to say that it would be a blessing if other Colleges could show an equally satisfactory administration.[132]

Elevation to the Episcopate

The bishops do not seem to have pressed the matter of the doctoral degree. They had been reminded, through the observations of the Apostolic Visitor of 1906, of what they owed the Roman rector. In the long run, the stand-off did Fraser no harm. After almost seven more years at the helm of the College, he became the first rector to be raised to the episcopate himself, succeeding none other than Macfarlane of Dunkeld. Sant' Andrea degli Scozzesi being too small for the occasion, Fraser's consecration took place in the convent of Tor de' Specchi on 25 May 1913. During celebrations in the College that evening, Bishop Fraser thanked everyone for their kind wishes and declared that, though Dunkeld would always now take first place in his heart, he 'would never forget the College and his old students, who would always find in him a friend and a support'.[133] But it was the College which was destined to have most cause to remember him. By 28 March 1914, Robert Fraser was dead.

Donald Mackintosh (1913–22)

Fraser's successor as rector was Donald Mackintosh, a former student of the College and vice-rector since 1901.[134] Born in the Lochaber district in 1876 (hence, a Gaelic speaker in his early childhood), and educated at Blairs and in Paris, he arrived in Rome in 1895 to study for the priesthood. Ordained in 1900, by the next year he had gained the second of his two Gregorian doctorates in philosophy and theology. In his later years, as Archbishop of Glasgow (1922–43), he had a reputation for being austere and phlegmatic – even his official obituarist remarked on these qualities.[135] However, in 1913, what counted was that he was perceived to be a safe pair of hands. He needed to be – for there were some trying times ahead.

First World War and its Aftermath

Within months of his taking office, in August 1914, the Great War broke out. Discussion in the Scots College reached fever pitch as staff and students anxiously awaited Italy's response to the crisis. Would she join forces with her partners in the Triple Alliance, Germany and Austria? In early 1915, a member of the College community looked back at that early period in the war:

> Those were exciting days; the war absorbed all our conversation and all our activity. The vineyard (at Marino) profited in consequence of a fever for spade exercise, and the more zealous went through a course of drilling with a view to future usefulness in the trenches on the plains of Flanders, should we be requisitioned.[136]

There is great poignancy in these words, so representative of the fancies of a generation of young men who left their towns and villages to the sound of bagpipes and drums, and ended their days face down in the mud of some field at the likes of the Somme or Passchendaele. The war, however, especially in those first intoxicating weeks, stimulated a heightened awareness of national identities amongst the belligerents. As a consequence of this, in the first week of the conflict, the Scots in Rome were placed in an invidious position. Taken for Germans because of their fair hair and pale complexions, they were catcalled and forced to applaud when patriotic processions passed through the city streets. Refuge was taken in their *British* identity, as subjects of the empire – they wore Union Jack badges on their soutanes as insurance against attack.[137]

The war hit the College hard. Correspondence from Donald Mackintosh to the bishops in Scotland consistently describes pressing economic needs. One of these letters, dated 8 February 1916, is particularly concise in its summing-up of the situation:

> Before the present hard times set in, I don't think the provision made for the students was ever on a lavish scale. The result of the limitations now in existence is that, I'm afraid, the provision made for them is below reasonable limits. They tell me they are almost constantly cold and hungry and, this year, there have been more cases of illness of one kind or another than there have been for any year within my recollection.[138]

Some students were caught up in the war.[139] The same letter, quoted from above, ends with the news that 'two more of the students leave for the army tomorrow – one is Aberdeen and the other Edinburgh – already one Aberdeen man has gone.' It was a student of former times, however, who made it into the newspapers for an act of bravery. Fr Stephen Thornton, in an inordinately long letter to Mackintosh of April 1917, described how he had led a small group of Dublin Fusiliers in the capture of around 450 German soldiers.[140] For this action, Thornton received the DSO.

With the war ended, there may not have been the immediate realisation that the world had been changed for ever. Some things remained the same, the financial appeals to the bishops on behalf of the College ever constant, including at one stage the (quickly rejected) proposal that the Scots College in Valladolid, Spain, be closed and its funds turned over for the maintenance of its Roman sister.[141] But the world *was* changing: for a start, it was getting smaller. There are reports from even before the outbreak of the war of streams of pilgrims, in groups or as individuals, arriving in the Eternal City, as railways brought the city's churches and shrines within the reach of many people for the first time. The Scots College became an obvious attraction for fellow countrymen and women and even the villa at Marino became part of a well-worn itinerary.[142] The students themselves partook of every opportunity to visit popular Italian centres of cults, such as Assisi (St Francis), Subiaco (St Benedict), and Genazzano (Our Lady of Good Counsel). Encounters with popular expressions of Catholicism, so publicly presented against the background of the beauty of the towns and countryside of an Umbria or Tuscany, must surely have made a profound impression on young Scotsmen whose faith required such large measures of discretion back home. A bond with Italy was forged. Scots, Romans, Italians: they were all of these.

On 21 May 1922, Donald Mackintosh was consecrated Archbishop of Glasgow in an impressive ceremony in the church of the Oblates of St Frances, in the Via Tor de Specchi. Amongst those present were the Count de Salis, Envoy Extraordinary of Great Britain to the Holy See, and Commendatore Zoccoletti, the Prefect of Rome. A large contingent of priests of Mackintosh's new archdiocese was present; so, too, were some eighty Scots pilgrims. The students presented their former rector with a missal and a set of silver Mass-cruets.[143] The picture suggested by the ceremony is of a Scots community confident and at ease in its Roman surroundings. By 22 June there were further grounds for optimism: on that day, the Protector, Cardinal de Lai, arrived at the College to announce the appointment of a young, upstanding priest, William Clapperton, previously the vice-rector, to the rectorship.[144] Clapperton would lead the College into the second half of the century and to the eve of the Second Vatican Council.

The world was changing. Some developments were more ominous than others. In the course of an innocuous account of a football match at Tivoli in 1922 involving a Scots College team, a student noted that 'an interesting feature of the match was the use, after half-time, of *Fascisti* music to urge the home team on to victory'.[145] One era was ending; another was about to begin.

NOTES

1. *SCD* 1849, 113–31.
2. D. McRoberts, *Abbé Paul MacPherson 1756–1846* (Glasgow, 1946), 19.
3. *SCD* 1849, 129.
4. *RSC* 146–7, nos 344–8.

5. See Christine Johnson, 'Secular Clergy of the Lowland District 1732–1829', *IR*, 34 (1983), 66–87.

6. *SCD* 1849, 127.

7. SCAR 11/85. Bishop Ranald MacDonald to Paul MacPherson, 1 February 1821.

8. See Christine Johnson, *Developments in the Roman Catholic Church in Scotland 1789–1829* (Edinburgh, 1983), 190, for reference to a letter of 23 May 1818 from MacPherson to Bishop Alexander Paterson in which he declares his inability to cope with regulating the affairs of the College *and* to act as Agent in Rome for the Scottish Mission.

9. SCAR 11/86. Bishop Ranald MacDonald to Paul MacPherson, 4 August 1821.

10. SCAR 14/116. Robert Gradwell to Paul MacPherson, 25 April 1822.

11. SCAR 11/94. Bishop Alexander Paterson, 9 September 1822.

12. SCAR 11/97. Bishop Alexander Paterson to Paul MacPherson, 9 December 1822.

13. SCAR 11/103. Bishop Alexander Paterson to Paul MacPherson, 6 January 1823.

14. SCAR 11/106. Bishop Ranald MacDonald to Paul MacPherson, 27 March 1824.

15. SCAR 31/55, paragraph 23. The suspicion that Neil MacDonald was anxious to depart from seminary life is given further force when one realises that he was sent out to Rome only six months after arriving from a period of seven years at the Scots College in Valladolid.

16. SCAR 11/116 (3 October 1825).

17. SCAR 11/126. Paul MacPherson to William Reid, 3 February 1826.

18. SCAR 11/117. Bishop Alexander Paterson to Paul MacPherson, 10 September 1825.

19. SCAR 11/120. Bishop Ranald MacDonald to Paul MacPherson, 16 February 1826.

20. McRoberts, *Abbé Paul MacPherson*, 16. The obituary writes of 'executing certain plans which had been revolving in his mind for the benefit of religion in his native country': see *SCD* 1849, 128.

21. *SCD* 1834, 48.

22. SCAR 12/5 and 12/6.

23. SCAR 11/127. Bishops Paterson, MacDonald, and Cameron to Cardinal Pacca, 1 May 1826.

24. See SCAR 31/55, paragraph 19, provides previously untapped background information on Angus MacDonald.

25. Many Lowland priests protested at the apparent appointment of a Highland priest to the position of superior of the Scots College. See Johnson, *Developments*, 240, which refers to a letter from Bishop Cameron to James Kyle from as early as 17 March 1826.

26. SCAR 29/25. Bishop Alexander Cameron to Cardinal Pacca, 13 May 1826.

27. F. Forbes and W. J. Anderson, 'Clergy Lists of the Highland District 1732–1828', *IR*, 17 (1966), 163. MacDonald's age at death is erroneously given as seventy-six; he was seventy-three.

28. SCAR 12/6. Angus MacDonald to William Reid, 10 August 1826.

29. Indeed, as early as November 1827, Angus MacDonald wrote in his turn that he did not keep good health and suggested that one of the students who had impressed him,

John Strain, be made assistant rector sometime in the near future (with probable right of succession). See SCAR 15/11. Strain would not, in fact, become rector; he *was* destined to become Vicar Apostolic of the Eastern District and, on the Restoration of the Scottish Hierarchy in 1878, Archbishop of St Andrews and Edinburgh.

30. SCAR 12/39. Angus MacDonald to Alexander Cameron (rector of the Scots College, Valladolid, and nephew of the bishop), 11 September 1827.

31. *Ibid.*

32. SCAR 11/128. Bishops Paterson and MacDonald to Cardinal Pacca, 2 September 1826.

33. SCAR 29/26.

34. SCAR 12/50. Bishop Ranald MacDonald to Angus MacDonald, 28 August 1828.

35. See Johnson, *Developments*, 219–30. Both the future Archbishop Strain and Bishop Kyle attended the Royal High School in Edinburgh.

36. SCAR 12/130.

37. SCAR 12/74. Paul MacPherson to Angus MacDonald, 1 February 1830.

38. SCAR 12/62. Bishop Alexander Paterson to Angus MacDonald, 7 February 1830.

39. SCAR 12/73. Bishop James Kyle to Angus MacDonald, 11 March 1830.

40. SCAR 12/75. Paul MacPherson to Angus MacDonald, 7 April 1830. It would seem that it was Angus MacDonald's accountancy skills which were suspect in the Cardinal's eyes. See SCAR 31/55, paragraph 19.

41. SCAR 12/64. Bishop Alexander Paterson to Angus MacDonald, 6 April 1830.

42. SCAR 29/77. Undated, but perhaps summer 1830.

43. SCAR 31/55, paragraph 2.

44. See *SCD* 1834, 48, and SCAR 31/55, paragraph 30.

45. See *SCD* 1879, 153. As a youngster, both Grant and John Strain had proven precocious and had been allowed to begin logic when still in their teens which presumably gave them time to complete doctoral studies in philosophy before going on to theology. This being the case, Grant would already have covered the final-year matter being taught at Propaganda College. See SCAR 15/11.

46. See Johnson, *Developments*, 191, quoting a letter of Angus MacDonald to Bishop Alexander Paterson, 1 August 1826.

47. SCAR 29/77. The letter refers to the pope's restitution of the *Collegio Romano* to the Jesuits, so the intended recipient must have been Leo XII who died in February 1829. Cardinal Pacca did not, in fact, resign as Protector until 1835 when he became Dean of the College of Cardinals.

48. SCAR 12/98. Bishop Andrew Scott (writing on behalf of himself and Bishop Kyle) to Angus MacDonald, 10 July 1832.

49. SCAR 12/93. Bishop Andrew Scott to Angus MacDonald, 19 September 1832.

50. SCAR 15/106. Bishop Andrew Scott to Paul MacPherson, 13 December 1833 (a copy of the letter from Propaganda is attached). Paul Cullen, the rector of the Irish College of whom Bishop Scott claimed never to have heard, went on to become Cardinal Archbishop of Dublin.

51. See *RSC* 151–4. Ordained a priest for the Western District, Daniel Gallagher (*RSC* no 372) was plagued by ill health for many years before dying in Partick on 8 March 1883. Gallagher's earlier claim to fame was that he had taught Latin to the young David Livingstone.

52. *RSC* 154–6, nos 379, 380, 385, 389, 393.

53. On Cowie, see *SCD* 1880, 146–50, and Maurice Taylor, *The Scots College in Spain* (Valladolid, 1971), chapter 15, *passim*. After leaving Rome and a short period teaching at Blairs College, Cowie ended his days as vice-rector (1843–73) and rector (1873–79) of the Scots College in Valladolid. He returned to Rome only once, in 1870, to act as an adviser to the Scottish bishops attending the First Vatican Council.

54. SCAR 16/1. Bishop Andrew Scott to Alexander Grant, 13 March 1841.

55. SCAR 13/114. Bishop Andrew Scott to Paul MacPherson, 6 March 1841.

56. SCAR 31/55, paragraph 6.

57. *RSC* 153, no 374. In fact, Angus MacDonald was ordained priest and left for Scotland in 1845, dying only five years later in Strathglass, aged thirty.

58. SCAR 16/6. Bishop Andrew Scott to Alexander Grant, 10 December 1841.

59. SCAR 16/16. Bishop James Kyle to Paul MacPherson, 4 April 1842.

60. SCAR 31/55, paragraph 29.

61. For a general overview of the pontificate of Pius IX, see Frank J. Coppa, *The Modern Papacy since 1789* (London, 1998), 84–116.

62. *SCD* 1879, 154. Grant's obituarist lamented that 'partly his delicate health, partly his innate modesty, prevented him from giving to the public other more extensive treatises on kindred subjects, a task for which his extensive reading, clear views, and logical judgement singularly fitted him'.

63. Two versions of the rules in Italian, apparently in Angus MacDonald's hand, exist from 1826. The rules for the Grant regime would have been essentially the same. See SCAR 29/22.

64. SCAR 31/55, paragraph 26. There is no indication of date or the name of the decano who braved the ire of his rector.

65. John Ritchie (*RSC* 156, no 392), who came to the College in 1841, must not be confused with the later John Ritchie (*RSC* 166, no 454) who wrote a memoir of College life in *Gray*, 91–100. William Mackay (*RSC* 154, no 377) joined the College in 1835 as a thirteen-year-old.

66. SCAR 16/85. John Ritchie and William Mackay to Alexander Grant, 6 September 1846. The students referred to are John Black (twenty-two years of age; joined 1842; *RSC* 157, no 395), John Carmont (twenty-two; 1839; *RSC* 155, no 386), John Ritchie (twenty-four), Roderick Chisholm (twenty-one; 1839; *RSC* 155, no 387), Francis McKerrell (twenty-one; 1840; *RSC* 156, no 391), Joseph Black (eighteen; 1845; *RSC* 158, no 400) and John Caven (twenty; 1843; *RSC* 157, no 397). One of the most famous of all Scottish prizewinners was John Dyer (1868–75; *RSC* 165, no 448) who won four gold medals.

67. The information which follows is based on a Calendar of the *Collegio Romano* for the session 1835–36, still extant as SCAR 29/95. The curriculum and timetable remained

remarkably similar throughout the nineteenth century, with the exception of the disappearance of the Lower Schools in the 1870s.

68. Alexander Grant claimed that the Abbé Paul MacPherson used to keep students in the Scots College and taught the philosophical matter of two years in one, presumably saving on a year's accommodation. See SCAR 31/55, paragraph 27.

69. Giovanni Perrone, *Praelectiones theologicae* (9 vols; Rome, 1835–42). Perrone's contemporary, Carlo Passaglia, had a more turbulent career, being caught up in the spirit of Italian *risorgimento* to such an extent that he spent his latter years suspended from the priesthood and lived life as a layman. He was reconciled to the Church before his death.

70. Several of the professors at the *Collegio Romano* contributed to papal doctrinal commissions and, during the First Vatican Council of 1869–70, acted as advisers. Perrone, for example, played an important role on commissions preparing for the definition of the Immaculate Conception (in 1854); Franzelin acted as consultor to the Holy Office and was a papal theologian throughout the First Vatican Council, being the principal advocate behind the dogmatic constitution *Dei Filius* concerning reason, faith, and revelation. See *Encyclopedic Dictionary of Religion* (Washington, 1979), 1404 and 2737.

71. The student was probably not too far wide of the mark. Three years later Ballerini published his *De morali systemate sancti Alphonsi M de Ligorio* (Rome, 1863). This was, in effect, a teacher's commentary on his students' main textbook in moral theology: the *Theologia Moralis* of Alphonsus Liguori (1696–1787), founder of the Redemptorists.

72. SCAR 30/48: *The Thistle*, no 1, 8 September 1860. This was handwritten by various anonymous student contributors during the community's stay at the villa at Marino. Five numbers were prepared (the last dated 7 October 1860) before it became defunct.

73. Another student in the same issue of *The Thistle* gave an account of why that name had been chosen: 'We have ventured to transplant the emblematic flower of Caledonia from its home on the stern mountains of the land of the 'mountain and the flood', where for ages it has braved the storm both 'black and grim': we have . . . removed it to the sunny clime of Italy. Here it may perhaps linger for a time, sickly and neglected, and then droop its withered head in death. It is only by assiduously tending it that we can hope to prolong its existence. It is only by affectionately cherishing it that we can prevent future generations from returning against us a disgraceful verdict, who, when collecting its scattered leaves, would say: the thistle was deliberately done away with for they had little respect for their national flower.' This is identifiably an eloquent metaphor for the challenge of preserving a Scottish national identity in the midst of the charm, distractions, and (not least) the education offered by the Eternal City. Indeed, long periods away from home had implications for the fluent command of the *English* language. Yet another student commented that: 'the introduction of a weekly paper . . . will, I am persuaded, both remedy a great defect in our social intercourse, and go far to take away from the sons of our 'alma mater' the too common reproach of

Scots–Roman students – ignorance of our native language . . . (It will) enable us to clothe our sentiments in a decent English garb.' See SCAR 30/48.

74. John Ritchie (Scots College 1874–81) seems to convey a genuine, long-held belief, and not just the hindsight of an old man, when he recalled at the age of seventy-two that 'every generation has its great professors that have their day and are then forgotten. However, I think that some of our day belong to the immortals: Franzelin, Ballerini and Palmieri. We older men were brought up in philosophy on Tongiorgi lines, scouting matter and form and the real distinction between essence and existence. Leo XIII changed all that; and Palmieri and Carretti had to go, orthodox Thomists taking their place.' See *Gray*, 96.

75. See H. McEwan, 'A Water-Colour of the old Scots College, Rome', *IR*, 15 (1964), 86–7. The purple soutane depicted in this watercolour of 1833, for so long associated with Scots College students, would appear to require a revision of David McRoberts' assertions that 'for the first two decades of the resumed life of the College (i.e. after 1820), the colour of the soutane, cincture and soprano, worn by the Scots students, was black' and that the traditional dress (including purple soutane) was restored by Grant after 1846. See D. McRoberts, 'Scots College, Rome: Students' Dress', *IR*, 2 (1951), 113–4.

76. SCAR 31/55, paragraphs 13 and 20. See also D. McRoberts, 'The Scottish National Churches in Rome', *IR*, 1 (1950), 120–30.

77. The invitation to Newman to sing the opening Mass of the restored College Church is especially revealing when one considers that Alexander Grant had the reputation (of which Newman himself was aware) of being a fierce critic of the English convert's writing on doctrinal development. Despite such differences, Grant was evidently quite happy to revel in Newman's celebrity status. His singing of the Scots' Mass was quite a coup – and Grant would have known it. See Hugh McEwan, 'Dr Grant and Dr Newman', *Scots College Magazine 1960*, 18–23.

78. SCAR 31/55, paragraph 24. Frances Plummer was, indeed, buried in Sant' Andrea degli Scozzesi when she died in 1860.

79. The historical record is confused over the actual amount donated by Frances Plummer. Grant's obituary (*CDS* 1878, 156) states 1200 Roman *scudi* whereas David McRoberts ('Scottish National Churches', 127) claims she gave 'over 12,000 Roman *scudi*'; the latter may be a typographical error.

80. SCAR 16/94. Bishop John Murdoch to Alexander Grant, 22 March 1848. There had been rioting in Glasgow with breaking of lamps and windows, and looting of shops until the police had opened fire.

81. Grant would later complain that not all the compensation money was received by the Scots College which he probably believed had broken the spirit of the pope's wishes. In fact, £2000 went to an orphanage for Catholic children being opened in Glasgow by Bishop Murdoch; £500 went to Murdoch himself to be used, no doubt, at his discretion. See SCAR 31/55, paragraph 11.

82. SCAR 19/9.

83. Anecdotal evidence reported by Monsignor John McIntyre.
84. SCAR 19/14.
85. Thomas Crumly (*RSC* 166, no 451) to his parents, 28 December 1869. See Appendix 3, letter 3.
86. *RSC* 164, no 441. Angus Macfarlane (born 1843) went on to become Bishop of Dunkeld (1901–12).
87. Thomas Crumly to his parents, 22 February 1871. See Appendix 3, letter 10.
88. It is interesting to note that the vice-rector, James Campbell, recorded a somewhat cooler version of the audience, suggesting that the Scots were disappointed by the brevity of the encounter. It seems that one of the students, Matthew Brady (*RSC* 165, no 444), had been primed to read the address to the pope, but Pius simply took the parchment from the nervous young man. Campbell claimed that the students would 'have nothing to swell their letters home' – he clearly did not have the measure of Thomas Crumly.
89. SCAR 20/1.
90. *SCD* 1879, 157.
91. SCAR 20/16 and 20/20.
92. Thomas Crumly to his parents, 27 October 1873. See Appendix 3, letter 14.
93. *RSC* 166-8.
94. SCAR 18/130. Alexander Grant to Valerio Cardella SJ, 22 October 1873.
95. SCAR 18/131. Valerio Cardella SJ to Alexander Grant, October 1873.
96. Gray, 92.
97. SCAR 16/92. Bishop John Murdoch to Alexander Grant, February 1848.
98. SCD 1854, 112; *RSC* 157, no 396.
99. RSC 163, no 433. See Campbell's obituary in *SCD* 1903, 246–8. Campbell became a Doctor of Theology in 1876.
100. SCAR 24/102. Undated, the document is probably from 1867 when, at one stage, Campbell had actually gone as far as requesting Bishop John Gray of the Western District to recall him (SCAR 24/101).
101. It is John Ritchie who refers to Campbell as 'rather choleric'. See *Gray*, 100.
102. After the Campbell kidnapping, which highlighted risks to the safety of the community, the Scots College community avoided Marino, travelling instead to a villa in Albano. They returned to Marino in September 1873. See Appendix 3, letter 13: Thomas Crumly to his parents, 2 September 1873.
103. Frederick Rolfe, *Hadrian VII* (London, 1904). In chapter 15, Hadrian visits 'St Andrew's College' and records characteristics of Scots College students from his time in the College: most have been identified. See A. J. A. Symons, *The Quest for Corvo* (London, 1934); A. S. MacWilliam, 'Fr Rolfe and the Scots College, Rome', *IR*, 21 (1970), 124–139; B. Sewell, 'Frederick William Rolfe at the Scots College', *IR*, 26 (1975), 20–26.
104. Alexander MacWilliam ('Fr Rolfe and the Scots College, Rome') uses quotations from Rolfe's *The Desire and Pursuit of the Whole*, *In His Own Image*, and *Hubert's Arthur*, all of which return to this theme.

105. *RSC* 189: Rolfe appears in the list of *convictors*, no 52.

106. John Crane, *Frank Baylis*, (London, 1903). MacVarish appears in *RSC* 174, no 498; he would end his life as an Anglican vicar.

107. *RSC* 189: Fortescue appears in the list of *convictors*, no 55.

108. A. Fortescue, *The Ceremonies of the Roman Rite Described* (London, 1917). The book went through several editions until the liturgical changes of the Second Vatican Council (1962–65) made it defunct.

109. SCAR 27/50. Adrian Fortescue to Robert Fraser, 20 February 1913.

110. *RSC* 170, no 475. Stack was at the College between 1881 and 1887.

111. *Gray*, 100; John Ritchie, *Reflections on Scottish Church History* (Edinburgh and London, 1927).

112. Denis Sheil, 'A Student of the Eighties', *Scots College Magazine* 1960, 9.

113. Paul Gardiner, *An extraordinary Australian: Mary MacKillop* (Newtown, 1993). Blessed Mary MacKillop was the daughter of Alexander MacKillop (*RSC* 149, no 358) who arrived at the Scots College in 1825 (leaving in 1831 before receiving sacred orders), and was one of the students who campaigned to retain Angus MacDonald as rector. Her father, therefore, had been a companion of Alexander Grant, but Campbell would not have had this personal link.

114. *SCD* 1903, 247.

115. *RSC* 171, no 484. Meany arrived in Rome in October 1884, aged twenty-four. Ordained in March 1887, he returned to Scotland where he served for many years in his native Diocese of Aberdeen. His extant diary (in SCAR R39) dates from 1886.

116. SCAR 32/16. The writer is Campbell's successor, Robert Fraser. He recorded in his rector's log for 1897 that 'when the finances of the College were examined into, they were found to be in a very wretched state. It was discovered that there were accounts amounting to over 97,000 lire unpaid, including the sums that Monsignor Campbell had borrowed to meet difference between income and expenditure in previous years; that monies given by Rev Louis Ferguson, Archbishop William Smith (of St Andrews and Edinburgh), and Monsignor Francis MacKerrell to found burses, instead of having been invested as permanent capital, had been spent to meet current expenses.'

117. Campbell's response is extant: SCAR 24/169. James Campbell to John Ritchie, 19 September 1901.

118. SCAR 32/16. All quotations from Fraser's log belong to this reference.

119. *RSC* 168, no 463. Fraser's obituary is in *SCD* 1915, 262-67. Aeneas Chisholm eventually became Bishop of Aberdeen (1899–1918).

120. Both Stuart (1877–83) and Rooney (1879–85) were Scots College Rome alumni. See, respectively, *RSC* 167, no 459, and 169, no 468.

121. SCAR 27/1. Robert Fraser to Cardinal Ledochowski, 2 April 1897.

122. SCAR 27/2. Cardinal Ledochowski to Robert Fraser, 18 May 1897.

123. *RSC* 181, no 545. Ordained priest for the Archdiocese of St Andrews and Edinburgh in December 1901, Gray remained at the College until May 1902. He spent some months of further study in Fribourg, Germany, before returning to Scotland. From

1905 to 1934, he was administrator of St Peter's in Morningside, Edinburgh. He died on 16 June 1934. See Brocard Sewell, 'Some memories of John Gray by the Reverend Dominic Hart', *IR*, 26 (1975), 80–8.

124. Lennon's obituary is in *SCD* 1909, 268–70.

125. SCAR 27/105. Pius X wrote: 'It is not unknown to us how disturbed were the affairs of the Scots College before you were granted first charge of the house, and how slight therefore the fruit it produced for the benefit of the dioceses. But the heart rejoices to see the fortunes of the College now restored, the number of students almost doubled, the well-formed piety of young men hastening towards sacred office, the aims of rector and students cooperating in wonderful harmony.'

126. Fraser shared the Victorian's love of pageantry and ceremony. His first birthday as rector saw the villa at Marino bedecked with banners and pennants like some medieval fortress. See *Glasgow Observer*, 14 August 1897, 5.

127. Robert Fraser, *The Scots College Rome* (Glasgow?, 1899). Fraser later contributed 'The Scots College' entry for *The Catholic Encyclopedia* (vol 13 of the 1912 edition) which emphasised that at the time of writing (1911) the College was 'proportionately the best attended of the colleges of Rome' – thirty-eight students out of a Scots Catholic population of 500,000. Fraser certainly knew how to reinforce the prestige of his institution.

128. SCAR 32/16. The College Song by John Gray and Augustine McDermott was published in 1900 by Enrico van den Eerenbeemt's establishment in the Via Clementino in Rome. McDermott (*RSC* 162, no 432) was a student at the College between 1858 and 1865. He was a professor at the Scots College Valladolid for many years, reputedly composing their 'College Song' also, *The Star of Ambrosio*. See Taylor, *Scots College in Spain*, 234, note 48.

129. *RSC* 177, 518. Bennett went on to succeed Aeneas Chisholm as Bishop of Aberdeen (1918–46).

130. On both Charleson and Grey Graham (who later became an auxiliary bishop in the Archdiocese of St Andrews and Edinburgh), see Hugh McEwan, *Bishop Grey Graham 1874–1959* (Glasgow, 1973).

131. SCA 27/44. Bishop Angus Macfarlane to Robert Fraser, 1 November 1906.

132. SCAR 27/45. Robert Fraser to Bishop Angus Macfarlane, 12 December 1906.

133. Arthur Wrightson, 'Consecration of the Right Reverend Robert Fraser, Fourth Bishop of Dunkeld', *St Peter's College Magazine*, 2 (June 1913), 22–3.

134. *RSC* 179, no 531.

135. *SCD* 1944, 344–8. Archbishop Mackintosh, as he became, died on 8 December 1943.

136. *St Peter's College Magazine*, 3 (1915), 48.

137. *Ibid.*

138. SCAR 34/22. Donald Mackintosh to Mgr John Ritchie, 8 February 1916.

139. An arrangement reached with the British Government meant that clergy were exempted from military service. In order to conform to this ruling, seminarians were ordained to the sub-diaconate a year early (i.e. after only two years' study of theology). See SCAR 34/170.

140. SCAR 34/95. Stephen Thornton to Donald Mackintosh, 2 April 1917. In 1917, Thornton was actually a naval chaplain, temporarily seconded to frontline troops. He attended the Scots College between 1891 and 1897; see *RSC* 176, no 511.

141. SCAR 34/200. Bishop John Toner to Donald Mackintosh, 3 May 1919. About this time, Pope Benedict XV had a strong letter in support of the College drafted with his full authority – but the pastoral letter produced by the Scottish bishops decreed a special collection for *all* the Scottish seminaries. This change irked Mackintosh a great deal. See SCAR 34/199.

142. The first recorded visit of a group of Scottish pilgrims to the villa at Marino, in June 1914, is recorded in *St Peter's College Magazine*, 2 (1914), 166.

143. *St Peter's College Magazine*, 5 (1922), 119.

144. *St Peter's College Magazine*, 5 (1922), 148.

145. *St Peter's College Magazine*, 6 (1923), 31.

CHAPTER 4

Challenges 1922–2000

John McIntyre

Expansion and Stability (1922–1940)

When Canon John Gray, Secretary of the Scots College Society, wrote to the rector in May 1929 to announce his purpose of producing a volume about the College for the Society's Silver Jubilee, he requested a contribution from Monsignor Clapperton and made a remarkable judgement:

> It will consist of six or seven items; and I earnestly hope that one of them will be a short account by you of this College in your time – I suppose the happiest period in three centuries of its existence.[1]

The 3000 words on his eight years' rectorship which Clapperton duly wrote 'as a Lenten penance' before Easter 1930 go some way to justify the secretary's words. The total number of students had risen from fewer than thirty to more than fifty; a complete new wing with extra rooms and a large refectory had been built along the Via Rasella; the seventeenth-century national church beside the college had become the College chapel; religious sisters were now in charge of the domestic side of things, with their own convent area and the old panelled refectory adapted as their oratory; and a central heating system had been installed. The appeals his predecessor as rector, now Archbishop Mackintosh of Glasgow, had made on the College's behalf had established a trust-fund which provided it with at least some independent finance. The vineyards at the country-house had been largely renewed, the track from Marino made *carrozzabile* and, after a series of rejected proposals, the old villa replaced by a magnificent new building. The whole piece is something of a litany of success.[2]

Other developments promised the College in the Via delle Quattro Fontane a future of solid progress. The report sent to the Protector, Cardinal De Lai, on 20 June 1927 on the visitation of the College carried out by Mgr Pasetti of the Congregation of Seminaries and Universities, was highly favourable as regards the spirit of the students and their relations with their superiors, the programme followed, and the economic standing and prospects of the institution. It recommended that a spiritual director and study tutor (*ripetitore*) be added to the staff of rector and vice-rector, but contains only one really negative judgement:

> The young men apply themselves to their studies, but the results are not commensurate with their goodwill: this follows from the mediocre ability of the majority.

108

Clapperton echoed this in 1930 – 'it must be confessed that we cannot compete with a college whose students are all picked men' – but discreetly omitted mention of the Visitator's suggestion that the bishops should be more selective. The new Constitutions of the College, issued in the aftermath of the visitation, established new demarcations:

> The powers which were formerly vested in him [the Cardinal Protector] have been transferred to the recently constituted Congregation of Seminaries, to which the College, like all pontifical seminaries, is immediately subject; whilst the right of granting dimissorial letters, and of deciding who are to be admitted to the College, is reserved to the bishops, who also have a voice in the appointment of the superiors, and are recognised as the legal representatives of the College in the civil courts, the rector being, *ex officio*, their procurator.

There was also provision for *delegati*, officially appointed consultors in matters of discipline and administration.[3] The change in the function of the Cardinal Protector was probably the most significant measure. It was not likely that another Protector would do what Ledochowski had done in 1901 and De Lai in 1923, demanding that an unwilling Scots bishop should release for the post of vice-rector the priest of the rector's choice. Yet it would be untrue to say that the holders of the office ceased to have influence or that the Congregation of Seminaries was to take less interest in College affairs than the Protectors of old.

The Rector

William R. Clapperton, forty-four in 1930, had a right to feel satisfied with what he had accomplished in eight years. Yet self-satisfaction was most untypical of him. Two years later, with Archbishop McDonald of Edinburgh in residence and very critical of the staff and the regime, he could write to Bishop Bennett of Aberdeen (his own bishop):

> Something will have to be done at once to waken things up in the College: a new vice-rector, and a new spiritual director, and then perhaps the greatest need of all, a rector who can get things done.[4]

Others had a higher regard for his qualities. Fr Donald Mathieson, also of the Diocese of Aberdeen, writing to Clapperton in May 1922 concerning Bishop Bennett's absolute refusal to allow the newly-ordained David Paterson to remain at the College as vice-rector, had this to say:

> I feel certain and confident that in you we have one of clear judgement and calm procedure in difficulty which will be recognised with pleasure from end to end of Scotland.[5]

The balanced and shrewd obituary his successor, Mgr Philip Flanagan, wrote forty years later puts that sort of enthusiasm in perspective. The question remains as to how far the cantankerous, idiosyncratic side of Clapperton detracted from his diligence, humble spirituality and deep human understanding. Perhaps a key to this paradox might be found in an examination of his background. He came of an old Catholic family of Fochabers in Banffshire, where his grandfather and father had built up a chemist's business. He had three priest-uncles, and his father was a JP and a director of Milne's Institute, the school young William attended before going on to Robert Gordon's College. Thomas Clapperton had been able to buy the house and small estate of Potterton near Aberdeen and the family snapshots – mostly William's own, since he was a keen photographer – reflect a comfortable middle-class milieu. From Robert Gordon's he went at fifteen to St Mary's College, Ushaw, near Durham, which was both Junior and Senior Seminary for the north-east dioceses of England. Whether he went there as a Church student is unclear; but around the time he began his degree course in Arts at Durham University (as an alternative to the seminary philosophy course) he accepted Tonsure and Minor Orders as a candidate of Aberdeen diocese.[6] A First in Classics was followed by the transfer to Rome in 1907 where he opted to do the philosophy course instead of starting theology, as he might have done. Ordained in 1913 before taking his theology doctorate *congruenter superata*, he moved straight from decano (head-student) to being vice-rector, a post he held throughout the rectorship (1913–1922) of Donald A Mackintosh.

A curious sidelight on his own character and the esteem in which he was held is the letter written by Mgr Robert Fraser (rector 1897–1913) to Clapperton, at home in Aberdeen for the summer, after the rector had returned to Italy in October 1910:

> Just a line to convey my warmest congratuations on your elevation to the priesthood. It has come to you out of due season but not unprepared and if God gives you length of days I hope for great things of you before I am gathered to my Fathers. Some day you may rule this College when Mgr Mac is at Oban and I am in the Campo Santo [the Roman cemetery].[7]

What seems to have happened is that Fraser, his vice-rector Mackintosh (later Archbishop of Glasgow) being home in Lochaber recovering from one of his many illnesses, saw the appointment to the decano-ship of Clapperton, with only a year's theology behind him, as the only way of keeping up student discipline. So he had arranged with Bishop Chisholm of Aberdeen to ordain him to the priesthood – as befitted a decano-elect – and imagined that the young man's own objections to taking the final step had been overcome. Hence the letter with its mistaken congratulations and not altogether inaccurate prophecy – one of the very few from that period which Clapperton preserved, perhaps because it tickled the dry humour which always lay not far below that craggy outward reserve which was his most obvious characteristic.

Since Clapperton as a person may become somewhat lost in the details of College history, it is worth recording two judgements which seem close to the truth. One is Philip Flanagan's:

To know him as he really was, one had to penetrate the brusque exterior. There, under the cloak, one found a man who longed to give and receive affection but whose shyness made him embarrassed at doing so.[8]

The other observation is from a letter written at the time of Clapperton's death by Mgr Sandy McWilliams, one of his oldest friends in the diocese he was destined to serve for only six of his long years of priesthood:

Monsignor never shoved himself forward – it wasn't in his character. He would have done with some self-confidence but what was lacking there was made up for by a tremendous fund of commonsense. Though there were times when he could be very aggravating![9]

Agent of the Bishops

Reading through the pre-war correspondence one notes how much of it does not directly concern the College. As agent for the bishops – the post which was first joined to that of rector in the person of Abbé Paul MacPherson – Clapperton was the normal go-between with the various Roman offices and Congregations on a wide variety of matters. In the course of 1937, for instance, a year before the appointment of William Godfrey as Apostolic Delegate in London provided an alternative method of recourse, Clapperton handled twenty-five items for Archbishop Mackintosh alone, from marriage dispensations involving the unbaptised to an indult for the provision of a private altar for Notre Dame convent in Glasgow.[10] There was far more to this task than filling with elegant Latin the signed blank sheets the bishops sent out with their requests. A separate account had to be kept with each bishop to cover the various taxes and fees, and they also often expected him to advise them on points of Canon Law and procedure.

The constant labour of dealing with not-always-sensible bishops and not-always-sympathetic Vatican officials was a background to all his other work and, occasionally, must have been quite distressing. Mackintosh asked him early in 1935, for instance, to go and tell Cardinal Rossi (the Secretary of the Consistorial Congregation) to reply to his letter of 1932 complaining about Edinburgh's use of the title 'Metropolitan'. Clapperton's reluctance to do such things annoyed the archbishop: 'Do not write to me to expostulate with these my direct methods, but, just carry out my instructions.' The rector declared that he had spoken to the Cardinal, but added firmly: 'You cannot expect more, since I am agent both to Glasgow and to Edinburgh.' In the end the archbishop followed Clapperton's suggestion and wrote himself to Rossi, at the same time rather lamely excusing himself: 'I never dreamt of the possibility of your thinking I wanted you to take sides in my difficulty with Edinburgh.'[11]

It must be recalled that Mackintosh was the man with whom Clapperton had collaborated as vice-rector for nine years and who, in the 1920s, had poured out his soul to the new rector in those difficult first years in Glasgow, when he was still at loggerheads with his fellow bishops about their interpretation of Benedict XV's letter in favour of the Scots College, and was finding the situation and personalities he had to work with difficult going. 'It is dreadfully lonely here and I am very Romesick every time I return from an expedition abroad,' he wrote in his first months as archbishop. Two years later, the mood had not changed so much: 'I find life here a terrible strain – between the bad climate, smoke, fog and the effort to overtake providing for the needs of the situation.'[12]

Vice-rectors

After he succeeded Mackintosh in 1922 it took most of a year for Clapperton to find a replacement for himself as vice-rector. He wanted, and ultimately got, David Paterson, a top-year student from his own Diocese of Aberdeen, but only after sustained resistance from Bishop Bennett had been defeated by a fairly peremptory letter from the Cardinal Protector, Gaetano De Lai.[13] In the long perspective of history it seems questionable whether a recently-ordained priest on very familiar terms with the students should have been promoted as the rector's deputy and consultant – yet this is what happened in 1901, 1913, 1922, 1933, and 1938. Clapperton provided a job-description for the vice-rector in December 1932, when looking for a successor to Fr Francis Magauran:

> Fr Sheridan [ordained that year] is doing very well as *ripetitore*. He has no time to do the work of vice-rector, namely to give a hand in helping to run the College, in looking after the discipline of the students, the servants, the accounts, the Agency work, the sermons and reading, the sacristy, the Archives, the Library (which wants a good overhauling and would be a whole time job for one man for two or three years), the vineyard, not to mention the various social duties which come one's way.[14]

The phrase 'to give a hand' perhaps indicates why Fraser, Mackintosh, and Clapperton, all strong personalities, were happy with young and inexperienced assistants whom they could mould to their ways. From the evidence available, Clapperton and Paterson cooperated well; the rector thought highly of him (he told Bennett he hoped to see Paterson a bishop some day) and obtained for him the honour of Papal Chamberlain before he left in 1930 to begin his years of honourable service in the Diocese of Aberdeen.[15]

Fr Francis Magauran had five years of parish work behind him when he succeeded Paterson. The rector was critical of him from the start – 'he is awkward and has a terrible voice; however he may turn out all right' – and by the time the *villeggiatura* (holiday time spent at Marino) came round, the first in the new villa and demanding new arrangements, Clapperton was glad to give him a long leave of absence 'because he is not much use at that sort of thing and I get on as well without him.'[16] It may be imagined that Magauran was at least as relieved as Clapperton when recalled a few months later to parish work, and felt sympathy for Dr John Sheridan when the young *ripetitore* (despite Clapperton's strictures) was asked to be vice-rector as well.

This appointment and that of Sheridan's successor, Fr Philip Ignatius Flanagan, in 1938 (Flanagan was a young priest-student who had just finished his theology doctorate) look like line-of-least-resistance measures, especially since the rector had sought for 'someone with a more practical turn of mind [than Magauran] and not too brainy.' Sheridan was, by all accounts, one of the 'brainiest' Scots priests of this century and carried out both his tasks of vice-rector and *ripetitore* (while also working for an advanced doctorate in philosophy!) most effectively. But one has the impression that his academic style and curious habit of incessant humming, and possibly his popularity with the students who appreciated his diligence and efficiency in helping them with their studies, did not endear him to the rector. When 'the Baxter', as he was always affectionately known by students (the reference is to Lord Emsworth's bespectacled secretary in the Wodehouse stories), finally left for Cambridge with a *summa cum laude* for his doctoral thesis, Clapperton's praise has a typically wry twist: 'Sheridan has brought great credit on himself and the College, but I hope the next vice-rector won't be such a devotee of the books.'[17]

Although Flanagan, recently awarded his doctorate *magna cum laude,* was another academic and one of the few Scottish priests who actually published books as well as reading them, he seems in his eight years of active vice-rectorship (1938–40; 1946–52) to have suited Clapperton rather well.[18] His obituary of Clapperton shows his real respect and affection for the older man but he was disinclined to defer to any superior and probably challenged Clapperton's indecisiveness at times – which may have made for a solid relationship. As described later in this chapter, he started off on the right foot by taking important decisions in Clapperton's absence during the Munich crisis of 1938.

Ripetitori *and Spiritual Directors*

The 1927 Visitation had proposed two other members of staff, namely a *ripetitore* and a spiritual director. When he wrote his account of the College in 1930, Clapperton already had on the staff a spiritual director, Dom Placid Turner OSB, as prescribed by the 1927 Visitation – but no *ripetitore* to help with studies. It was five years before Sheridan was appointed to this post, in time to answer the new academic demands made in the Vatican's reforming document *Deus Scientiarum Dominus* (1931). Because the professors themselves could be consulted in difficulties and assisted in the College's system of internal mock exams, there had been doubts about the need for someone in this role. Later rectors would see the value of a 'third voice' in the assessment of students but, even where *ripetitore* and vice-rector were the same person, someone like Sheridan could and did give the young philosophers great help. His work involved giving seminars, tutorials and mock orals on the current material, and acquainting himself with the courses on scientific questions the Gregorian University had begun to demand in 1932.[19] He carried this on with unrelenting industry while adding an advanced philosophy doctorate to the two he already held, making him a *magister aggregatus*. There was, however, a new arrangement after Sheridan left in 1938: the vice-rector, Flanagan, tutoring the philosophers and a *ripetitore*, Michael Connelly, another postgraduate student, assisting in theology.

When, in 1939, sterling for the second time in a decade dropped heavily against the lira, Clapperton proposed as an economy that the posts of spiritual director and *ripetitore* should be left unfilled and argued with some cogency that spiritual guidance and tutoring could be provided from outside the College. Fr Connelly did not return for the 1939–40 session, but the spiritual director, Canon Gillon, did. Gillon came home with the students when politics put an end to the session for them in May 1940.

The students themselves seem to have asked for a spiritual director during the 1927 Visitation. The English College in Rome had had one for several years and the idea must have been in the air since Mackintosh – perhaps facetiously – had asked Clapperton in 1924 if one of his own *bêtes-noires*, Fr Gerard Stack, might not make a good spiritual director.[20] There has always been difficulty in finding someone of pastoral experience to act as spiritual director in foreign colleges: he necessarily shares the life of the superiors but, in order to deal in the internal forum with students' lives and problems, must be seen to stand apart from staff tasks of discipline and assessment. A religious like Turner (the representative in Rome of the English Benedictines who also had parish experience) might seem likely to fulfil the role well. But Clapperton's enthusiasm for the cheerful little monk waned rather quickly and Turner himself clearly felt inadequate:

> Fr Placid wrote to me some time ago saying that he felt himself unfitted for the post and begging me to find someone else. He is in fact practically useless, and is too old to change his ways: he hears confessions occasionally, but that is all. He has agreed to stay on until I can get someone to take his place.[21]

From his letters, Dom Placid appears as a cultured and magnanimous man, generous in praise of the Scots College regime and realistic about himself. He stayed for another year or so because his intended replacement, Fr Edward Stephens from Ushaw, refused to come on condition of a year's probation, which was what the Scottish Bishops wanted. Only in 1933 did Fr Coogans from Dunkeld take up the post, and within a few months his health and nerves were so poorly that he had to go home.[22] With the coming of Canon Gillon of Edinburgh, a person of quiet disposition and deep spirituality, the College got someone who better suited the bill. He wished to resign after five years but, as noted above, remained for the 1939–40 session.[23]

Students

The student body as pictured in the group-photos of the 1930s looks remarkably like that of the 1880s and the 1960s, not only because the uniform of purple cassock with red buttons and sash remained the same (though pudding-basin hats and the odd sleeveless cloak called the *soprana* had disappeared in the 1960s) but also because their age-range and background were basically similar.[24] Most would have attended the Scottish National Junior Seminary at Blairs, near Aberdeen, and followed a timetable as boys not differing greatly from that of senior Colleges. The nineteenth-century groups would have had a higher proportion of older students, often English, but even in our period we find the former History lecturer (at the University of Glasgow) W. E. Brown, the convert J. K. Robertson, and Wilfrid Johnston, an Englishman with legal reasons for visiting home each year – something Clapperton would concede and Godfrey at the English College would not.[25] Another notable element in the student body was the Maltese candidates sent by their archbishop who had been a monk of Fort Augustus. Despite the great difference of culture, the Azzopardis and Grimas and Lupis were very acceptable to the other students, often gave an example of ferocious devotion to study and, in one or two cases, were destined for very important service in their own part of the Church.[26] Not so numerous were the Americans and Canadians whom Clapperton accepted from time to time and who generally kept a link with the College in later years.

Then, as now, the students' timetable was governed by that of the Gregorian University (or 'Greg' as it was popularly known). Meditation, Mass and breakfast had to be fitted in between a 5.30 a.m. rise and first class at 8 o'clock. Lunch, after a period of spiritual reading or a talk, had to be early enough to leave a bit of time before afternoon classes. Outdoor recreation, except on Thursday and Sunday, consisted typically of a walk from the 'Greg' to the Borghese gardens and back by the Via Sistina or the Via Veneto, with tea, study, rosary and supper following before the time of evening recreation. After night-prayers the monastic Grand Silence was expected to be observed; lights-out was at 10 o'clock. There were variants in the summer months and at the villa and on Sundays and feast-days when students would receive communion at an early Low Mass before donning *cotta* and *biretta* for the solemn sung (High) Mass. But this stable framework, hedged around with rules about going out in groups of three unless by permission (and wearing a black soutane), not entering one anothers' rooms in the College or shops and bars outside, and so on, made the task of the superior in charge of discipline a fairly uncomplicated one. Expulsions seem to have been very few and far between and clearly justified. According to Flanagan:

> To Monsignor Clapperton the rule was very important indeed. Having drawn up the rules, he put them before the students as an ideal to be aimed at. He knew they would not be kept perfectly. And the students knew that he would not expel them or keep them from ordination because of trivial breakages of the rules. He treated his students as adults. Of the men trained by him there is not one who will not agree that under his direction life in the College was exceedingly happy.[27]

A little hyperbole is allowed in an obituary but the picture of the relationship between rector and student in Clapperton's time is true enough. All the more startling is the occasional story which tells the other way – as when a student shortly to be ordained priest, and anxious for a decision from the rector about the form of the post-ordination celebration, dared to express impatience and was promptly told his ordination was postponed.[28]

What is really surprising to find is that at the moment he was writing his account of what John Gray called 'the happiest period' a dispute with a student appeared to be threatening his future as rector. When Andrew Joseph McDonald, the new Archbishop in the Scottish capital, suggested that after his success with John Ogilvie (beatified, with Clapperton as postulator, in late 1929) the rector should take on the cause of the Edinburgh working-girl, Margaret Sinclair, he was not unwilling but added: 'Of course this presupposes that I am to remain rector, a point which is rather doubtful in the meantime.'[29]

The dispute was with W. E. Brown, biographer of John Ogilvie and now an ordained top-year student, and the point at issue was astonishingly trivial. Brown had written to his ordinary, Archbishop Mackintosh of Glasgow, complaining about Clapperton expecting priest-students to dispense after-lunch coffee to guests. (In particular, he was unhappy about not being invited when the two archbishops were the guests – the rector, of course, had reason to be wary of McDonald.) Mackintosh upbraided Clapperton with going back to the autocratic style of Mgr James Campbell (rector 1878–97), insisted the matter be on the bishops' agenda for May 1930, and asked others' judgments. In the course of such deliberations, Dr Laydon, the Glasgow archdiocese's treasurer, was quite incensed about Mackintosh quoting him against Clapperton: 'I was most emphatically on your side. Do not worry, old man. You will leave Rome, or rather the College, when the Holy See has a bigger job for you.'[30]

Clapperton, though he talked gloomily about 'going home to do some useful work', fought his corner and saw the funny side. If the bishops wanted a tactful rector, he would argue, they should have made another choice in 1922; the bundle of letters being passed round concerning the matter 'reads like something out of Gilbert and Sullivan.' Finally, 'after long discussion' (Parkinson's law at work!), the bishops felt they could not usefully circumscribe the rector's authority but recommended he use tact in dealing with senior students.[31] Clapperton tried to mend bridges with Mackintosh – 'I know your Grace loves a fight above all things! I hope at any rate you have not been disappointed in your adversary as my one desire is to oblige you' – and the whole thing disappeared into a corner of the archives.[32]

Studies

Clapperton in his 1930 account had spoken of 'new regulations' soon to be issued concerning studies. *Deus Scientiarum Dominus*, promulgated in 1931 and coming into operation in session 1932–33, put an end to the old doctorates which represented only three years' study in philosophy and four in theology. The bench-mark degree became the licentiate, qualifying the holder to teach at seminary level, so that for the next half-century most students would go home after seven years with this degree both in philosophy and theology. As anticipated by Clapperton, a number would move into the *cursus minor* which did not provide a teaching qualification. Some of good ability would stay for at least a further year and defend a thesis to gain the new doctorate or look for qualifications in other disciplines like scripture or canon law.

Clapperton's original plan was for a 'propaedeutic year' of scientific and language studies followed by only two years of philosophy (which would still qualify for entry into theology) but this turned out to be a good idea that did not work and was dropped after a year's trial. Once again, youths straight from Blairs or a secondary school were dropped in at the deep end of lectures in Latin on scholastic metaphysics and cosmology, not to speak of the dreaded *quaestiones scientificae*. The main examinations were orals and the marking system was a classical and sensible six-grade assessment, five or under being a fail and six, seven, eight, nine, and ten representing a bare, adequate, good, praiseworthy and excellent pass.[33]

Space does not permit a full discussion of the system and, perhaps, it is more to the present purpose to listen to a critic. The Benedictine Archbishop McDonald of St Andrews and Edinburgh, appointed in 1929 in preference to the Roman-trained auxiliary Bishop Henry Grey Graham, cast a very cold eye on the education offered at the Scots College. His ideal of the cultured priest, equal to the challenge of the times, was an English-educated Oxbridge graduate, and he had a general policy of using English seminaries for his students and sending bright young priests to Cambridge – something which was of undoubted benefit to the Scottish Church. He did send students to Rome, especially when his legal right to use Roman bursaries for British seminaries was challenged by Mackintosh and Clapperton. But he did so in the explicit hope that defects could be remedied and twice, in 1936 and in 1939, set out his specific objections. Their acerbic tone should not distract the reader from the genuineness of McDonald's concern – indeed, friendlier critics have made similar points right down to the present day. In 1936 he wrote:

> As you have taken such strong action in the matter of the Taggart bursaries, I think it is only fair to both of us to state quite frankly my reasons for my attitude towards the College in Rome. The major course, as now organized in Rome, presupposes students of outstanding ability and, even in the case of these, the course to be effective demands ample individual tutorial repetition.

McDonald adverted further to the impossibility of teaching being relevant to particular countries, to the poor standard of public-speaking and reading in the newly-ordained, and doubted whether studious habits and a keen taste for serious reading were deeply implanted in students. When he returned to the attack in 1939, he deplored the proposal to manage without a spiritual director and *ripetitore* in order to save money. He again emphasised the need for tutorial help if the Rome courses were to be effective, made unfavourable remarks about the poor training in plainchant, the 'truly lamentable' waste of time at the villa, the 'pernicious habit' of a summer siesta, and the standard of Italian which was very poor compared with the St Sulpice (Paris) students' mastery of French. He praised Clapperton's earnest care for his College, but would have liked to see him display 'a like zeal in remedying defects in the training of these students which are such a cause of anxiety to some who are constrained to send several subjects to Rome.'[34]

The rector's painstaking replies to these diatribes are too long to quote in full. He pointed out that Rome was full of able priests willing to act as spiritual guides. It was not true that the degree course presumed exceptional ability – all were agreed, and results indicated, that hardworking students of normal ability could cope with it. The great number of lectures, in a system where the professor was expected to cover all the material, limited the time for 'repetition' and, besides, the professors themselves were there to be consulted. For years he had enlisted expert help for plainchant and had recently had the very competent Fr Francis Duffy (whose bishop now refused to send for further musical studies) in charge of practices. He had brought in Italian teachers and supplemented their work himself at the villa but, obviously, to match the Saint-Sulpice standard (where French was the language of daily discourse) students would have to go to an Italian, not a Scots seminary. He did demand that students make use of their time at the villa for broader studies. At each point he accepted that there was room for improvement. There is no doubt, however, that he found the attacks wounding: 'If I fail in my chief work, which is that of training the students, there is no use of my being here, and I have no desire to remain longer than I am wanted.'[35]

The point that the students could match the demands of the courses seems confirmed by the results-sheets prepared each year by Sheridan or Flanagan. Fewer and fewer students did not sit the licentiate and even in 1934 there were only twelve failures out of 210 examinations with an average passmark of 7.2.

A student's-eye view from a diarist of the late thirties should not be overlooked in this section. An Edinburgh student, he was not unaware of his Benedictine archbishop's attitudes towards his College:

> 10th December, Friday. He sent for us before first class. He'd only about seven minutes to speak to us and in it he told us we had to become holier than ever in order to combat the growing menace of Communism. He also wanted to know how much literature we did and so on, and praised up the Oxford education.

The diary also allows the reader some idea of what it was like at the age of barely eighteen to face a Latin oral exam – the final one of the first year – in epistemology, cosmology and metaphysics:

> 2nd July, Friday. Jock and I and an American McGlynn were the first three. Arnou, Morandini and Abelé came in and Arnou told some of the 'dagos' they were up to spy.[36]

I wanted Arnou first but we'd no choice and I'd to go to Morandini first. He gave me thesis 5 on scepticism and relativism. I seemed to forget all about it but struggled through with the help of the leading questions he asked me. Then I went to Abelé and he hit me with thesis 20 about *Praedicamentum Ubi* of which I knew practically nil. I got a bad rumbling and he spoke most of the time trying to explain things to me but in vain. Then to Arnou, and he gave me thesis 32 on the analogy of ens. I got on quite well with him but missed one question. He helped me out a bit at another and I thought he was very decent. So were the others if I'd known more. We'd a beer afterwards of course.[37]

He passed – but only just.

Events and Crises: a College in Fascist Italy

Mussolini marched on Rome six months after Clapperton's installation in 1922, so the Fascist *Ventennio* coincided closely with the rector's first twenty years in office. For the first seven years they actually lived within 100 yards of one another, Italy's Prime Minister finding it convenient to have a flat in the Via Rasella, near to Ministry offices and not too far away from the Parliament which he so rapidly made an instrument of his will. There is remarkably little reference to politics and the change to a totalitarian regime in the College records of those years, though a remark in a Mackintosh letter of 1922 shows that the nature of the dictator was early understood: 'I learn I have been dubbed "Mussolini" – with reference to the shorthand methods I have used in dealing with three or four cases.'[38]

Indeed it was the Glasgow Mussolini who dominated College events in those first years when his enthusiasm for the College where he had spent most of his adult life was still undimmed. The new wing on the Rasella had really been his project but in his first years as archbishop he seriously thought the plan should be shelved, a palazzo bought over in central Rome and a college for 100 students established with money obtained by realising the assets of the College in Spain. This idea he quietly abandoned without, it would seem, even his fellow bishops realising what he was up to. But the impression that the major works of those years were paid for by the trust fund set up with the proceeds of Mackintosh's earlier national appeals, plus residual monies willed to the College by Henry Stuart, Cardinal Duke of York, would be false. Even the final stage of the Rasella project was subsidised from Glasgow. Indeed, it was only because Mackintosh convinced his finance board that the villa was a legitimate use for the annual seminary collections (and got the support of his fellow-bishops by what was suspiciously like a ruse) that that fine building saw the light.[39] At the time construction was starting (1928), Clapperton was still worried about the status of the Glasgow contribution: his other masters at the Congregation of Seminaries would never have allowed him to borrow such a sum on the College's behalf and, in fact, the Glasgow treasurer, Dr Laydon, apologised when he inadvertently used the term 'loan' with regard to one of the instalments.[40] Mackintosh's solution was to act on the assumption that Glasgow was spending the money (including contributions from other bishops) with Clapperton as agent. He further proposed that the bishops become legal proprietors of the villa, both in Scots and Italian law. Clapperton and his lawyer Pacelli were luckily able to convince the other bishops that this would endanger rather than safeguard the property in a political crisis.

Apart from the W. E. Brown affair, trouble over David Paterson's monsignorship and a passage-at-arms with Bisleti of the Congregation of Seminaries who wanted the Scots College to apply for permission to use the age-old title of 'Pontifical' (it was duly confirmed), one could argue that there were no dark clouds looming as the rector wrote his piece for Gray in 1930. But when the Duce's fiscal policy began to bite in the early thirties and the pound slid within a year or two from being worth 100 lire to an exchange of sixty-seven, the College – basically dependent on boarding fees, a few bursaries, and a very limited trust-fund income invested in Britain – began to feel the pinch. Clapperton had to beg for help: an extract from the bishops' meeting of 10 May 1932 permitted him to transfer one of the six bursaries to general revenue and agreed to supplement the half-yearly payments to make the yield in lire equivalent to what it had been in previous years. The cost per student moved steadily upward and the critical moment was reached in 1935 when a letter from Mackintosh, which began with a gossipy reference to Hinsley's appointment to Westminster, ended with an almost casual bombshell: 'If it [the lira] remains as it is, I am afraid I shall have to withdraw all my students from Rome.' A typed note the following day requested details of all twenty-nine students:

> . . . in view of my purpose of withdrawing from the Scots College, Rome, all Glasgow students. Possibly the other dioceses of Scotland may find it possible to keep the Scots College in Rome going. I – *omnibus perpensis* – cannot.[41]

Clapperton knew Mackintosh far better than most people, and he did not treat this as some kind of monstrous joke. From the diary he kept as rector we know that he immediately consulted Fr Welsby SJ (a College consultor) as well as the Cardinal Protector Marchetti-Selvaggiani who suggested he go to Scotland to debate the matter personally ahead of the bishops' meeting scheduled for 25 April. But there was nothing frenzied about Clapperton's reply to the archbishop. Business matters are dealt with first, including the suggestion that Mackintosh come out personally to speak to Cardinal Rossi about the Edinburgh metropolitan dispute. Eventually Clapperton turns to the thorny issue at hand: 'I cannot refrain from expressing the hope that you will not carry into effect your startling proposal to remove all your students.' This urgent statement is followed by carefully marshalled arguments suggesting such an action would be a disaster for the men's studies and for the College. Having only fifteen–twenty students would have its repercussions:

> [It] would mean the closing of the College and I am sure Your Grace could not contemplate such an event with equanimity; it would mean the undoing of all your great

work for the College and, I am sure you will agree with me, it would be a national misfortune.[42]

The letter ends with the hope that Clapperton would soon hear that the proposal has been abandoned. Later, with time running on, he wired Mackintosh for a definite response which came in a two-word telegram: 'PROPOSAL DROPPED'.

Mussolini's Ethiopia adventure and sanctions changed the economic picture over subsequent years: in 1937 a student noted in his diary that he was getting over 102 lire to the pound. So, with student numbers reasonably sustained, there was less worry for the College until the outbreak of war in 1939 sent sterling down again and Clapperton sought to economise by limiting his staff. Mussolini had long since moved from the Rasella to the Villa Torlonia and adopted the image of a family man with respect for that Church whose priests he had once called 'black germs as fatal to mankind as the germs of tuberculosis'.[43] The Concordat of 1929, effected between Mussolini and the Vatican (creating the independent Vatican City State), had been welcomed even by the Duce's critics. An extant note acknowledges Clapperton's congratulations on the Concordat from Avvocato Francesco Pacelli whose late-night discussions with Mussolini had moulded the treaty.[44]

In general, the political events of the thirties affected the College community only indirectly. Students were not molested even when League of Nations sanctions were provoking anti-British demonstrations. Writing to a rather jingoistic Mackintosh, Clapperton insisted that nobody in Europe considered Britain's attitude disinterested, that the Italians would fight and that, in fact, the sanctions were causing irritation rather than hardship.[45]

But 1938 brought two moments when the College was truly threatened in different ways. The first burst upon Clapperton when he opened his *Tribuna* newpaper at the villa on 18 July to find a full plan of Mussolini's latest project in Rome, a great new street sweeping up from the Piazza Dodici Apostoli to the Piazza Barberini and passing right through the College and the Church of Sant' Andrea degli Scozzesi. An interview with officials at the city offices on the Campidoglio in the afternoon confirmed that the whole project was sealed and delivered. When he saw the Cardinal Protector and the Congregation of Seminaries the following day they took the line that a new College built with compensation money would be no bad thing and that he should immediately look for a site.[46] The fact that Archbishop McDonald was in Rome with a pilgrimage and busy with the Congregation about his own agenda of forging ahead with a single regional seminary in Scotland (with the corollary of the closure of the Scots College in Valladolid and a much reduced operation in Rome) was a complication he could have done without; but within a day or two the rector and his lawyer, Serafini, had looked at six or seven possible sites. At some point they seem to have had word that the plan had been re-scheduled and Clapperton went home to

Scotland without taking any decisive action. His new young vice-rector, Philip Flanagan, had private information in early October that the street-project had been shelved indefinitely.[47] 'If I were you I'd keep this bit of news up your sleeve until after the bishops' meeting,' he told Clapperton – the idea being to let the rector see how the land would lie if some day he did have to build a new college.

'If I were you.' The words suggest a new kind of relationship between rector and deputy. Flanagan had a right to a certain self-confidence because in Clapperton's absence had come the second great danger-point of 1938 – the Munich crisis – and he had dealt with it very competently, taking the best advice, checking on passports and visas for hurried departure and wiring instructions to Clapperton to open an account in his name in Scotland so that the friendly banker at Barclays, Rome, could give him sterling to cover immediate needs.[48] In the event, however, the crisis passed, ingloriously enough, with Mussolini able to pose as the broker of peace.

Much more could be related of the life of the pre-war College – other details of student life and minor but significant events – but space is limited. There were the sad events of the 1930–31 session when one of the sisters, so seldom mentioned but so important to the smooth running of the College, was drowned near Ostia; the College tomb received, a few months later, the remains of Mgr Hugh Cameron of Argyll and the Isles who had been holidaying in Rome and assisted at the deathbed of a friend just days before the illness which ended his own life. There was the proposal, turned down it would seem by Clapperton, to appoint him Apostolic Delegate in Africa in succession to Hinsley in 1934. There was the visit of two young Scots cycling round Europe in 1933 who stayed weeks longer than Clapperton expected and later put the College into a book.[49] There was the arrival as a student in 1938 of a celebrated singer, Sydney McEwan, who made the Gilbert and Sullivan of that Christmas a very notable occasion but, like other University graduates before and after him, found the Gregorian's course heavy going.[50] There was the death in early 1939 of Pius XI and the election of the Secretary of State, Cardinal Pacelli, as Pius XII, all interestingly chronicled in a student's diary, as is the visit to the College of the Irish Premier Eamon De Valera when he came out for the new pope's coronation.

The Quattro Fontane was on the main route to the royal palace of the Quirinal, so students of those days had memories of watching Hitler and Goebbels and the rest passing below their windows – the student diarist remarked that he could easily have lobbed a bomb! – as well as of walking over to the Piazza Venezia to hear the Duce in full flight:

> Then out onto the balcony strode 'Muss' himself. Oh boy, what a swagger! He started talking about the criticisms of his journey [to Libya] in foreign papers and 'l'oratoria isterica e ipocrita di certi pulpiti anglicani'; 'who see the mote in another's eye', etc. They called him back seven times and each time he marched out, had a look round and gave the Fascist salute.[51]

It was a spectacle to fascinate and amuse the foreign students in their purple soutanes at the edge of the surging crowd. The menace it represented to their lives and their world, and to the College in the Via delle Quattro Fontane, they would learn only too soon.

War and Peace (1940–60)

Unlike the English College in Rome, Clapperton's community did not continue to have an independent existence between 1940 and 1946. All philosophy students studied under Drs Flanagan, Sheridan, and Cahill in part of the massive junior College at Blairs, near Aberdeen; for theology they transferred to St Peter's College in Bearsden. Still, Clapperton kept the title of rector – he was administrator, not parish priest, at Banff – and reported regularly to the bishops on the administration of the College and villa in Italy and on his own handling of College funds at home.

Departure from Rome

Clapperton, however, had not foreseen such an enforced return to Scotland quite so soon. As late as his report to the bishops of April 1940, he was still echoing the common assumption that Italy would wait for a long time before entering the war. But a month later things looked black and a chance meeting with the British Minister to the Vatican, Sir D'Arcy Osborne, decided Clapperton to evacuate the students even before he had authorisation from the bishops. In later years he would imitate Osborne's plummy tones: 'The situation has deteriorated considerably: I should go!'[52]

The students left on 16 May with the vice-rector, spiritual director and some of the sisters on the same train as the English College party. Obtaining French visas for a sister at the Scots and students of the English College who had Irish passports preoccupied Clapperton and Mgr MacMillan of the English College for the following fortnight, during which Clapperton transferred the final heritage items to the Vatican, paid off servants, made necessary arrangements with his employees Valentino Pinci at the villa and Lorenzo Martinelli in Rome and briefed the administrator appointed at his suggestion by the Congregation of Seminaries, Monsignor Fidecicchi, an old friend. Flanagan reported safe arrival in Scotland and ended with the words: 'knowing you as I do I shall be surprised if you come soon. You will never be able to convince yourself that all that is possible has been done for the College. But take care you don't get caught.'[53]

He almost was. With MacMillan, the sisters and those English students whose Irish passports had caused complications, Clapperton (who had earlier turned down the chance of a direct flight) set off on 29 May and after some anxious days in Paris finally reached Britain on what must have been one of the last planes out of Le Bourget. Within ten days Italy had declared war.

Preserving the College

A notice at the College entrance declared the building 'Property of the Scots College under the protection of the Holy See'. Like Paul MacPherson before him, though with misgivings, Fidecicchi leased the College property to people acceptable to those in control. The Via delle Quattro Fontane building first housed children of Italians who had emigrated to new lives abroad but had been caught by hostilities on holiday in the fatherland, and later, at some point (judging by a press photograph taken in the refectory), returned emigrants drafted into the services. Then the Ministry for Italian Africa, dealing with refugees from the defeat there, took over. After Mussolini's fall some of Badoglio's troops were billeted, leaving weapons and equipment which found their way in time to the partisans. During the German occupation there were Franciscan sisters with war-orphans as well as a soup-kitchen to help in the general distress. After the coming of the Allies, the Catholic Women's League set up a social and chaplaincy centre for British troops which operated almost until the return of the students.

Fidecicchi, in the reports he sent via the Apostolic Delegate in London to Clapperton in Banff, was pleased to have got a good rental for the Rome building but unhappy about the villa and vineyard costs and, within a year, he had replaced Valentino with someone of his own choosing, Sebastiano Bartelucci.[54] He found buyers for the wine and could assure the rector that income in Rome covered costs. Although there was some sort of coolness after the war over remuneration from the bishops and the final accounting, Monsignor Augusto Fidecicchi served the College well and his name should not be forgotten.

In due course Clapperton learned that the villa, occupied by the Brazilian College for three summers and then rented by the Italian Air Force, had become a German headquarters centre important enough to be visited by Field-Marshal von Kesselring, and later housed hundreds of local families bombed out of their homes by the Allies. Clapperton's main joy, however, lay in knowing that the College buildings in the city itself had survived the war – though not without one very close shave. The blowing-up by partisans of a German platoon in March 1944 close to the trades-entrance in the Via Rasella was a very dangerous moment. It is said Hitler intended to destroy the whole quarter and, certainly, Lorenzo was lucky to escape with his life in the wild shooting which followed the blast and the round-up of victims for reprisal executions.

Return to Rome

Archbishop Mackintosh's death in 1943 left McDonald of St Andrews and Edinburgh by far the strongest force among the bishops and Clapperton, shrewdly aware that the College's Italian administrator would have the ear of Cardinal Pizzardo at the Congregation of Seminaries, communicated his forebodings to Fidecicci at the war's end:

As far as I can see the bishops are in no hurry to see it [the College] reopened. The Archbishop of Edinburgh has never been enamoured of Rome and has never sent students to the College if he could send them elsewhere, as Mgr Ruffini well knows. At present he is pushing his project of having in his diocese one interdiocesan major seminary for all Scotland. At the most in Rome we would have a small house for priest-students.[55]

Clapperton was riled at McDonald's claim to be representing the mind of the Holy See: he had no recollection that reducing Rome to a postgraduate house was part of the recommendation of the pre-war visitator of the Scottish seminaries, Abbot Aloysius Smith CRL (Canons Regular of the Lateran). Now Fidecicchi assured him that the Congregation wanted the College to continue as before.[56] Clapperton knew that the firm letter Pizzardo sent him in March 1946, declaring that the Congregation wanted the College re-opened and asking what he was doing about it, would not in itself win the kind of support the College would need in the future. He wrote to Fidecicchi asserting that the bishops needed reassurance about living conditions in Rome and suggested a letter to the bishops – or to His Grace of Glasgow (Archbishop Donald Campbell) – raising the question of a single region-al seminary and suggesting the adaptation for the purpose of Glasgow's diocesan seminary. At the same time, this would be the chance to insist that the Scots College in Rome be maintained as before.

But a meeting with Archbishop Campbell and the English rector, MacMillan (recently returned from Rome), left Clapperton feeling optimistic. His interesting project of using the Congregation to outflank Edinburgh's *'grandioso progetto'* was quietly buried. He reported to Cardinal Pizzardo a favourable decision of the bishops at their May 1946 meeting and, in July, went out to Rome on a flight of Transport Command to talk to Pius XII, the Cardinal Protector and the Congregation and to start preparations for the return.

The Re-opening

On 18 October 1946 Clapperton was at Rome station with two former students, Fr Gerard Rogers and Mr John McCaffery, to meet Fr Flanagan and a larger number of students (thirty-one at that point) than he had dared to hope for.[57] Life for the time being would be fairly spartan, with water and electricity problems, food-shortages and a cost of living in real terms three times higher than pre-war. But in his first report he struck a note of optimism about the spirit and co-operation of the students and the way everyone was coping.

Clapperton had Flanagan again as vice-rector as he had wished but it would be some weeks before Archbishop Campbell agreed to allow Fr Michael Connolly to take up the task of *ripetitore* which he had had in 1938–39 and several months before a student of the thirties, Fr Denis Meechan, was appointed spiritual director. When Mgr Flanagan – as he became in 1949 – went to Spain as rector in 1952 and Dr Meechan returned to parish work a year or so later, their successors, Fr John

Gogarty and Fr Thomas Murray (and Fr Murray's successor, Fr Matthew Kinsella), were students of the same era. Possibly Clapperton felt most at home with the generation he knew when he was in his prime.

Students and Student Life

Although only one of the students to have attended the pre-war College of 1939–40, Fr Eugene Mathews, returned 'as a venerable postgraduate' in 1946, Clapperton could declare in his letter of 1948 to the Scots College Society that 'one would have thought that there had been no break with the past but only a rather prolonged vacation.'[58] And, indeed, the community, which within a year or two had increased to more than forty, lived, prayed, studied and enjoyed itself very much as it had done in the thirties. Students still had to go through the process of requesting – after three and five years – to spend a summer at home, though the day when bishops like Grey Graham would demur was long past. Close inspection is necessary to spot differences in the daily timetable. Almost at the end of his time Clapperton was persuaded by a decano to delay the morning-rise by a quarter-of-an-hour – so that the bread on the breakfast table would be fresh. Much earlier the University decided to crowd main lectures into a longer morning; thus, for all except those attending special courses, there would be recreation and an hour's study before the compulsory walk and tea. This gave more opportunity for rehearsal of the Savoy operas and the plays which were a constant and time-consuming activity: thus it was that, in the tiny theatre restored to use with money gifted by the Scots College Society in 1949, much of the fixed recreation time was passed. Otherwise people gravitated to the common-room (the venue also of regular and generally well-attended debates and talks from visiting speakers) where Clapperton too would spend part of his evening away from his accounts and agency work. With increasing deafness he must have found such dutiful socialising with the post-war generation rather purgatorial, unless able players were available to make up a four at bridge. It could be a struggle for students too, of course – especially on the night of a film when he wanted his neighbour to explain the plot.

As ever the majority of students would have come – though often a year or two younger than in the past – straight from their Highers year at Blairs. Most brought with them good study-habits and acquitted themselves reasonably well at the 'Greg'. One or two students at most would at any time be following the *cursus minor* (referred to irreverently as 'the fresh-air course'). Three or four a year would 'return to their own people' but very few were asked to do so. The most notable difference was the increased proportion of postgraduate students. Seven came out with the first batch (all, except Eugene Mathews, 'first-timers' at the College), five still too young to be ordained, and though this group brought credit to the College by performing well in degree courses in theology, scripture and canon law (in which discipline John Barry distinguished himself as the sole gold medallist of his year), Clapperton found difficulty in coming to terms with them and their successors. The rules imposed were irksome, according to young Fr Barry who claimed to have the bishops (perhaps he meant his own, McDonald) on his side.[59] Clapperton was transparent in his comment:

> It is not very satisfactory having two sets of students in the house subject to different rules. One or two do not make such a difference in the College, but it is undesirable to have many.[60]

Another tension, not perhaps obvious to students, was the fact that by nature Flanagan had not quite the flexibility he saw in Clapperton. In later years the former vice-rector would remember threatening to have nothing more to do with College discipline if his judgements were to be countermanded.[61]

The Pre-conciliar Church

During those post-war years there was no sense of impending change in the Church of the sort which would be ushered in with the Second Vatican Council in the sixties. Two new dioceses (Motherwell and Paisley in 1947) and scores of new parishes were established in Scotland; hordes of pilgrims came out for the 1950 Holy Year to be guided around by students and cheer a pope who seemed to have been reigning forever. Of course, ripples from the currents of new ideas were felt at the Gregorian but the core theses were the traditional ones, even if taught by original thinkers like De Finance, Lonergan or Alfaro. One was only occasionally startled by Flick conceding that a suspect thinker called Teilhard de Chardin had asked some good questions; or a Scripture professor being hissed at – *Razionalista!* – because he dared teach a critical view of Genesis. Even when the bouncy figure of Pope John XXIII entered the scene in 1958 the changes seemed more a matter of personal style than anything that would rock the Church. In the College diary there is a somewhat hilarious account of Pope John's synod for the Diocese of Rome where College superiors joined the Roman clergy to hear documents rapidly read through, followed by a roll-call of names, a chorus of *placet*s and an exhortation to anyone wanting something modified to be sure and let the Vicariate know.

A Time for Change

Although the post-war period, like the twenties, could have been described as happy for the College, for Clapperton himself there was a lot of worry and foreboding and perhaps some disappointment as well. The deep traditional piety Flanagan described as supporting him in times of difficulty and rebuff left little room for clerical ambition. But both his predecessors had been appointed bishops, and there is anecdotal evidence that he felt a little saddened at being passed over in the early fifties, when Gordon Gray was appointed to Edinburgh and, for the second time, his own Diocese of Aberdeen went to one of his former students.[62]

Clapperton's main concerns were material ones. Once the lira had stabilised, the rise in costs and boarding fees was gradual and the bishops voted extra sums – £2000 in 1947, £5000 a little later, £10,000 in 1951 – to make good the wartime damage.[63] On the one hand, the regime was economical to a fault: the sisters never returned, young country lads being employed instead to help Lorenzo and Costantino the cook, and food costs were closely watched. But his architect, Pocci, advised that the piecemeal repair subsidies were merely postponing the day when either repairs of the order of £50,000 would have to be carried out or a radical solution found. Clapperton was 'not constitutionally opposed to change', as Flanagan put it, and the series of reports in which the former dealt with these matters is remarkably objective. In the early fifties, villa repairs were costly and the vineyard was not making a profit: Clapperton thought it might be best to sell both and get a smaller place.[64] Three years later, in a careful position paper, he returned to this villa project but with the need for major expenditure in Rome in mind. He and Pocci concluded that the £60,000–£70,000 they might get for that large communal building on a remote site would either pay for Rome repairs or replace the villa, but not both. The bishops having refused a national appeal in Scotland, the sale of the College itself on its city-centre site had to come into the frame: if it realised £350,000–£400,000 that would pay for a suburban site and a new building with something, perhaps, to spare. Clapperton wrote to the bishops in August 1957:

> But if you should decide to sell the present College and build a new one elsewhere, I hope you will not ask me to put the plan into execution. I am too old and out of date for such a job.[65]

The resignation he had proposed in similar terms ('getting stale and into fixed ways') in 1954 was this time approved 'as from the end of this year [1957–58]', but there was a delay in the matter being finalised, apparently because the bishops failed to inform Cardinal Protector Pizzardo officially. It was not till 30 June 1959 that Clapperton petitioned John XXIII:

> . . . that Your Holiness kindly deign to release him from the office of rector, and allow him to return to his native land where he will be able still, God willing, to fulfil for a few years some ministry more suited to his powers.[66]

Letters passed between Clapperton and Bishop Walsh of Aberdeen on the matter of a suitable parish, but the decision (apparently the pope's) was that he should remain in Rome and take up a canonry at St John Lateran.

Meanwhile the bishops asked the rector to explore other avenues of funding a major repair – by now his own preferred strategy – and in September 1958, in his usual businesslike way, he let them know that the Congregation of Seminaries was against his cashing in the trust-fund, the College's major independent income, which would anyway generate only £16,000. Moreover, he argued that a quick sale of the villa or the raising a long-term loan on it were impractical ideas given the current state of Italian business. He added that:

> The Cardinal [Pizzardo] did not approve of the idea of mortgaging the villa, nor did the College lawyer. If the money cannot be raised in Scotland, either by loan or otherwise, we should give up the idea of renovating the College and seek another solution.[67]

Everything pointed to a sale of the College and, given Clapperton's distaste for the idea and impending departure, it is not surprising to find that the bishops took things into their own hands. Although the expert quantity surveyor from Scotland who arrived rather unexpectedly may have given too pessimistic a view of the College's dilapidation, there was a clear case for following the lead of the Beda College and others which had moved to the suburbs.[68] The decision was taken and negotiations begun with a reputable firm who would buy over the old College (despite planning restrictions and a feu-burden) and leave the community in occupation while the new institution was built on the Via Pisana, some miles out on the Via Aurelia side of Rome. In February 1960, the appointment of Mgr Flanagan, then rector in Valladolid, to the Rome rectorship was announced and he was invited to a meeting in Glasgow between the bishops' representatives, the College lawyer, and the head of the company which was to be charged with this historic relocation of the College.

The End of the Clapperton Era

On Wednesday, 24 February 1960, Mgr Flanagan arrived: at supper Clapperton insisted on Flanagan taking what had been his place for so many years at the head of the table. The new canon of the Basilica of St John Lateran took a month to make his arrangements and then wrote a final entry in his diary:

> On March 21st I left for good and went to stay in the Villa San Francesco, a guest house in the Parioli district under the management of German Franciscan lay-brothers, where a number of clerics, as well as laymen, stay. And so, at last, my sojourn in the Scots College, Rome, came to an end. It was a wrench leaving the place that had been my home for so many years, but I had realised for a long time that it was time for me to go and it was a relief to have the suspense and uncertainty of the last year or two brought to an end. Now the die was cast and all I had to do was to make my exit with as much grace as I could muster! I shall continue to pray, as I have done continually since I became Rector, that God in his inscrutable wisdom will find a way to bring good out of all my mistakes and my sins of commission and omission; and will see that under the new rector the College will enter upon a period of increased prosperity, spiritual and temporal, and in the years to come will send forth many devoted priests to work for the spread of the Faith and the good of souls in Scotland and elsewhere.

A New College in a New Church (1960–82)

This important period in the College's history will be dealt with more briefly than it deserves. The three rectors nominated by the bishops for appointment by the

Holy See were men of strong personality and solid experience. Mgr Philip Flanagan (1913–83), besides his long years under Clapperton, had been quasi-rector of the Philosophy house in Blairs and for eight years in charge of the College in Valladolid. Canon Daniel P. Boyle (1916–84), a Sulpician dedicated to seminary work, outstanding among the priests sent to Cambridge by Archbishop McDonald, had been both spiritual director and rector in Spain and latterly rector at Blairs. Mgr Sean O'Kelly (1931–81), a Limerick man and Galway graduate who was working in Edinburgh when attracted to the priesthood, had (like Clapperton) eight years as vice-rector behind him when appointed in 1973.

The duty entrusted to these men was to build and consolidate a new community in a new location. Providence, however, had another task for them, unforeseeable in 1960: to bring the College into the new world of the Second Vatican Council. Given the inhibitions imposed when dealing with matters so close to our time, it seems best to say that in the judgement of the present writer neither Flanagan nor Boyle was well suited to the second task. O'Kelly understood better the changing times yet the model of seminary formation he followed was perhaps already outdated. All accepted changes in externals. Before Flanagan left in 1967, the students were permitted to wear suits outside the College and had elected their first decano (curiously enough an American, Daniel A. Helminiak, ordained for the Diocese of Pittsburgh in December 1967). Time-table changes, introduced by Boyle and O'Kelly in the early 1970s, abolished fixed study-periods and gave students considerable discretion about the disposal of their time, especially on free days. But the impression remains of men somewhat at odds with the vision many students had of what the Church and their own community ought to be.

The New College Plan

Flanagan had protested before his appointment against the idea of moving from the Via delle Quattro Fontane and only after his arrival in Rome did he become convinced that it was the right thing to do – and that the plan he had been given to execute at the Glasgow meeting was the wrong way to do it.[69] His advisers, Spani (the lawyer), Dr Marenda (the Congregation's business adviser) and John McCaffery thought the £250,000 offered for the College building was a poor price. Moreover, the proposed new site on the distant Via Pisana should never have been contemplated.

Having two sets of superiors worked to the College's advantage. Flanagan was able to report to the bishops Cardinal Pizzardo's distress that he and his Congregation were rumoured to be behind a project which they were willing to agree to but which they did not like.[70] To the credit of the bishops they agreed to abandon the plan and, at a time when there were several costly seminary projects in the offing, consented to finding £120,000 to buy the site on the Via Cassia where the College now stands. Flanagan, aware that there was £250 of College income annually for each student in Spain against £70 in Rome, naturally wondered if he could emulate what Mgr Humble had done in Valladolid forty years before. He seriously discussed with John McCaffery the feasibility of borrowing to develop the Quattro Fontane site and, in time, generating rent-income to pay off all debts and give the College long-term financial independence.[71] But Flanagan had to put the dream aside, borrow to extinguish the feu-burden which was depressing the asking price, and wait for a buyer who would make a proper offer for the building despite the need to preserve Poletti's façade and the seventeenth-century church.

The offer of £390,000, made in late 1961 by the bank CARIPLO (*Cassa di Risparmio delle Provincie Lombarde*), fulfilled the requirements and Flanagan saw himself building at the Via Cassia in accordance with his new architect Renato Costa's plan, investing the surplus, paying off the bishops' site-loan over a period of years and giving the College in time some further endowment income. He seems to have been genuinely taken aback when the bishops insisted the loan should be repaid immediately and the plans modified to minimise any danger of overspending. The covering letter with the bishops' instructions was uncompromising:

> I would suggest you keep within the limit of £190,000 so that we do not have to discuss how further economies can be effected. You will note what is said with regard to the repayment of the loan – all the more necessary as we are going to run up a large bill for the new wing at Langbank.[72]

Marino and the New College Opening

The bank took over the old College building in summer 1962 and for two years the community lived in the villa Clapperton had built at Marino in 1930. With heating installed, life there was better than expected and being 'bussed' to and from the University suited all but those (like postgraduates) who might want to be in libraries or at seminars at odd times. A surprising number of activities, theatre performances and Holy Week services in a Roman church were kept up, but many would have looked forward keenly to the great flitting to the Via Cassia. In the midst of all his work, the search for grant-aid to cover the inevitable shortfall and for patrons and artists to adorn the new College with suitable artefacts, Flanagan managed to find Italian Sisters, the *Suore di Bethania*, to take charge of domestic needs.[73]

The formal opening by Pope Paul VI on St Margaret's day, 16 November 1964, had wide media coverage. Some ex-students may have felt a twinge of embarrassment at the rector on television referring to the purple-clad students as 'boys just like boys anywhere' – but the whole thing went off well and less-knowing people, watching Flanagan chat with the Pope and the aged Cardinal Pizzardo, may have thought they had before them one of Scotland's future bishops.

The Second Vatican Council

The Scots bishops attending sessions of the Second Vatican Council (1962–65) were frequent visitors at the villa and used staff members – Drs Hugh McEwan (vice-rector), Thomas Winning (spiritual director) and Fr Foley (*ripetitore*), as well as the rector – as theological advisers. It is said that Scotland's bishops were a little shocked when the Council's draft document on Revelation, approved by Flanagan, was flatly rejected by most of their fellow-bishops. Like many others, they probably learned from the Council rather than contributed to it.

One student, John Fitzsimmons, was a stenographer during one Council Session – as Angus Macfarlane had been a century before. But one has a general impression that the Council did not impinge too much on life until, in its aftermath, the rector loyally began to follow the new ways in liturgy and to invite speakers like Gregory Baum (whose ideas he privately attacked) to address the students.[74] Admired like Clapperton for his meticulous rubrics in an age when slipshod celebration was commonplace, Flanagan was irritated by the freer style beginning to appear. But when he wanted the liturgist J. B. O'Connell to condemn those who were 'separating what the Church had set together' by pausing between the end of the Prayer over the Offerings and the Eucharistic dialogue, he was firmly told that it was 'absurd to make no distinction between two quite separate parts of the Mass.'[75]

Studies

Where Flanagan did want to see change was at the Gregorian University. In a telling letter to the theology Dean, Fr Dhanis SJ, he expanded on what he had said at a stormy rectors' meeting about the need he and his students felt for a system where lectures would be fewer and more emphasis put on private study stimulated by short-term goals like essays and seminar presentations.[76] He was aware of 'a strong current of criticism of Rome. There is a great danger that in a few years the Gregorian will be considered old fashioned and out of touch.'

The updating of *Deus Scientiarum Dominus* (1968) a year after Flanagan left Rome fulfilled these desires to a remarkable extent. Later, Italian would be adopted as the language of lectures and orals held in the main European tongues. The total course remained at seven years, but philosophy would only last two years, and the three years to the theology baccalaureate would be followed by a two year specialisation – in dogma or related disciplines – for the licentiate qualification.

Administration

There are many excellent aspects of Flanagan's work, too numerous to record comprehensively here. His indexing of the College archives, for example, leaves historians in his debt. Another achievement, which was of lasting value, was accomplished in co-operation with Bishop Francis Thomson of Motherwell (appointed with Bishop Michael Foylan of Aberdeen just after the new College's opening in 1964, to produce a hierarchy – for the first time since 1878 – without a single College *alumnus*). This was a financial arrangement whereby the fixed College costs were paid *pro rata* by the dioceses whether or not they had students there, while costs like food and tutorial fees, which varied with the number of students, were paid by the student fees. It worked imperfectly – the *pro rata* element would be static for years at a time – but did encourage bishops to send students and cushioned the effect when they did not do so.

Other Events

Mention, at least, should be made of the tragic event of October 1968 which clouded Flanagan's last year in office: the death of two students, Hugh Graham and John McMahon, in an accident with a hired car. The families were brought out to Rome for the funeral and a meeting with the Pope, arranged by Flanagan, helped them through the days of grief before the burial in the Campo Santo tomb.

New Attitudes and Problems: Canon Boyle

> Assuming that a Roman education should be reserved for the academically gifted, the College is much too large. To restrict entry to the fully qualified is to compromise the College economically, to increase the numbers … is to weaken the College academically.[77]

To find that Canon Daniel Boyle, Flanagan's successor, had been infected by Archbishop McDonald's attitudes is not surprising, but it is strange that he should trumpet this view (including a future vision of 'a small house in the city centre') in his first Report to the bishops, with Flanagan's last academic report – showing three failures out of 158 exams and an average pass of 7.9 – before him. It is a relief to find that his second Report talks of 'genuine hard work, crowned (on the whole) by successful exams' and mentions the high regard in which the University and other Colleges held the Scots.

In fact, he was to become very attached to the College and its traditions. Moreover, he achieved acceptance – due largely to his sharp mind, fluency in languages, and entertaining style – among the circle of friends of the College he inherited from Flanagan and the academics with whom he very actively cooperated.[78] He was also close to Clapperton as he moved into his eighty-fourth year and the mercifully short final illness. Boyle gave the Scots College Society a touching account of the former rector's last hours:

> When Mgr Rogers had said that the pope was praying for him, he had replied: 'You tell the pope I'm praying for him,' with the Clappertonian nuance. Very gently, at 7.52 a.m., he breathed his last.

In the same year (1969), the College was in the public eye when Archbishop Gordon Gray of St Andrews and Edinburgh came out to be made Cardinal. With the help of Frs O'Kelly and Jamieson (vice-rector and *ripetitore*), Boyle got to work to organize things for bishops, press and visitors, interviewed Vatican officials about the choice of titular church and other matters, and set up a final reception at the College where Gray and the other Scots (though Rome-based) Cardinal, Theodore Heard, met hundreds of pilgrims individually.

Administration

Boyle was bent on making savings where he could, which was an understandable policy when the student population was slipping towards its low point of twenty-two in 1971. Where Flanagan had adorned the College with outstanding artwork, he made £19,000 by creaming off and selling the best of the engravings Grant had collected in the nineteenth century. Where Flanagan had made the villa pay for itself by renting it to a religious community and taking the irreversible step of sending all students home in summer, Boyle sold it, for a price which some thought disappointing but which was not much lower than that anticipated by Clapperton's and Flanagan's advisers, for use as a recovery hospital for stroke victims. He dropped an employee on the grounds that the community could cover his tasks in spare time and, at the end of Fr Jamieson's time as *ripetitore*, did not press for a replacement.

The Community

There was a strong argument for having someone like Jamieson on the staff. Flanagan had asserted the need for someone 'still young enough to appreciate the new ideas and sympathise with the youth of today'. Nevertheless, the contention that a *ripetitore* or his likes could provide a 'third voice' with rector and vice-rector in matters of assessment and discipline was not a view which would have appealed to Canon Boyle.[79] It is interesting, at least, that the session following the *ripetitore*'s departure (1970–71) was reported to the bishops as 'a most disturbing one from the point of view of general discipline'. Boyle blamed the general disposition of modern youth, bad example (there had been '68-type demonstrations at the Gregorian) and the character of some individuals. But the fact is that, for the first time in generations, the general body of students protested to the rector about relationships in the community and his personal style. As usual there was a catalyst – an incident in which the rector publicly stopped a Christmas performance which was running late – and this pointed the contrast with Flanagan, a naturally peppery man who had learned (perhaps from Clapperton) to walk away from situations and in a subsequent confrontation to leave students feeling no smaller for the encounter. Those who helped to calm the situation, the vice-rector, spiritual director and the external confessor, Fr Patrick Treanor SJ, seem to have felt that the protest was understandable but the method wrong. Nonetheless, despite such incidents, it must be emphasised that Canon Daniel Boyle was one of the most able and energetic men to have filled the post of rector and one who, from cool beginnings, became one of the College's strongest supporters.

A College Prospering

Within two years of Mgr Sean O'Kelly taking over the rectorship in 1973, the student population had risen to over forty and, before his tragic death, corridor alcoves were being converted to cope with an increase which continued after his time. Other factors, no doubt, helped the situation but the trust the bishops felt in a rector who was at once confident and good-humoured, widely cultured, very hospitable and a writer of meticulous and respectful reports, undoubtedly contributed. While he made sure that the student diet was equal to anything elsewhere, he was a constant entertainer at the top table of members of the expatriate, diplomatic, and academic circles among whom he was notably popular. Busy with many things, including work for the Congregation for the Causes of the Saints, he ceased to keep the College Diary in 1978 and, more than once, replaced the customary letter to the Scots College Society with a greetings telegram. Students he treated as adults – he would not, like Flanagan and Boyle, have used 'docile' or 'mild and obedient' as terms of high approval – but liked them to keep their place.[80] They generally enjoyed him, as everyone did, and laughed at his snuff-taking and other idiosyncrasies; but some were critical and few would conceive for him the kind of exasperated affection his hero Clapperton had inspired.

Administration

Sharp rises in food-costs, wages and state insurance, sewerage problems and one or two large severance claims must have given the new rector some uneasy moments in his first years; in 1975 a deficit of over £12,000 was recorded. Yet his reaction was not the penny-pinching one of Clapperton or Boyle but insistence that fees should rise realistically, a further land-sale at Marino and the acceptance that, like other institutions, the College could work for itself in summer. The September 'refresher-courses' for clergy, initiated by Archbishop Thomas Winning of Glasgow and led by Roman academics, brought many priests to Rome and augmented income. Other notable measures were the introduction of Croatian sisters – Franciscans of the Immaculate Conception – when the *Suore di Betania* left.[81] Most valuable of all for his successors in office, with the bishops' approval he brought out an accountant from home each year to give a clear picture of the financial workings of the College and its future needs.

Changes and celebrations

The change in style of the academic system led the students after some years to vote against continuing the Savoy Opera tradition with its demands on free time and to issue a duplicated newsletter rather than the printed magazine which had demanded much commitment and speedy learning of publishing skills. Diary entries suggest that O'Kelly, who had strong interests in the theatre and literature and desired a rounded priestly culture, found such decisions deplorable. Circumstances led to difficulties with staff: Fr Hugh McEwan, his first choice as vice-rector, and later the spiritual director, Fr John Ramsay, had to go home for health reasons. After Fr John Sheary's four years as vice-rector, there was a return to 1930s style with Fr Philip Tartaglia (who already had a tutorial role) and, later, Fr Thomas Magill taking the responsibility while still post-graduates. Fr William Anderson would be spiritual director for several years but O'Kelly's desire for a full-time *ripetitore* – for community as well as academic reasons – was only satisfied towards the end of his time with the appointment of Fr James McNeil as Dean of Studies (the preferred modern title) in 1980.

The pressures that had been felt at the 1950 Holy Year were allayed to some extent during the 1975 Holy Year by the provision of an office for Scots pilgrims managed by a former student, Fr Michael Woodford; even so, the College welcomed an estimated 9000 visitors. It was a year later, at the canonisation of John Ogilvie in 1976, that the demands on the talents of the rector and his College were greatest. He was involved himself in a number of potential saints' causes (notably that of his countryman Edmund Rice) so he knew what would be required. But, as he collaborated in the tasks of the various committees and successfully organised the papal and cardinalatial Masses and the College reception which followed, he might have thought wistfully (though wistfulness was hardly a habit of his) of the 1929 beatification of Ogilvie where the papal photographer got all the notables, the visitors, the students and the Scout pipers into one photograph.

All the Scottish bishops were in Rome two years later (1978) to combine their *Ad limina* visit (a five-yearly consultation with the pope) with the commemoration, by way of a papal audience and celebratory Masses, of the centenary of the restoration of the Scottish hierarchy in 1878. O'Kelly was unhappy about having to invite the bishops' press-officer to the celebratory meal, and about other things:

> After tea [next day] the bishops held a meeting in the *salone* to discuss the affairs of the College. The meeting was at my suggestion – a mistake not to be repeated.

Requiescat

It is an odd note for a rector to strike who seemed then and later to have enjoyed – deservedly – the confidence of his bishops. In his last Report (on the 1979–80 session) he asked them 'to begin thinking of a successor'. How he would have managed the change after 16 years of priesthood in the Roman *milieu* he fitted so well there is no means of knowing. The shock of his tragic death, struck by a car within a few yards of the College with which, more than anyone since Clapperton, he had become identified, affected great numbers of people who held Sean O'Kelly and his College in affection. This sad juncture in the life of the College closed the era about which anything can be said in genuinely historical terms.

The Present Day (1982–2000)

A future historian of the College may find the last eighteen years of the twentieth century as significant, perhaps, as the period William Clapperton sat down to describe in 1930. All that may be attempted here is a brief and factural account of the events and changes in those years.

College Staff

The vision Clapperton had in the forties of rectors serving a five-year term has largely been realised.[82] Since Mgr O'Kelly's sad death there have been four rectors: Frs James Clancy, John Fitzsimmons, John McIntyre and Christopher McElroy. There have also been four successors to Fr Thomas Magill as vice-rector: Frs William Nolan, John Tormey, Christopher McElroy and Raymond Breslin. Those following Fr William Anderson in the post of spiritual director have been Frs Peter Lennon, George Bradburn, Gerard Conroy and Stephen Robson. When Fr John Tormey, after several years as *ripetitore*, became vice-rector in 1990, he was not replaced.[83]

Major Events

A period of College history which began in sadness – within a few months of the obsequies for Mgr O'Kelly, a student, John Lavelle, also died tragically – reached something of a symbolic peak two years later when Pope John Paul II paid a special visit to the College. He said Mass with the forty-seven-strong student community, was introduced to everyone individually, and had breakfast prepared by the Franciscan sisters from Croatia before returning to the Vatican.

The other occasion which brought the College very much into the eye of the public media was the nomination to the Cardinalate of Archbishop Thomas Winning of Glasgow in November 1994. The new Cardinal had been a student, postgraduate and spiritual director at the College, and his titular church of Sant' Andrea delle Fratte had had connections with the ancient Scots Hospice and lay close to the original College site. As in 1969 (with Cardinal Gray), the College cooperated in the arrangements made at short notice for media representatives and hundreds of Scots visitors who met the new Cardinal at the College in the days following the consistory.

Two beatifications which should not go unnoticed were those of John Duns Scotus – though this was primarily a Franciscan celebration – and of Mother Mary MacKillop, an educational pioneer, during the pope's visit to Australia. Daughter of a former student of the College, she visited the College and corresponded with

Mgr Cambell who appears to have been a confidante and supporter at a trying time in her life.[84]

Visits by bishops, priests and others to the College have, if anything, multiplied; in the case of bishops, Synod and Commission meetings, as well as the four *Ad Limina* occasions have often called for their presence in Rome. There were, of course, special occasions: Bishop Mario Conti's visit in 1983 to celebrate his priestly Silver Jubilee and the Cardinal's in 1996 to commemorate his twenty-five years as bishop; and a major occasion in 1997 when many priests came to celebrate the fiftieth anniversary of the College's post-war re-opening.

Apart from such occasions, items mentioned in the annual letters to the Scots College Society meeting tend to repeat themselves and to be similar to those of thirty or sixty years before: the rise or fall in student numbers; the year's ordinations (to the priesthood nowadays in the new priest's home parish, to the diaconate in the College Chapel with a bishop from Scotland as ordaining prelate); distinguished visitors; performance in studies; theatre items – making something of a come-back now; exceptional matters, such as the hospitality extended to small groups of Ethiopian refugees for over a decade; and the result of the all-important soccer match with the English College.

Administration and the Student Community

For several years now – with the cooperation of the sisters and priests at home – the College's income has been boosted by opening its doors to parish pilgrimage groups in the summer. Increased knowledge of and interest in the College has led to the opening of a Trust fund and the establishment of a *Friends of the Scots College* society. As in previous periods, the financial well-being of the College is much affected by fluctuations in the value of sterling.

The general drying-up of vocations and the demise of the National Junior Seminary at Blairs had their inevitable effect towards the end of the '80s when large ordination years were not replaced and the College population dropped by 50 per cent. As in previous eras, this made it expedient to accept applications from non-Scots. Where the forty-seven students the pope met in 1984 were exclusively for Scots dioceses, by 1990 candidates and post-graduates from Namibia, Mozambique, Italy, Canada, USA and El Salvador had entered the College at different times. In the following years the lists would include Iceland's sole seminarian and men from Poland, South Korea, Ghana, Peru, Tanzania, Rwanda and Malta. The small number who joined the main 'formation' community have generally integrated well; given the much relaxed general programme in the College, the community involvement of postgraduates has largely been left to themselves.

Formation

Alumni of previous generations who visit the College are probably most struck by the relative lack of regulation. Prayer of the Church, community Mass and meals have their fixed times but there is no bell to summon the community, no *Benedicamus Domino* in the grey dawn; there are no purple soutanes except for liturgical or special occasions, no assigned places or top table at meals; students have keys to the door and the use of a car. There is an obvious social and cultural benefit from the mixing at meals of Scots and non-Scots students, visitors, superiors and other resident priests working at the Vatican. But the superficial differences are less important in themselves than as a reflection of post-Vatican II attitudes to priestly formation.

There has certainly been in this time a development of theory and practice of priestly 'formation' – not an ideal term for the process by which an individual aspiring to serve the Church is accompanied by those in his community, his academic teachers, those who supervise pastoral experience and impart particular skills, and his spiritual guides, to the point where he can make a humble and unconditional commitment of his life to the priesthood. Perhaps a seminary constrained by the work-programme of a central academic institute loses something by being limited in the time devoted to pastorally-directed learning and experience, but gains by being insulated against exaggerated experiment.

What can be asserted is that in the modern Scots College students are expected to take a more conscious and focused attitude in preparing for their future work; at the same time, superiors have tried to become more thoughtful guides through attendance at preliminary courses and exchange of views with seminary rectors and staffs elsewhere, both within Rome and on a broader geographical basis. The constant in the situation is a group of men who have come a long way to live and pray together and to discern God's purpose. Their influence upon each other is an essential part of that process. Things have not changed so much.

NOTES

1. SCAR 44/97. John Gray (student 1898–1905) was a convert, former Foreign Office official and once a member of the literary circle of Oscar Wilde. He wrote the words of the College song (to music by Canon Augustine MacDermott) in honour of the tercentenary in 1900.
2. *Gray*, 70–90.
3. The report to Cardinal De Lai on the visitation of 20 June 1927 is in SCAR 39/1; the comments on the new set of constitutions are Clapperton's in *Gray*, 87.
4. SCAR 45/147 (December 1932).
5. SCAR 43/25.
6. His private papers show that Clapperton kept up connections with all these schools in later life. He visited Ushaw when he could and, in the thirties, tried to get an Ushaw teacher and friend of his youth, Fr Edward Stephens, to become spiritual director at the Scots College.
7. SCAR WRC 6 (uncatalogued). The College had its own plot in the Roman cemetery at Campo Santo from the 1870s; Alexander Grant (rector, 1846–78) was the first to be buried there.

8. *SCD* 1970, 314.

9. SCAR 100/10.

10. SCAR 48/324.

11. SCAR 46/214; 46/386; 46/218.

12. SCAR 43/15; 43/102. No historian of the Archdiocese of Glasgow can afford to neglect this correspondence where Mackintosh is brutally frank about the senior clergy of the archdiocese (who had regarded him as 'an inexperienced scholastic bookworm'), about Bishop John Toner's administration in the last years of Maguire's illness, about his local seminary and its staff, and about his own joy in combat: '*Come si fa?* They have chosen to fight – and they shall get a fight, until they put up their hands and forget their game!' With reference to Benedict XV's support of appeals for the Scots College Rome, see SCAR 36/40–47.

13. SCAR 43/30, 33, 34, 36, 37. In September 1922 Bennett had told Clapperton to take it as certain that he would not release Paterson: 'so the sooner you make other arrangements the better'. Mackintosh prevailed on Bishop Donald Martin of Argyll and the Isles to release Dr Donald Campbell (a future bishop and archbishop) to replace Paterson in Aberdeen.

14. SCAR 45/147.

15. SCAR 44/214; 39/32. Clapperton confided to Bishop Bennett that Cardinal Pomphili, Rome's vicar-general, was blocking Paterson's *onorificenza* on grounds of scandal: the vice-rector, years earlier, had helped and visited an expatriate lady who was in difficulties and gossips had been at work. The fighting tenacity of Clapperton and his strong loyalty to a friend comes through well in this episode. He spoke to Cardinal Protector Merry del Val, Bisleti of the Congregation of Seminaries and Pomphili himself. To Merry Del Val's successor, Cardinal Ehrle, he wrote a long *esposto* on the matter in which careful argument barely hid his seething anger. Ehrle showed the *esposto* to the pope who was impressed but reluctant to intervene. However, Clapperton won the day in the end.

16. SCAR 44/506.

17. SCAR 45/75. A student diarist of the time showed more enthusiasm: '7th April. Baxter's mark came out today – 10, *summa cum laude*! Boy! We got a bick for it [a *bicchierotto* was a glass of red wine] at supper to drink his health and called for a speech.'

18. J. Darragh, *The Catholic Hierarchy of Scotland* (Glasgow, 1986), 85. The published version of Flanagan's thesis has its modest niche in the vast Newman bibliography: P. I. Flanagan, *Newman, Faith and the Believer* (London, 1945).

19. Writing to Clapperton in Scotland shortly before the 1936 exams, Sheridan joked that he would have to ask for a special course in mathematics for himself since Fr Soccorsi's new notes for the course *On scientific questions related to philosophy* were 'really terrible . . . the reasoning is very hard to follow, but I can follow it, so I am going over these sheets with the students'.

20. SCAR 43/101 (November 1924). Stack founded the Scots College Society.

21. SCAR 44/506: to Mackintosh (22 October 1931).
22. SCAR 55/40.
23. SCAR 46/53. An anecdote about Canon Gillon illustrates the hazards of the spiritual director's trade. He centred a 'What is the world coming to?' talk on the *graffito* to be seen everywhere – *Evviva Guerra!* – without realising that, besides meaning 'war', *Guerra* was also the surname of a champion Italian cyclist. (Interview with Mgr Francis Duffy, Nazareth House, Kilmarnock. Mgr Duffy studied at the Scots College Rome before being ordained for the Diocese of Galloway in 1939.)
24. The bishops concurred in 1931 with Clapperton's decision, on practical grounds, to abolish the uniform in favour of a black cassock and red sash. Why the decision was not implemented – Clapperton claimed the Congregation of Seminaries supported the change – cannot presently be established. Signor Rocco, who started tailoring the soutanes in 1937, was still making them in the 1990s.
25. Interview with Mgr Francis Duffy who was Wilfred Johnston's classmate.
26. Articles in the *Scots College Magazine* by Fr Hector Scerri, a Maltese postgraduate at the College in recent years, deal interestingly with some of these figures. See, for example, the edition of 1997.
27. *SCD* 1970, 316.
28. Interview with Mgr Francis Duffy. Clapperton duly changed his mind – but at the last moment.
29. SCAR 44/327.
30. SCAR 44/274 (3 April 1930).
31. SCAR 39/28 (14 May 1930).
32. SCAR 44/307.
33. In recent times professors have been at liberty to introduce intermediate gradings which has had the interesting effect of bunching marks upwards rather than downwards as in percentage systems. The average marks reported to the bishops by Flanagan in the 1960s were generally between seven and eight; ten years later they were between eight and nine.
34. McDonald references to be found in SCAR 47/12 (6 August 1936) and SCAR 48/205 (14 October 1939) respectively.
35. SCAR 48/279 (23 November 1939).
36. Major exams were strictly speaking public. Examinees would not be happy to have spectators and neither, it would seem, was the Professor of Metaphysics.
37. SCAR R40B.
38. SCAR 43/16 (11 November 1922).
39. Mackintosh was keenly interested at all stages of the villa project: the purchase of a new site, the search for a water-source, the improvement to the road and the consequent decision to demolish and rebuild on the site of the old villa. He warned Clapperton to parry questions from the bishops about the source of the large low-interest loan he claimed to have obtained for the construction. See SCAR 43/175 (13 October 1926).
40. SCAR 43/352 (1 February 1928): 'I and the whole Board with me look on this money

as a pure gift to the College.' However, because some school rents money was being used, Mackintosh was representing it as a loan 'for the time being'. Put not your trust in princes: at the beginning of the Second World War Mackintosh would remind Clapperton 'that Glasgow had a heavy loan without interest at the college.' Mackintosh's accountant calculated the liability at over twice Clapperton's figure. See SCAR 48/357 (8 January 1940).

41. SCAR 46/218, 219 (30 and 31 March 1935).

42. SCAR 46/387. Mackintosh's eventual reply is recorded in SCAR 46/223 (17 April 1935).

43. L. Fermi, *Mussolini* (Chicago, 1961), 258.

44. SCAR 44/124. See Fermi, *Mussolini*, 260.

45. See SCAR 46/226 (31 October 1935) and 46/392 (31 November 1935).

46. College Diary 1938. There had been a brief official visitation of the College a fortnight before, part, it would seem, of a general inspection of Roman seminaries. No student had taken the option of a private talk with the apostolic visitor whose remarks on the too great freedom given to senior students Clapperton was later to resent. But there and then the visitor had criticised the Via delle Quattro Fontane site and suggested that the College should be moved. The Irish College rector of the time resigned on account of criticisms made on this occasion by the apostolic visitor.

47. It appears that the objections of the College's neighbour, the widow of Signor Tittoni (a former President of Senate) who had provided quarters for the Duce in the twenties, may have saved the day.

48. In Flanagan's long letter about all this to Clapperton there is a slight sense of gloating when he finds Godfrey at the English villa moneyless and unprepared. In the final crisis of May 1940, Clapperton found the man at Barclays 'full of jitters and of little use'. See College Diary 1940, 111.

49. Hunter Diack and R. F. MacKenzie, who became a noted educationist.

50. See Sydney McEwan, *On the high Cs* (Glasgow, 1973) for description of the Scots College in 1938 when he arrived and the warm description of Clapperton as 'this gem of a rector'. McEwan eventually transferred to St Peter's College, Bearsden, and spent his priesthood in the service of the Diocese of Argyll and the Isles.

51. SCAR 40B [date uncertain].

52. It was Osborne who had arranged for the original Stuart tombstones in the Vatican to be gifted to the Scots College (with King George VI's approval) when a new sarcophagus was provided in St Peter's Basilica in 1939 by the Royal family. See SCAR 48/266, 323. In general, the wartime period at the College has been dealt with at length elsewhere, in articles by Clapperton in the 1950 and 1955 editions of the *Scots College Magazine* and by Christopher McElroy in 1996.

53. SCAR 49/14.

54. Valentino Pinci was the brother-in-law of the very able *vignerolo* Eugenio Rossi, who died in 1927 leaving a widow and three small children. The family remained at the villa, first on a temporary and then on a more permanent contract and took on the work

of the vineyard throughout the 'thirties, while Signor Rossi, always referred to as 'Sor' Emma' saw to the domestic side of things. Writing to the Scots College Society after the war, Clapperton simply stated that Sor'Emma and her family, with Valentino, had returned to their home town. He asked prayers for Valentino who had died in the meantime. Sor'Emma and her son Augusto Rossi remained close friends of the College. Augusto was at Clapperton's deathbed and the link with the family has continued to the present day. Augusto's brother Gaetano, after a period studying at the seminary of Anagni in the thirties, was accepted by Archbishop Mackintosh as a student for Glasgow. Mgr Rossi, as he now is, suffered wartime interment and has since served the Archdiocese and the Scots–Italian community in many offices.

55. SCAR 49/173.

56. SCAR 49/175. Aloysius Smith CRL was abbot of San Pietro in Vincoli, Rome. His report is in SCAR 48/131 (31 August 1938).

57. The destruction by fire of the newly-renovated seminary in Bearsden, just after the bishops' meeting in May, may have had some influence here. Rogers and McCaffery were among Clapperton's closest friends. Rogers became vicar-general in the new Diocese of Motherwell and spent his later years in Rome as a Rota judge; he died in Glasgow. McCaffery, a former lecturer at Genoa and, in wartime, Director of Special Operations (Europe), was in business in Milan and had the distinction of introducing Clapperton to Padre Pio, for whom the rector developed a great devotion. See John McCaffery, *The Friar of San Giovanni* (London, 1978), 98-100.

58. Report to Scots College Society 1948.

59. College Diary 1948 (3 January).

60. Report to bishops (April 1949).

61. Interview with Canon Michael Meechan, a colleague of Flanagan's in Valladolid.

62. Interview with Mgr Francis Duffy.

63. The transfer of the £2000, really a subsidy from Glasgow alone, aroused the interest of the Custodian of Enemy Property who was charged with applying the legislation of 1942 under which (he maintained) this sum could not be given to an Italian institution; moreover the investment income Clapperton had passed on to Blairs in the war years ought to have been forfeited. The appeal for exemption was successful. Clapperton had had an earlier brush with British authorities over an attempt to transfer funds to a religious order in Rome. See SCAR 50/134, 49/177; also GAA CE6/6/3, 10.

64. See SCAR 56/12, 56/13, and 56/8 (10 April 1954).

65. SCAR 56/12 (30 August 1957).

66. '. . . *ut Sanctitas Vestra eum ab officio Rectoris liberare, et in patriam reverti sinere benigne dignetur, ubi aliquod ministerium suis facultatibus magis aptum, per aliquot annos, si Deus concedat, adhuc explere poterit.*'

67. SCAR 56/13.

68. SCAR 83/21 (23 January 1959). The report suggested a total repair cost of £70,000 which the surveyor considered uneconomical. Some of the structural weakness noted, for example in the Staff wing, proved to be less critical than at first appeared.

69. SCAR 83/4.

70. Cardinal Pizzardo, besides being Prefect of the Congregation of Seminaries, had been Cardinal Protector since 1951 – the last appointed.

71. See SCAR 84/50–51 (both from 1960). Something rather like this was being done for the Lombard College by Marenda. For Mgr Humble's experience in Valladolid, see Maurice Taylor, *The Scots College in Spain*, (Valladolid, 1971), 252–6.

72. SCAR 84/177. Langbank was a junior seminary which provided education for boys in their first two secondary years before moving on to Blairs to complete their education.

73. A generous Columba Trust grant came through the good offices of Michael Crichton-Stuart, a friend in whom Flanagan confided: 'The College suffers through having no effective friend on the Hierarchy.' The ex-Roman Campbell had twice said publicly that the College in Rome need not look for his money which was needed for the seminary at Cardross. See SCAR 89/243.

74. See SCAR 90/327: Flanagan to J. McKee.

75. SCAR 90/294, 327.

76. SCAR 81/103.

77. SCAR 80/42B: rector's report of April 1968.

78. On Boyle's departure in 1973, Fr Latourelle SJ, Dean of Theology, spoke of the 'constant, generous, and intelligent collaboration' he had given the Gregorian University. SCAR 100/213 (7 June 1973).

79. See Flanagan's Report, April 1965. Boyle seemed non-plussed about handling postgraduates; latterly they lived elsewhere. See SCAR 80/42B.

80. See SCAR 90/294 (5 February 1965), Flanagan to Boyle: '. . . of course our boys are still very mild and obedient and sane compared to those in some other places'.

81. In a General Chapter of the *Suore di Betania*, superiors had reversed the decision that seminary service could be part of the Italian order's vocation.

82. Clapperton's comment is in his 1948 report to the Scots College Society. See SCAR 56/51 (8 July 1948).

83. Fr Tormey succeeded Fr Aidan Martin. Like Dr Sheridan in the thirties, he carried both burdens for some time; later, outside tutorial help had to be sought as in the past.

84. The letters quoted in Paul Gardiner, *Mother Mary MacKillop* (Newtown, 1993) appear to have been taken from SCAR before Mgr Flanagan catalogued the collection.

Appendix 1: A British College in Rome?

Michael E. Williams

Those not conversant with the history of the Catholic Church in the British Isles are sometimes surprised to find that in Rome there are three separate institutions for the training of priests to serve in the dioceses of Scotland, England and Ireland, each with its own distinctive history and traditions.[1] Certain tendencies towards a homogenisation of culture which seem to be making the cities of London, Edinburgh and Dublin and their inhabitants less foreign to each other might suggest that some sort of amalgamation of Catholic effort in the field of clerical training might be both appropriate and opportune.[2] However, over the years, even at times of extreme pressure on both human and financial resources, each College has gone its own way and struggled for independent survival. The factors that have kept them apart stem not only from the legal, social, cultural and temperamental differences of three nations but also from the various ways in which the Early Modern Reformation movement affected different parts of these islands. Unfortunately, this has had an adverse effect on Catholic historiography since historians have sometimes tended to focus their attention on their own particular bailiwick and paid less attention to important common concerns. Looked at from the mainland of Europe there has at times been disappointment or even dismay that persecuted Catholics did not make common cause and overcome the national and tribal differences of English, Scots and Irish. It must be recalled that the recovery of the whole British Isles for the Catholic cause was the concern of both the papacy and the Catholic powers. Pope Gregory XIII (1572–85) not only approved of the transformation of the English pilgrim hostel in Rome into a seminary, but he also supported both the Scots and the Irish by providing funds for Colleges.[3]

However, the situation was more complex than at first supposed. As Hugh Fenning has observed, Propaganda Fide soon realised that the affairs of the three nations, England, Scotland and Ireland, had to be treated separately since the demands made on the missionary priests differed from place to place.[4] England experienced a series of Reformations: Henrician, Edwardian, Marian and Elizabethan. In the process the bishops followed their rulers and the links with Rome were broken and this gave the religious orders an unusual importance. (Although the orders have a presence throughout the universal Church, it is through the local episcopate that the link between the apostolic college and its head, the pope, finds the clearest expression. This no longer existed in England. The later appointement of Vicars Apostolic did something to remedy this.) Moreover, in England the priests coming from the seminaries abroad were faced with a populace that was predominantly hostile. Scotland, a separate Kingdom to begin with, later shared its monarch with England (after 1603) and the Scots Catholics, being a less numerous community than their neighbours, suffered even fiercer persecution. Added to this, the exceptional conditions in the Highlands and Islands provided particular difficulties. Ireland, on the other hand, managed to preserve a hierarchy and, on the whole, the people remained loyal to Catholicism, but they had to contend with colonising and protestantising rulers from across the sea. All three nations had their Catholic networks abroad providing opportunities for schooling and religious life that were not possible at home. Each had its agents in Rome, cultivated its own patrons, had distinct Cardinals Protector and was prepared to fight its own battles. But this lack of uniformity did at least have one advantage since it meant that the Church never lost sight of the different situational needs and aspirations of each particular nation.[5] From within the Colleges themselves there is not much evidence of any desire for a closer association. Nevertheless, the idea of a British College is not entirely unheard of.

At the end of the seventeenth century, the administration of all three Colleges was in the hands of the Jesuits.[6] As superiors they were often criticised by those on the mission for the way in which they were failing to prepare future priests for pastoral work at home. For their part, some Jesuits were inclined to lay the responsibility for any shortcomings on the fact that the Colleges were directed by English, Scots and Irish nationals. This they considered to be unsuitable for Jesuit Colleges in Rome under the direct eyes of the Father General.[7] The year 1701 was an important date for the Scots because in that year the Jesuit General removed Fr Forbes SJ from the rectorship of their College and put an Italian Jesuit in his place. The alleged reason for this change was the poor administration and financial state of the College. In his account of the College history, the Abbé MacPherson makes reference to a scheme of the Jesuits in 1704 to unite the three Colleges into one.[8] It would be much more convenient administratively to have one set of superiors and one establishment instead of three distinct institutions. The Abbé saw this in a sinister light: 'the mutual antipathy of the three nations would be a lasting and insurmountable obstacle to national superiors as none of the three would submit to be governed by any of the other two.' This would mean that a non-national, an Italian perhaps, would be called in to keep the peace. He then goes on to tell of how the Vicars Apostolic, Thomas Nicholson and James Gordon, put forward an alternative plan. This was to unite the Scots College to the College of Propaganda Fide. This would not only be of benefit for the Mission; it would avoid any association with the English or Irish and it would mean, in effect, that Propaganda would take charge and there would be no place left for the Jesuits.

This explanation of Macpherson, however, is not satisfactory and it does not take into consideration some of the materials that have come to light in the Archives of Propaganda Fide.[9] It would appear that the idea of amalgamating the three Colleges into one did not originate with the Jesuits from the base motive suggested by MacPherson. Mention of uniting the Scots with the English occurs in a reference to the visitation of the Scots by Cardinal Barbarigo in 1693. At this time the Scots College was a very small community of six or seven students at most, the accommodation was poor and this drew unfavourable comparisons with the English College which had recently undergone extensive rebuilding undertaken by the Protector, Cardinal Howard.[10] At the end of his visitation Barbarigo declared that it would be a waste of money to continue to maintain a separate Scots College. Rather, one ought to consider uniting the Scots and the English. This would increase the total number of students and satisfy other Scots' requests such as a better provision of travelling expenses (*viaticum*).[11] Moreover, he stated that both the Pope and the Congregation of Propaganda Fide were resolved to bring about this union. This elicited a strong protest and the Scots were opposed on many grounds, saying that it would be prejudicial to the Mission and shameful to the Scots nation.[12]

In these years preceding the Act of Union, the Scots were especially hurt by the sharp contrast between the state of their College in Rome and that of the English. To incorporate the two would be nothing less than a further slight on the Scottish Mission and nation. Even though they might come to recognise that a union with some other College might be necessary both for the cause of religion and the honour of the nation, it certainly could not be with a people to whom they had the most antipathy. The College would have to be one where their students could live in peace and unity with their fellow students. This was possible with any nation except the English and more easily with remote peoples with whom they had no quarrel. The Scots would have to follow the same way of life as other students with no conflicting views on liberty, with their honour respected and independence recognised.[13]

There was unanimity among the Scots that there should be no union with the English but most of the attention now becomes focused on a possible alternative union with Propaganda Fide College. Many pleas were directed to the exiled Stuart Court at St Germain.[14] The idea was strongly supported by James Gordon on his being appointed coadjutor Vicar Apostolic to Thomas Nicholson.[15] He wrote to Propaganda in favour of such a union – not simply for the good of a financially embarrassed College in Rome but for the benefit of the Mission in Scotland. Although not entirely closed to the possibility, the Jesuits were against any deeper ties with Propaganda and they feared a break of the link with the *Collegio Romano*. In the end, the matter was resolved in a rather unexpected way. In 1706, Cardinals Protector were appointed to the posts vacant since the death of Howard: Caprara for the English, Imperiali for the Irish and none other than Sacripanti, the Prefect of the Congregation Propaganda Fide, for the Scots. He was the one to whom both Nicholson and Gordon had written about their troubles. Sacripanti took possession of the College in September 1706 and later he was able as part of his office to conduct a visitation in which he could make reforms yet retain the existing relationship with Propaganda. There was no need to dismiss the Jesuits.

But neither the Scots of the day nor later writers like John Thomson and Paul MacPherson realised the matter was not yet concluded. Before Sacripanti made his visitation, a meeting was summoned of the Particular Congregation of Propaganda Fide for the affairs of England, Scotland and Ireland which took place on Monday 28 November 1707. Present were Caprara, Imperiali and Sacripanti as well as Cardinals Colloredo (an Oratorian), Paolucci (former Nuncio in Paris), Fabroni (former Secretary of Propaganda Fide), Pamfilii and Barberini (who had made a visitation of the English College in 1702). Acting as secretary was the recently appointed Cavalieri. The first item on the agenda was the union of the English, Irish and Scots Colleges under the single title of The British College with rules laid down by Propaganda.[16] Each member spoke in turn and we have Cavalieri's brief jottings on what they said. Except for Barberini, they recognised that the royal opinion had to be taken into consideration (i.e. that of the Court of St Germain). Colloredo called attention to one of the main requests of the Scots, namely the need to cater for younger students under the age of seventeen who were not yet ready for the study of philosophy and also to difficulties that might arise from having several nations living together in one house. There was a need for a very prudent rector. Fabroni was for avoiding any suspicion of slight to the Jesuits. Caprara was for delaying the matter. But in the end the motion was carried and the secretary was to secure the reports of previous visitations that had been made to the Colleges. At the beginning of the following year, 14 January 1708, it was recorded that although the constitutions were available and various other decrees concerning the Scots College, the official report of Barbarigo's 1693 visitation could not be found, either the visit to the Scots or that to the Irish. It was two months later, on 13 March, that Sacripanti made his own visitation. His brief was to examine the situation obtaining in the College since Barbarigo's visit of 1693 and up to the end of the year 1707. The Rector was the Italian Jesuit Naselli but the former Scots Rector, James Forbes, was now Prefect of Studies. The Agent of the Scots, William Stuart, was present at this visitation.[17]

It was an extremely thorough examination and detailed instructions were laid down as to the future conduct of the House; the Agent promised to send more students to Rome; it was recommended that visits should be made to the German-Hungarian College to see the correct way of performing the sacred ceremonies; and the system of accounting had to be improved. But there was no mention of any union with the English or Irish, nor indeed with Propaganda College, unless one understands the visit of Sacripanti and his regulations as an indication of a closer link with this institution. Two years later, in 1710, the visit was followed up by another visit whose purpose it was to inspect the progress made by the Scots in their College from 1708 up to the end of 1709. But from now on there is no more reference to a united British College.

The idea of a union between the three Colleges arose out of the Holy See's concern for the plight of the Scots College and its apparent non-viability as a separate institution. The Scots, aware of the difficulties of their own situation, were willing to entertain the idea of a union with another institution if necessary to preserve their continued existence. But they were totally opposed to a union with the English on the grounds that it was not possible to form a harmonious community with these people. At the time when this question arose feelings were aggravated by the prospective Act of Union (1707) between England and Scotland.

To sum up: neither English, Irish or Scots proposed the setting up of a British College in Rome. There is no evidence that such a united College was initially proposed by the Jesuits as a convenient administrative solution. The exiled Jacobite Court at St Germain was not in favour of the scheme. The idea came originally from the pope and the Congregation of Propaganda Fide and it was first disclosed by Cardinal Barbarigo at the visitation of the Scots College in 1693. It was rejected outright by the Scots and not even discussed, being replaced by a consideration of the possibility of a union with Propaganda Fide College. Nevertheless, it remained on the Roman agenda up to and including the meeting of the Particular Congregation in November 1707. After that meeting something happened preventing the decree from taking effect. A narrow escape!

NOTES

1. More accurately four Colleges. But the Pontifical Beda College also provides for English-speaking countries other than those in the British Isles.
2. In 1998 the Catholic Bishops' Conferences in England & Wales, Scotland and Ireland in *One Bread, One Body* (London, 1998) set out general norms concerning the reception of the Eucharist for the whole of the British Isles.
3. Money was given to the Scots College on condition that six Irishmen would also be

provided with pensions at Pont-à-Mousson in 1584. See ARSI, Rom 156, f 334.

4. Hugh Fenning, 'The Three Kingdoms, England, Ireland, Scotland', in *Sacrae Congregationis de Propaganda Fide Memoria*, II, (Rome – Freiburg-Wien, 1973), 604–29.

5. The only real losers were the Catholics of Wales who as a result of the troubles on the change of the Hospice into a seminary found themselves excluded. See Williams, 2–6.

6. The Jesuits had administered the English College since 1579, the Scots College since 1615 and the Irish College since 1635.

7. The removal of Forbes in 1701 and the substitution of an Italian rector coincided with similar manoeuvres at the Jesuit-run English College where there was an attempt to introduce Italian priests as prefects to supervise discipline. See Williams, 49–50.

8. *MacPherson*, 98.

9. APF, CP 34A, *Anglia, Ibernia, Scozia dal 1702 al 1712* is a large bound volume although the documents are not always found in a good chronological order.

10. The Dominican Philip Thomas Howard, although for a time Protector of all three Colleges, was often a disappointment. He improved the buildings of the English College and made it a suitable palace for himself in Rome but he also bequeathed his bills to the College.

11. It was pointed out in an (undated) reply to some objections against the union of the Scots College with the College of Propaganda Fide, that such a union would help to solve two of the outstanding problems of the College: namely (i) the inability of the College to defray the heavy costs of travel from Scotland to Rome; (ii) the lack of provision for the tuition of those students who were not yet ready to study philosophy. (APF, CP 34A, ff 166–170.)

12. APF, CP 34A, ff 166–70: 'At the conclusion of his visit to the Scots College in 1693, Cardinal Barbarigo (of happy memory) . . . said that it was a waste of money to maintain a separate Scots College where there are as many superiors as there are students. Consequently the Scots College should be united with the English College so that the number of students would be increased and travelling expenses provided. Both the pope and the Sacred Congregation were determined to bring this about were it not that the Scots were opposed to it for many reasons, especially because it would prejudice the mission and be an affront to the Scottish nation. But at the same time the memorial presented by the Scots against such a union makes it clear that union with some College other than the English was considered necessary for the sake of religion and the honour of the nation . . . So it remains to set up a union with a college other than the English where Scots can live at peace, preserve charity and not suffer dishonour to their nation.' The document goes on to say that the memorial of the Scots was presented by the 'Queen of Great Britain' (Mary of Modena, regent for James III) to Monsignor Gualtieri, the nuncio in Paris who sent it on to Cardinal Paolucci in Rome in 1704.

13. These sentiments are almost identical with those of William Leslie: see *Gray*, 37.

14. The Stuart Court in exile claimed privileges in regard to the overseas Colleges. Many still regarded James II as lawful King and when he died in 1701 his widow Maria

Beatrice of Modena became Regent until her son James Edward became of age. The Jesuit fathers were influential in the Court.

15. APF, CP 34A, ff 121, 123.

16. APF, CP 34A, ff 91r, 91v, 92r, 109v.

17. APF, Collegii Vari 63 (Collegio Scozzese di Roma 1600–1842), ff 75–91, 100–108.

Appendix 2: Clement VIII's Bull of Foundation (1600)

The Bull of Clement VIII which formally constituted the Scots College Rome was promulgated on 5 December 1600. It is a long, wordy text, replete with legal formulae. It is principally concerned with establishing the rights and privileges of the College, bequeathing in the process the original building on the Via del Tritone. The following is a paraphrased extract prepared by the editor, based on a literal translation (of SCAR 59) by the Rev Victor T. Boyle, a priest of the Diocese of Paisley, presently working in the Congregation for Catholic Education, Rome. The value of this particular passage rests in the light it throws on official papal justification for the foundation of the College; it also shows that a Cardinal Protector was appointed from the very outset. The editor is in Fr Boyle's debt; the editor alone is responsible for any errors.

CLEMENT BISHOP
Servant of the servants of God
For everlasting memory

We have learned that in the most noble Kingdom of Scotland – numbered among the first to have accepted the Catholic faith, but now for many years violently disturbed by heresy – there are many Christian faithful who, though afflicted by the greatest calamities, outlawry, or liability to punishment, hold on to the Catholic faith and persist in their obedience and devotion to the Holy Roman Church. These same faithful are accustomed to journey to Rome and to visit the tombs of the most holy apostles, in token of their respect and love for the Roman See. But until now in this city there has been no place for the receiving and educating of boys and youths of the Scottish nation who, as orphans or exiles or robbed of their goods, have lacked the means of sustaining life and spiritual growth – in sum, a place dedicated to the promotion of piety and Christian living, and the study of letters. However, there is a building close to the church of Our Lady of Constantinople, in the Trevi region of the city. It was gifted by our beloved son, Michele Sebastiani, a native of this city, and now belongs to the Apostolic Camera, the responsibility of our beloved son, Andrea de Spinosa (who shares our table and is our constant servant). This property may usefully serve for the foundation of a College, and for the reception of the aforesaid boys and youths. In imitation, therefore, of Popes Celestine and Honorius, and the other Roman Pontiffs who had special care for this nation, we wish to commend this outstanding work of piety in the hope that, in the future, the students of this College may save many souls in the Kingdom of Scotland. May they, when all heresy has been eradicated, work towards the restitution both of Catholic worship, which has fallen into abeyance, and the ancestral religion of their homeland. By our own initiative, therefore – not at the instance of a petition of the Scottish nation nor of any other brought to us concerning this matter on behalf of this nation – and with the fullness of Apostolic power, we erect and institute in perpetuity in the aforesaid building, a College, to be called of the Scottish Nation, in which well-fitted youths and adolescents of Scotland might become familiar with good traditions, true piety and sound doctrine, and be instructed in other virtues worthy of the Christian name . . . We furthermore constitute and appoint our beloved son Camillo Borghese, called Cardinal Priest of the Title of Saints John and Paul, as Protector and Defender of the same College by whose counsel and aid all matters pertaining to its scholars may be ordered . . . Given at Rome at Saint Peter's, in the Year of the Incarnation of Our Lord 1600, 5 December, the Ninth Year of Our Pontificate.

Appendix 3: The Letters of Thomas Crumly

Thomas Crumly (1851–1930), a native of Govan, was educated at St Aloysius' College, Glasgow, and Blairs College, near Aberdeen, before setting out for the Scots College Rome in 1869. There he opted to be ordained for the Eastern District in 1874 and became a priest (and, later, canon) of the Diocese of Dunkeld when the Catholic hierarchy was restored in Scotland in 1878. He served in Dundee, Blairgowrie, Doune, Crieff, Lochee and Wellburn.

From the outset of his time as a student at the Scots College Rome, the young Thomas Crumly kept up a correspondence with his family and with the priest who had influenced him in discerning his own vocation, the Rev Walter Dixon of Govan. Twenty-seven of those letters are extant and in private hands. A good deal of what Crumly wrote is typical family gossip and there would be little of lasting historical value if that was all these letters had to offer. But Crumly was studying in Rome during the heady days of the First Vatican Council and the surrender of papal Rome and he could not resist recounting adventures and experiences to his Govan family which emphasised the proximity of their Thomas to danger and events of great import.

Crumly's letters offer the unique perspective of a Scottish student in Rome during the momentous period of Risorgimento, as well as interesting vignettes of College life. They are windows to the prejudices, dreams and hopes of a former age. They deserve a wider audience. This appendix publishes an edited selection.

1

To Rev Walter Dixon of Govan

Scots College Rome – July 1869

Journey to and arrival at College

The last news that I gave you was that we arrived in Paris all right. We arrived on Saturday evening and put up at the Hotel St Joseph, Place St Sulpice. I will not attempt to describe my thoughts and feelings on entering that city of grandeur and magnificence. The buildings, the manners, ways and language of the people were so strange and new to me that I could almost fancy myself in another world. The next day was Sunday and we attended a Grand High Mass in the parish of St Sulpice. Here I was lost in amazement; I cannot express what I felt. My uppermost thought was, well, since the worship of God is so magnificent and grand on earth, what must it be like in heaven . . . We visited several famous places during the short time we had to stay. We took the train for Marseilles on Monday evening and reached it on Wednesday morning after 36 long hours travelling. The country all along is very beautiful but the train went as slow almost as it possibly could go. On Wednesday evening we took the boat from Marseilles to Civita Vecchia. We were two nights and a day at sea and reached port on Friday morning. We had a magnificent passage and no one was sea-sick. The food and bedding were excellent. From Civita Vecchia we took a train for

153

Rome . . . When we reached the Scots College everything was in confusion. The students were engaged in removing from the old to the new College.

2
To his parents
Country House, Albano – 27 August 1869
Description of country house at Albano

I received your pleasant letter in due time, and I am glad to inform you that your letters always come safe and in due time. I am now in perfect health, feel no inconvenience from the heat and enjoy myself immensely. On the 16th August, the students left Rome and went to their country house at a place called Albano, about 16 miles from the Eternal City. It is beautifully situated among the hills and is a place famous for the beauty of its scenery and the purity of its air. As I sit at my window I have a beautiful view of the Mediterranean Sea. It seems to be quite near to us, but it would be a walk of at least thirteen or fourteen miles to reach it, across a dry and barren country, as flat as the palm of your hand, almost uninhabited, and which stretches for miles and miles along the sea coast. We have a very fine country house and attached to it is a garden full of shady walks and figs and grapes and all sorts of fruit trees and beautiful flowers. The country about us where we go for walks is really delightful. It is covered with finely wooded hills and summer houses beautifully situated, vineyards and olive yards with everything in fact that would please the eye. Outside the town a little is the beautiful lake of Albano which is six miles in circumference, and along whose pleasant banks we often take our walks. However, although we are so near the lake, we are not allowed to bathe in it because it is considered unbecoming in this country for ecclesiastical students to bathe: the same can be said of the sea; we have a splendid view of it, but that is all, is it not a pity? But, in spite of this, you may easily perceive from my poor description that if we are not in paradise we are in the next best place to it. A thing very remarkable here, as well as very edifying and beautiful, is the great devotion of the people to the Blessed Virgin. In the town and along the roads in the country, little oratories or chapels are to be met with where there is a beautiful statue or picture of the Virgin and Child, or perhaps a large Cross, and these are on the public roads and in the open air, a thing which very forcibly reminds us that we are in a Catholic country. It was once the case in poor Scotland I have no doubt, and I hope the day is not far distant when it will be so again.

3
To his parents
Scots College Rome – 28 December 1869
Opening of new Scots College; Popular acclamation of Pius IX; Opening of the First Vatican Council; Christmas in Rome

Your last letter came in due time and was all the more agreeable to me as I had been expecting it for some time. You need not be astonished at my tardiness in replying for, as you know, it is only at festive times like this that we are allowed to write. At other times we are too much taken up with our studies to have leisure for letters. But now I must try to give you some news about Rome and the great events that daily take place in it. Towards the end of November, Bishops Strain and McDonald arrived in Rome from Scotland and took up their residence in our College. Besides these, there were two bishops from Nova Scotia residing with us. On November 30th, the feast of St Andrew the Apostle and Patron Saint of Scotland, our new Scots College was solemnly opened. High Mass was sung in the forenoon at which the bishops resident in the College attended. At one o'clock we had a grand dinner in honour of the occasion, at which were present Dr Manning, Archbishop of Westminster, Dr Spalding, Archbishop of Baltimore, America, and several other Scotch and English bishops, several rectors of colleges in Rome, besides a great many of the most respectable English gentlemen in the City. Cardinal Cullen and the Marquis of Bute were invited but, unfortunately, they had not as yet arrived in Rome. The Marquis did his best to be on time for the opening of the College and would have arrived before the day appointed had it not been for a trick played on him by the Keeper of the hotel in which he was living at Marseilles. The Marquis asked the hotel-keeper on a certain day whether the ship would sail for Civita Vecchia, the seaport town of Rome. As I might say, the Keeper, whether through ignorance or for his own private ends to make more money by the presence of such a noble guest, told him wrong, and the consequence was as I have stated. However, the night after his arrival he came to see the new College and was shown over it by the rector, Dr Grant. He has the reputation of being a very sensible and pious young nobleman and already the fame of his extensive charities has spread far and near.

On Tuesday, December 7th, our holy father the pope gave solemn Benediction in the church of the Twelve Apostles and was attended by a great number of Cardinals. Long before the pope arrived the large square in which the above named church stands was crowded with people and the square was lined with soldiers on either side to keep back the crowds and keep a clear passage for the pope's carriage. Many bishops and priests were to be seen among the rest, and an immense number of English, French, Americans and strangers from almost all nations were all anxious to catch a glimpse of His Holiness the pope. The windows and balconies on both sides were tastefully and richly decorated with red hangings so that the whole square presented a grand and splendid appearance. Before the pope appeared the people were quiet and orderly and I heard some English ladies near me contrasting the behaviour of the crowd with that of an English mob in terms not very favourable to the latter. But when the pope appeared the enthusiasm of the people knew no bounds. Thousands joined in one grand shout of welcome, handkerchiefs were waving on all sides, while the air was rent with shouts of 'Long live our Pontiff King', 'Long live Pius the Ninth'. When his carriage stopped and the pope was getting out, he stood upright, smiled with pleasure upon the people and blessed them all. He then entered the church which was crowded to the doors. The whole people joined with one voice in singing the *Te Deum* and it was something wonderful and beyond all description to hear that solemn hymn of thanksgiving sung in unison and perfect harmony by thousands of pious worshippers. It was enough to put one in mind of the heavenly choirs who sing day and night before the throne of God. When all was over, the pope departed amidst the same enthusiastic demonstration of loyalty and warm attachment. I must not forget to tell you that the military bands played at his coming.

On Wednesday, December 8th, in St Peter's, the largest and grandest church in the world as you know, the first Council of the Vatican was opened. I was at the opening along with my fellow students and, after making our visit to the Blessed Sacrament and paying our devotions at the tomb of the Apostles, we tried to get as good a place as possible to see the procession of the bishops. There were about 800 I believe, all dressed in copes and mitres. They moved on in slow procession to the Council Hall, where Solemn High Mass was sung. After Mass the assembled bishops were addressed in a Latin sermon by one of the bishops appointed for that purpose. There were about 70,000 or 80,000 persons present, and the crush was so great that several people fainted away and had to be carried out, while the desire of the people to see the bishops was so intense that the soldiers could scarcely keep back the multitudes that were pressing forward. The whole ceremony took up about six hours. Oh! What a grand and noble thing it was to see Christianity, if I may so speak, to see the bishops of the whole world assembled around the Chair of St Peter, showing by their very presence the Oneness and the Universality of the Church of Christ. Such an august assembly could be seen nowhere else; no, it is only the Bishop of Rome, the successor of St Peter, who could gather together from all parts, by his only word, so great a body of venerable bishops and holy men. But why should I say more about the General Council? You hear of it from the altar, you read of it in the newspapers, the whole world is full of good and evil reports about it. We have only to pray God to bless and protect the Fathers of the Council and to humble and confound all the enemies of the Church, and then to rest assured in the firm faith and confidence that God will direct the bishops in all that is for His own glory and the salvation of men.

I hope you and all my friends have had a Merry Xmas and I wish you all, both great and small, a Very Happy New Year and a large share in the abundant blessings of God showered down upon the good at this joyful season. Before speaking of Xmas day in Rome, I will take notice of a beautiful custom which exists here. At the beginning of Advent, pipers come into Rome from the mountains in its neighbourhood to welcome the infant Saviour into the world and during the whole of Advent they go through the streets piping and singing litanies. When Xmas comes they return to their mountains and you hear no more of them. On every Sunday of Advent there was a sermon in English delivered in a church set aside for English-speaking people alone by the Revd T. Burke, an Irish Dominican Father of great reputation as a preacher. In the Scots College on Xmas night, exactly at 12 o'clock, Bishop Strain commenced Mass. He said three before leaving the altar, and at the first he gave holy communion to the Marquis of Bute and to some other Catholic Lord whose name I did not hear. In the forenoon we went to St Peter's where the pope himself sang High Mass. In the afternoon we went to one of the grandest churches in Rome to see the crib in which our Saviour was born. What a glorious sight it was to see there exposed to the veneration of the faithful, and enclosed in a beautiful shrine and surrounded with burning lights, the holy crib of Bethlehem. On Sunday, the day after Xmas, we went to a church called *Ara Coeli*, that is Altar of Heaven, where there was a most beautiful crib. In the front part there were the Divine Infant, His Mother and St Joseph and the shepherds kneeling in adoration; there were there also the ox and the ass. In the background there was a representation of the country about the stable, and you could see people coming with baskets on their heads to make offerings to the new born Saviour. Overhead there was heaven; you saw the heavenly Father looking down on his Son with pleasure, and all the choirs of angels looking down with admiration. The whole was beautifully lit up so as to give it the appearance of heavenly glory. In this same church I saw what I never saw or heard of before. On a raised platform in front of the crib, but at a good distance from it, little children were holding forth and preaching with all their might to a large and very respectful audience in which there was a great number of priests, if not even of bishops. Some of the children were not more than three or four years old, but still they shouted at the top of their voices so as to make themselves heard, they gestured right and left without end, sometimes they raised their little eyes to heaven, other times they stamped their feet on the floor when they were giving forth something very important, and sometimes they threw themselves on their knees in prayer to the little Babe of Bethlehem. They exhorted all to be glad and rejoice at this happy time; and it was wonderful to see children so young with so much sense as to stand up and preach to a large number of people. Whenever they mounted the platform they blessed themselves and made a bow to all and then began. As soon as one came down another mounted and, although their sermons were not long, they were in general given with equal grace and energy.

4

To Rev Walter Dixon of Govan

Scots College Rome – 26 April 1870

Holy Week and Easter in Rome

I will now relate some of the wonderful things which happen here at this glorious time of Easter. On the eve of Palm Sunday we entered Retreat and came out on Holy Thursday. The retreat was conducted by a Jesuit Father, a very holy man, of great experience and full of unction and of the spirit of God. Such was the opinion formed of him by us all. After finishing the retreat, we spent the remainder of that happy day in visiting the holy Sepulchres in the different churches which were beautifully decorated with flowers and lit up with numerous lamps and candles. On Good Friday we assisted at the Mass of the Pre-Sanctified in the morning and in the evening were present at the Office of Tenebrae in St Peter's. On Holy Saturday morning the pope assisted at the Mass in St Peter's and, at the intonation of the *Gloria*, the artillery of the Castle of St Angelo thundered forth and were answered by all the church bells in the city which, after their short silence, sent forth their joyous peals once more to welcome the approach of the Paschal Solemnity. On Easter Sunday the pope himself sang Mass and after it gave his blessing from a balcony in front of St Peter's to Rome, to Italy, and to the whole world. The whole piazza was filled with people from all parts of the world and, in the centre, was the papal army, several thousand strong in their gayest uniforms. At night the dome and façade of St Peter's were illuminated. On Monday night there was a grand display of fireworks and on Tuesday the whole city was illuminated in commemoration of the return of the pope from Gaeta. On Low Sunday the public session of the council was held, the pope presiding in person.

5

To Rev Walter Dixon of Govan

Scots College Rome – 8 July 1870

The curriculum at the Roman College

Our onward march in the paths of science this year has been rapid and steady. The professors at the Roman College, men of great learning and abilities, lead us on at an astonishing pace. In Mathematics we have got through Arithmetic, Algebra, Plane and Solid Geometry and Trigonometry; while in the other branch of our studies we have gone through all Logic, and a great part of Ontology, Natural Theology, Psychology, and

Cosmology. The *concorsi* or concurring for prizes will take place in July, and the examinations in August.

6
To Rev Walter Dixon of Govan
Country House, Albano – 8 September 1870
Albano, Examinations and Premonitions of Risorgimento

If I remember well the last time I wrote you was when the greatest heats were setting in and the harvest study beginning. Since that time there has been a good deal of hard work which has at length given place to the repose and quiet of a country life. I am happy to say that although several of my fellow students broke down under the terrible heat of July, I remained strong and healthy throughout.

At different times in July we had to write *concorsi* or compositions on the different matters we were studying and the best of these are awarded with prizes on the Premiation day. The prizes are always a gold or silver medal. After these *concorsi* were over we left Rome for Albano early in the morning of the 1st August in a pair of *vitture* or carriages, each drawn by two horses. As it was a fine fresh morning and the journey was only about fourteen miles, we much preferred the mode of travelling to going by rail and, strange to say, it was much cheaper to hire private carriages in this way than to travel by the railway.

Albano is a favourite country residence of the Romans at this season on account of the beauty of the surrounding scenery, its pure air, and lofty situation. It is about 900 feet above the level of the sea which is only 12 miles distant. On the south-east side is Monte Cave which rises to the height of 3,000 feet above the sea. At the top, and on the ground where once stood a temple of Jupiter Latialis, is a Passionist convent. At the foot of the mountain is the lake of Albano, one of the most beautiful pieces of water in the world. It was once the crater of a volcano, and the immense layers of lava which surrounded, now hard and solid stone, show how active it must have been at one time. It is 6 miles in circumference and is said to be fathomless and, on account of its sombre appearance, is called 'the Philosopher's lake'.

After coming here we continued our studies until the 13th when we went into Rome to pass the examination and take the degree belonging to those finishing the first year of philosophy, *vis* that of Bachelor of Philosophy. All those who pass receive the degree. There were 5 of us: we all passed successfully and returned to Albano the same night with lighter hearts, you may depend, than we had in the morning when all was doubt and anxiety. The consequences of not passing are fatal for we have a rule that says that he who does not pass must immediately leave and return to Scotland as one unfit to remain in the College. This rule we owe to Bishop Gillis and, with it before his mind, even the best student may not be without his apprehensions when the result is so uncertain. However the examiners were easy and no one had any difficulty in passing.

The premiation, or distribution of prizes, took place on the 2nd September and after it commenced the real country (vacation?). Up till this time we have had as long hours of study as we had in Rome, but now the play day is from morning until night and we have many liberties and amusements which we had not before. We have long walks and sometimes go on long expeditions (not on donkey back as formerly) to visit the most famous places round about. There is no talk of brigands this year – everything is quiet and we are in perfect security. In short, we have everything to make our vacations very happy and if we do not become strong and healthy, it is not for want of the means. I hope, dear sir, you will not be displeased with these frivolous details; a student's life is not one which is marked by many adventures.

But here I am at the end and have not said one word about the march of the Italian troops against Rome with their pontoons and boats to cross the Tiber in case they should find the bridges blown up; of the fortifying of every gage and hill in Rome; of the determination of the pope to hold out to the last. On all this I must be silent.

7

To his father

Country House, Albano – 10 September 1870

Spectre of Garibaldi

This part of the country is perfectly quiet and we expect to have a peaceful and happy time of it – there are no brigands to frighten us as there were last year. Rome has been put into a posture of defence for fear that the Italians, taking advantage of the withdrawal of the French troops which were defending the pope, might wish to do what they have often tried before, that is, to take possession of Rome for themselves. But the pope will defend himself and, if they come, will give them a warm reception. For fear the pope should be driven from Rome, there is an English frigate of 16 heavy guns at Civita Vecchia ready at his service.

8

To his parents

Scots College Rome – 27 September 1870

Surrender of Rome

Having heard news of the approach of the Italian army to take possession of Rome, we left the country house in Albano and fled to Rome as did all other colleges and people who, like ourselves, had left Rome to enjoy the country for a few months. In another week the Italians were gathered round the walls of Rome and on Tuesday the 20th, at 5 o'clock in the morning, they commenced the grand attack with heavy cannon at several gates at once. After five hours constant firing and hard fighting, the pope, to save all further bloodshed, ordered all fighting to cease and surrendered the city. During the cannonading many houses were riddled with cannon balls or burnt to the ground with bomb-shells but, thanks be to God, our fine college has not been touched. After the surrender was made the Italians entered by the thousands in great triumph. For very obvious reasons I cannot enter into particulars as I would wish and give my own thoughts on matters. Just now the less that is said the better. For several days after their entry there were public rejoicings and great disorders prevailed amongst the people. I heard that 500 people have already been sent to prison for their excesses. Things are quieter now and we have the prospect of returning to the country in a few days. Amidst all the public excitement no one has offered to molest us. The English Union Jack was flying on top of the College and under its protection we have been saved from all danger; no one dared to dishonour it.

9

To his parents

Scots College Rome – 4 November 1870

Disorder in Rome

Now that our vacations are ending and our studies about to commence I think it a fit time to write you a few words on my thoughts of the past and my prospects for the future. Our vacations have been long and, under the circumstances, they should scarcely have been more agreeable. We have had three full months of it and the only unfortunate thing was that, on account of the invasion of the pope's states and the taking of Rome, we had to fly to town in the beginning of September and stay there until the end of the same month. In Rome great disorders have taken place and all sorts of crime have been committed. Among other things three priests were stabbed, one after the other, by the same man. Here in the country, however, the people have been well disposed towards us and, to show their sympathy for our character, are more eager than they ever were to do us reverence. Only now and again we meet with some scoundrel who cries out 'Down with the priests' and blasphemes the Blessed Virgin; others again say when they pass us, 'Poor youths, you will soon come under the conscription, you will make fine soldiers for Victor Emmanuel.' The law in Italy is that all, even students for the Church, must take their chance of becoming soldiers and, as they do not know us to be foreigners, they think that we shall have the fate of the rest. One evening in Rome after it was taken, when we were returning from our walk, we met in with a mob in the midst of which there was a man holding forth with great eloquence and, as it seemed, to their no small amusement. As we passed by the crowd in ranks, the orator addressed his speech to us which began thus: 'Gentlemen, the guns are all ready for you; you are all just so many soldiers of Emmanuel.' This speech was received by the people with cheers, but no person offered to do us any harm. Immorality and vice prevail in Rome to a great extent. But one great blessing is that they have not driven away the Jesuits, as most people expected, and that these good Fathers will open their schools at the usual time which is the 5th or 6th November. The Italians have already turned the lecture halls and school rooms into barracks for their soldiers, but the Jesuits at the Roman College will hold their classes in the interior of their own house. We left Albano and returned to Rome on Saturday the 29th October.

10

To his parents

Scots College Rome – 22 February 1871

An audience with Pius IX and a description of the Roman Carnival

On 4th January we had an audience of His Holiness the dear old pope. The poor old man, amidst all his sorrows and afflictions, has always a saintly smile and seems as cheery and well-looking as ever. When he entered the chamber where we were waiting we all knelt down and, passing amongst us, he gave us his hand to kiss. He asked how numerous we were and the rector, telling him that we were only nine, he said 'Oh, then you must at least be the nine choirs of angels.' He then blessed our rosary beads and whatever we had to be blessed and said to us, 'May the Lord bless you and preserve you from all evils and may he grant you to persevere and to become good priests in your own country.' He then began to joke about Scotland and asked us if we had brought him a piece of Scotch marble, meaning granite. We then returned home after having given him a written address of sympathy and a present in money, rejoicing to have thus shown in common with all good Catholics our feeling for our persecuted Father and Head, and received his blessing at this time of his deep distress. He bears all his sufferings with wonderful patience and calmness of mind, and his confidence in God is unbounded, well knowing that the Church and its Head must triumph over all their enemies and, if that triumph is delayed for a time, it is only that in the end it may be the more glorious. In fact, he said one day to a bishop who was paying him a visit, 'It may be a dream but I think I shall sing the *Te Deum* in St Peter's this year as yet.' God grant that it may be soon. With my own eyes and to my great grief I have seen the exaltation of his enemies in the Holy City itself. I hope I shall have the unspeakable satisfaction of witnessing also their downfall and humiliation. The pope never leaves his palace but is there visited daily by crowds of good Christians who go to console with their Father and offer him their sympathy and contributions. Long live the good old pope! Long live Pius the Ninth, the Pontiff King! Death to his enemies!

This is the time of the Carnival or farewell to the flesh before the penance and fasting of Lent begin, and it is in fact the festival of sin and the devil, a time when the people give themselves up to all kinds of excesses. Even the public newspapers tell us that they could not defile their sheets with the mere account of the immorality and debauchery which take place, especially at night. This festival is perhaps the greatest in this country and lasts for seven days before Ash Wednesday during which the people take to singing and dancing and drinking; horse races take place every evening and the streets are filled with people who have masks on their faces and wear buffoonish dresses of all sorts, sizes and colours just like so many clowns or play actors. In fact the city becomes like one big circus or show where everyone tries to be more ridiculous than his neighbour. Prince Humbert, the eldest son of Victor Emmanuel and heir to the throne, and his consort the Princess Margaret are now residing in Rome and show themselves no less eager for the fun than the rest of people. They live in the Quirinal Palace which was taken from the pope for their accommodation. It is at no great distance from our College so that at night from our windows we can see the ballroom magnificently lit-up where the Prince and his court go on dancing till all hours of the night. The princess is so fond of this pastime that she is not content unless she can continue it till three or four in the morning. But some people are not content to enjoy themselves in this way but wish even to outrage religion and those who practise. Some have been known to go into churches in the time of the sacred services and stand there with their hands in their pockets, their hats on their heads, and cigars in their mouths, mocking and staring at everything and disturbing the pious people at their devotions. But this is not all. In two different churches the tabernacles were broken open and the Blessed Sacrament scattered about and the ciboria and pyxes stolen. The same thing happened at the Roman College within the very walls of the private chapel. In another church a man was attempting the same sacrilegious robbery when he was seen by a woman who raised a cry and alarmed the sacristans. The man threw away the ciborium which he had and tried to escape but was seized and taken into custody. These are a few of the enormities and impieties which are of so frequent occurrence in Rome.

Bishop McDonald of the Northern District, having heard that the pope expressed a wish to have a piece of granite or Scotch marble as he called it, has ordered a collection to be made in the parishes of the North in order to make a present to His Holiness of a fine piece of granite.

11
To Rev Walter Dixon of Govan
Scots College Rome – 14 February 1872
His first sermon

Whenever you speak of your new chapel, you are pleased, I notice, to allude to my first sermon in it. I thank you for the kind allusion and I only hope that my poor endeavours will in some measure answer your desires and expectations. But you must know that I have already made my first attempt at preaching a sermon. It is a rule with us that the students of theology preach a sermon once a year. It lasts only a quarter of an hour, is delivered in the church at the foot of the altar of the Blessed Sacrament, and in the presence of the rector, vice-rector, and all the students. It is therefore no sham, but a very solemn affair. My subject was 'Devotion to our Guardian Angels' and my text from Psalm 90th, verse 11: 'He hath given his angels charge of thee that they keep thee in all thy ways.' I fear, however, that whatever merits the piece may have had as a composition, it had not many as a sermon for it was spoiled by a bad delivery. I did not know it well enough by heart and the consequence was that some hesitation was visible in my manner and I made some rather long pauses but – true to your principle of, above all things, never coming to a stand still – I soon recovered the thread of my discourse. As it was my first attempt, I am not at all dismayed.

12
To his parents
Scots College Rome – 6 April 1872
The Mission Oath

In Holy Week we had a short retreat of three days which passed away very pleasantly and, I hope, also profitably. Easter Sunday passed very quickly and happily with us; and I hope that you, too, had a large share in the joys and blessings which this great and glorious day is always sure to bring to every truly Christian family. We have a week of playtime after Easter and that is the reason why I am able to write to you at this time. But perhaps the best piece of news I have to give you is that on Easter Sunday I got married and am now fairly settled in life. You must not be astonished, for it is not to some beautiful Italian that I have engaged myself but to the Church and to the Scotch Mission; and all I mean to say is that, on Sunday last, I had the happiness to take the Mission Oath, that is, I have bound myself by a solemn oath, as all the priests in Scotland do, to receive Holy Orders at the proper time, to return to Scotland when ordered by my Superiors, and there employ myself, as long as I live, in promoting, to the best of my power, the greater honour and glory of God and the salvation of souls by the faithful discharge of all the duties of a good priest and missionary. This is, as it were, the first step in a priest's career and a very important one, for by it he is obliged to take all the rest, when it will please God and his Superiors.

13
To his parents
Country Villa, Marino – 2 September 1873
Return to the Scots' villa at Marino

We left Rome on the 15th of August and have returned to our own country house and vineyard after an absence of four years. It is beautifully situated amongst the hills which are covered with vineyards and olive yards, not far from the city or, rather, village of Marino. The house was abandoned as a country residence since the year 1868 when brigands broke into the house, demanded a large sum of money and, not finding any, carried away the vice-rector as security for the future payment. These Italian brigands have a very strange way of extorting money. They kidnap some wealthy person, carry him away to the woods, and they detain him till their demands have been satisfied by the friends or relations of their unfortunate prisoner. If speedy payment is not made, the brigands cut off the nose and ears and other members of the unhappy man and send them by letter or other means to the friends of the prisoner to induce them to pay the sooner. But, happily, our vice-rector got safe out of the hands of his captors, who were brought to justice, and not with the punishment they deserved. Since that time Marino has not been considered safe and we have not ventured back until this year. Even now we have a guard of two soldiers or royal carbiners every night to secure us from harm. When the Italians throw off religion, they become a lawless set of people, and there is not much security for life and property among them. Last Sunday night our two policemen were much later in coming than usual. When they were asked the cause, they said there was a stabbing match in Marino and they were detained longer than usual to make peace between the contestants. These folks seem not to know how to use their fists for in every bit of a brawl which the boys at home would settle with their fists, the Italians immediately pull out their knives and daggers and make at each other just like so many Turks. But you need not be afraid for us; they will not touch a hair of our heads.

14

To his parents

Scots College Rome – 27 October 1873

Jesuits' philosophy classes in Scots College

At present the persecution against the Church in Italy and especially in Rome is fiercer than ever. The monks and nuns are being sent adrift upon the world and their lands and houses are confiscated and seized, as it is said, for the good of the state. As I said before, old Harry the Eighth might learn a lesson from these scoundrels as to the best way of robbing the Church; I am sure he would not hold a candle to them. The Jesuits fare worst of all. All their chief houses are to be seized and, amongst the rest, the Roman College which we attend. But this will not interrupt our studies for the schools will be opened elsewhere, those of theology in the German College and those of philosophy in our College. You need not be at all afraid for us, because both the English and the Italian governments have declared that the British Colleges will not suffer.

Appendix 4: Register of the Scots College Archives

The document archive of the Scots College Rome is relatively small in comparison with many other institutions of similar antiquity. What now exists of pre-nineteenth-century material is only a remnant of what must have existed before the troubles of the Napoleonic invasion. The archive takes the form of box files with ribbon ties. Supplementing these is a heterogeneous collection of account-books, diaries, photograph albums, and so on. All of this material is on high shelving in the working office used for College administration. Mgr Philip Flanagan, rector between 1960 and 1967, completed the burdensome task of re-filing and re-numbering the whole collection. He also produced a comprehensive handwritten list of items, as well as an index of names.

1. Varia, 1605–1727
2. Abbadia di S Mennato, 1067–1617
3. Leslie Papers, 1643–1711 and undated (these belonged to or are connected with the Agent, Mr William Leslie, who died in 1707)
4. Varia, 1600–90
5. Varia, 1690–99 and undated seventeenth century
6. Varia, 1700–36
7. Varia, 1737–83
8. Varia, 1784–99 and undated eighteenth century
9. Manoscritti di D. Mauro Cappellari che fu poi Gregorio XVI
10. Manoscritti di D. Mauro Cappellari
11. Paul Macpherson: Agency Letters, 1811–26
12. Aeneas Macdonald: Agency, 1826–32; Macpherson and Macdonald, Canadian Agency, 1819–32; Macdonald: Miscellaneous Letters, 1827–31
13. Paul Macpherson: Agency, 1834–46
14. Macpherson: Miscellaneous Letters, 1811–26
15. Paul Macpherson: Miscellaneous Letters, 1827–46
16. Alexander Grant: Agency, 1841–66
17. Alexander Grant: Agency, 1867–78 or undated
18. Alex Grant: Miscellaneous Letters, 1842–77; Plummer Letters and Will
19. Fabbrica del Nuovo Collegio, 1863–73
20. Collegio Romano and 1870 Troubles, 1870–88
21. Rev James Hamilton: Papers and Letters, 1841–51
22. James A. Campbell: Agency, 1870–82 (1889)
23. James A. Campbell: Agency, 1883–87 (1878–89)
24. James A. Campbell: Agency, 1888–96 (1886–96); Miscellaneous Letters, 1867–1901
25. Restoration of the Hierarchy in Scotland: Financial Questions between the Dioceses, 1877–92

26. Fort Augustus Agency, 1882–98
27. Robert Fraser: Agency and Letters, 1897–1913
28. Varia, College or Agency, 1800–20
29. Varia, College or Agency, 1820–40 (1856)
30. Varia, College or Agency, 1840–69
31. Varia, College or Agency, 1870–90
32. Varia, College or Agency, 1890–1900 and undated of nineteenth century
33. Varia, not of College, 1800–1900
34. Donald Mackintosh: Agency and Letters, 1914–1922
35. Varia, College or Agency, 1900–17
36. Collections for the College, 1916–17 and 1919–21
37. Varia, College or Agency, 1918–23
38. Varia, College or Agency, 1924–26
39. Varia, College or Agency, 1927–33
40. Beatification of John Ogilvie, 1923–32 (mainly 1929)
41. Varia, College or Agency, 1934–38
42. Varia, College or Agency, 1939–46
43. Mgr William Clapperton, Letters to and from, 1922–28
44. Mgr William Clapperton, Letters to and from, 1929–31
45. Mgr William Clapperton, Letters to and from, 1932–33
46. Mgr William Clapperton, Letters to and from, 1934–35
47. Mgr William Clapperton, Letters to and from, 1936–37
48. Mgr William Clapperton, Letters to and from, 1938–40
49. Mgr William Clapperton in Scotland, Letters to and from, 1940–46
50. Mgr William Clapperton, Letters to and from, 1946–50
51. Mgr William Clapperton, Letters to and from, 1951–54
52. Mgr William Clapperton, Letters to and from, 1955–59
53. Varia, College or Agency, 1947–52
54. Varia, College or Agency, 1953–59
55. Reports to Bishops, Congregation of Seminaries, and Scots College Society, 1926–46
56. Reports to Bishops, Congregation of Seminaries and Scots College Society and Examination Results, 1947–60
57. Lists of Students, Timetables, Prospectus, etc, 1928–59
58. Baptismal and other Certificates, Mission Oaths, Dimissiorials, *Fides Ordinum*, Student Bursar Lists, etc., 1744–1940
59. Bull of Foundation, 1600. Rules and Constitutions of the College: preparatory drafts and approved text
60. Catalogue of Priests from Dr Grant's Collection in the possession of the College
61. Bequests, Foundations and Trusts, A to L
62. Bequests, Foundations and Trusts, M to P
63. Bequests, Foundations and Trusts, Q to Z
64. Scots College (Rome) Fund, 1920–62
65. Taggart Burses I, 1888–1958
66. Taggart Burses II, 1918–62
67. Marino: Varia, 1700–1864

The Scots College Rome

68. Marino: Varia, 1859–1882
69. Marino: Varia, 1900–65
70. Marino: Terreni, 1924–63
71. Marino: Nuova Villa, 1921–33
72. Marino: Acqua e Strada (Acqua = 72/A; Strada = 72/A)
73. Sample Receipts and Accounts, 1789–1879
74. Sample Receipts, 1880–89
75. Accounts and some Receipts, 1891–97
76. Sample Receipts, 1897–1922
77. Sample Receipts, 1922–30
78. Sample Receipts, 1930–50
79. Sample Receipts, 1950–56
80. Reports on the College to the Bishops and the Scots College Society: Reports to the Bishops on their students
81. Varia, College or Agency, 1960–67
82. Varia, not of College or Agency, 1900–
83. New College: Pisana and other Proposals, 1956–60
84. New College: Cassia Site and Building, 1960–62
85. New College: Documents, 1963–65
86. Photographs of Old College and of Laying of Foundation Stone of New
87. Photographs of New College and Inauguration Ceremonies
88. Mgr Philip Flanagan: Letters to and from, 1960–62
89. Mgr Philip Flanagan: Letters to and from, 1963–64
90. Mgr Philip Flanagan: Letters to and from, 1965–67
91. New College: Impresa Castelli: Preventivi, Disegni, Corripondenza
92. New College: Impresa Castelli: Disegni dell'Impresa
93. New College: Impresa Castelli: Contabilità
94. New College: Dita Trinello: Impianto idrosanitario: Riscaldamento
95. New College: Opere Scorporate (Minor Contracts) I
96. New College: Opere Scorporate (Minor Contracts) II
97. New College: Varia (Comune, Dazio, ENEL, ANAS, etc)
98. New College: Receipts for all payments from 1960 to end of 1965
99. Canon Boyle: Varia, 1968–70
100. Canon Boyle: Letters and Documents, 1967–73
101. Mgr Gerard Rogers (died 1975): Varia
102. Mgr Sean O'Kelly: Letters to and from, 1973–75
103. Mgr Sean O'Kelly: Letters to and from, 1976–78
104. Mgr Sean O'Kelly: Correspondence with bishops and others, 1973–81
105. Mgr Sean O'Kelly: Varia
106. Fr James Clancy

Books of the Archives

AB1–AB102	Account Books, 1762–1960
R1–R5	Constitutions and Rules, 1617–1951
R6–R8	Prayer Books, 1896–1933

R9–R12	College Register, 1602–2000
R13–R17	The Mission Oath
R18–R20	Ordination Register, 1703–
R21–R35	Mass Registers
R36–R38	Necrology of the College
R39–R40	Diaries

Appendix 5: Cardinal Protectors of the Scottish Nation

1. Camillo Borghese (1600–05)
2. Maffeo Barberini (1607/8–23)
3. Francesco Barberini (1623–79)
4. Philip Thomas Howard (1680–94)
5. Archbishop Alessandro Caprara (1694–1706)
6. Giuseppe Sacripanti (1706–27)
7. Alessandro Falconieri (1727–34)
8. Domenico Rivera (1734–52)
9. Giuseppe Spinelli (1753–63)
10. Gianfrancesco Albani (1763–73)
11. Mario Marifoschi (1773–74)
12. Francesco Caraffa (1774–80)
13. Gianfrancesco Albani (1780–1803)
14. Charles Erskine (1803–11)
15. Bartolomeo Pacca (1814–35)
16. Giacomo Filippo Franzoni (1835–56)
17. Alessandro Barnabó (1856–74)
18. Alessandro Franchi (1874–78)
19. Giovanni Simeoni (1878–92)
20. Miecislas Ledochowski (1892–1902)
21. Gerolamo Gotti (1902–16)
22. Domenico Serafini (1916–18)
23. Cajetano de Lai (1918–28)
24. Raffaele Merry del Val (1928–30)
25. Franz Ehrle (1930–34)
26. Francesco Marchetti–Selvaggiani (1934–51)
27. Giuseppe Pizzardo (1951–70)

Appendix 6: Rectors of the Scots College Rome

1. Bernardino Paolini (1600–15)
2. Patrick Anderson SJ (1615)
3. Carlo Venozzi SJ (1615–19)
4. Giovanni Marietti SJ (1619–22)
5. George Elphinstone SJ (1622–44)
6. William Christie SJ (1644–46)
7. Francis Dempster SJ (1646–49)
8. Andrew Leslie SJ (1649–52)
9. Adam Gordon SJ (1652–55)
10. Gilbert Talbot SJ (1655–58)
11. Francis Dempster SJ (1658–63)
12. Gilbert Talbot SJ (1663–70)
13. John Strachan SJ (1670–71)
14. Hector de Marini SJ (1671–74)
15. William Leslie SJ (1674–83)
16. Andrew MacGhie SJ (1683–90)
17. William Leslie SJ (1692–95)
18. James Forbes SJ (1695–1701)
19. Diego Calcagni SJ (1701–04)
20. Giovanni Naselli SJ (1704–08)
21. Thomas Fyfe SJ (1708–12)
22. William Clark SJ (1712–21)
23. Alexander Ferguson SJ (1721–24)
24. Luca Gritta SJ (1724–29)
25. Francisco Marini SJ (1729–31)
26. Giovanni Morici SJ (1731–38)
27. Livio Urbani SJ (1738–47)
28. Lorenzo Alticozzi SJ (1747–66)
29. Giovanni Corsedoni SJ (1766–73)
30. Vincenzo Massa (1773)
31. Lorenzo Antonini (1773–74)
32. Alessandro Marzi (1774–77)
33. Ignazio Ceci (1777–81)
34. Francisco Marchioni (1781–98)
35. Paul MacPherson (1800–26)
36. Angus MacDonald (1826–33)
37. Paul MacPherson (1834–46)

38. Alexander Grant (1846–78)
39. James Campbell (1878–97)
40. Robert Fraser (1897–1913)
41. Donald Mackintosh (1913–22)
42. William Clapperton (1922–60)
43. Philip Flanagan (1960–67)
44. Daniel Boyle (1967–73)
45. Sean O'Kelly (1973–81)
46. James Clancy (1981–86)
47. John Fitzsimmons (1986–89)
48. John McIntyre (1989–95)
49. Christopher McElroy (1995–)

Index

Acquaviva, Claudio   3, 16
Albani, Cardinal Gianfrancesco   52, 54, 56–61, 168
Albert, Archduke (Netherlands)   4
Alexander VII, Pope (1655–67)   30, 38
Alfaro, Juan   127
Allen, Cardinal William   2, 4–7, 39
Alticozzi, Lorenzo   50, 52, 169
Anderson, Patrick   20–21, 169
Anderson, William   136–137
Anne of Denmark   7
Antonelli, Cardinal Leonardo   55, 58
Antonini, Lorenzo   54, 55, 169
Aquhorties   63, 66
archives   22, 116, 132
Argenti, Signor   75
Arnou, Rene   118–119

Badoglio, Field-marshal   124
Baillie, Alexander   21
Ballantine, William   29, 31–32, 38
Ballerini, Antonio   82, 102–103
Banff   43, 123–124
Barbarigo, Cardinal Gregorio   13, 38–39
Barbarigo, Cardinal Marcantonio   35
Barberini (junior), Cardinal Antonio   22
Barberini (senior), Cardinal Antonio   22
Barberini, Cardinal Carlo   27
Barberini, Cardinal Francesco   22, 27, 33, 168
Barberini, Cardinal Maffeo   20, 22, 27, 168
Barclay, Robert   34
Baronius, Cardinal Cesare   3, 10
Barra   71–72
Barry, John   126–127
Bartelucci, Sebastiano   124
Baum, Gregory   132
Bearsden   123, 142, 143
Beaton, Archbishop James   41
Beda College   129, 148
Belgium   21, 25
Bellarmine, Cardinal Robert   3

Benedict XIV, Pope (1740–58)   50
Benedict XV, Pope (1914–22)   107, 112, 140
Benedictines   19, 22–23, 34, 114
Bennett, Bishop George   95, 106, 109, 112, 140,
Berthier, General   61
Bisset, George (alias Gilbert Talbot)   32, 41, 169
Black, John   81, 101
Black, Joseph   81, 101
Blairs College   xv, 78, 92–93, 101, 153
Blairs Letters   29
Bologna   36
Borghese, Cardinal Camillo   5, 20, 152, 168
Boyle, Canon Daniel P.   130, 133–135, 144, 170
Bradburn, George   137
Braunsberg   19, 24
Brazilian College   124
Breslin, Raymond   xiii, 137
Brest, Union of   10
Brown, William E.   xi, 31–32, 40, 115–116, 120,
Bruno, Giordano   9
Bute, John Patrick Crichton-Stuart, Third Marquess of   86, 155

Cahill, Hugh   123
Calcagni, Diego   36, 169
Cambridge   2, 113, 117, 130
Cameron, Bishop Alexander   62–63, 66, 69, 71–72, 99, 100
Campbell, Archbishop Donald A.   125
Campbell, Colin   43, 47, 48, 49, 64
Campbell, James   47
Campbell, James (rector)   87–92, 104–105, 116, 164, 170
Campidoglio   121
Campo Santo   88, 110, 133, 139
Cappellari, Cardinal   77
Caprara, Archbishop Alessandro   36–37,

147, 168
Caraffa, Cardinal Francesco   54–56, 168
Caravaggio, Michelangelo Merisi da   10, 17
Cardella, Valerio   87–88, 104
CARIPLO   131
Carmont, John   81, 101
Carnegie, James   45
Carruthers, Bishop Andrew   79
Carthusians   25
Cassedi, Andrew   24
Castel Gandolfo   11
Catholic Relief Act   43
Catholic Women's League   124
Cavalieri, Cardinal   10, 147
Caven, John   81, 101
Ceci, Ignazio   55, 169
Cenci, Beatrice   9
Chalmers, Thomas   23
Charles I, King of England and Scotland 23
Charleson, John M. M.   95, 106
Chisholm, Bishop Aeneas   92, 105–106, 110
Chisholm, Bishop William   20, 39
Chisolm, Alexander   66–67
Christie, William   23, 29–30, 32, 169
Civita Vecchia   153, 156, 159
Clancy, James   137, 166, 170
Clapperton, Mgr William R.   85, 98, 108–135, 137, 139–144, 165, 170
Clapperton, Thomas   110
Clark, William   45, 169
Clashinore   47–48, 164
Clement VIII, Pope (1592–1605)   xi, 3–6, 8–11, 20, 151
Clement X, Pope (1670–76)   34
Clement XI, Pope (1700–21)   36, 47
Clement XIV, Pope (1769–74)   13, 54
Clermont College   30
Collegio Romano   vii, 2, 4, 20, 33, 69, 76–82, 85, 87–88, 95, 100–102, 147, 164
Colloredo, Cardinal   147
Columba Trust   144
Colville, David   21, 40
Conn, George   23
Connolly, Michael   114, 125
Conroy, Gerard   37
convictors   38, 105
Cornely, Rudolf   91
Corsedoni, Giovanni   52–53, 169

Cowie, John   78, 101
Crichton, William   4, 6–7, 16, 19–20, 24
Crichton-Stuart, Michael   144
Cruickshanks, Charles   49
Cruikshank, William   46
Crumly, Thomas   xiii, 86–87, 104, 153–163
Crusan, Patrick   24, 40
Cullen, Cardinal Paul   77, 86, 100, 153
Curle, Hippolytus   24

D'Arcy Osborne, Francis   123
De Finance, Joseph   127
De Lai, Cardinal Gaetano   98, 108–109, 112, 139, 168
De Valera, Eamon   122
Dempster, Francis   23, 169
Dempster, Thomas   2, 4
Dhanis, Edouard   132
Diack, Hunter   142
Dilworth, Mark   19, 39–41
Dominicans   21, 24
Douai   x, 2, 4, 7, 19, 23–25, 27, 29, 33–34, 38, 72
Drummond, William   49
Duff, Thomas   21
Duffy, Francis   118, 141, 143
Duke of York (Cardinal Henry Stuart) 77, 119
Duns Scotus, John   137
Durham, Sir Thomas   49

Edinburgh   xi, 43, 55, 59, 68, 70–71, 79, 89, 97, 100, 105–106, 109, 111, 114, 116–120, 124–125, 127, 130, 134, 145
Ehrle, Cardinal Francis   140, 168
Elizabeth I, Queen of England   4, 6
Elphinstone, George   22–23, 169
Emsworth, Lord   113
England   2, 5–10, 16, 110, 145, 147–149
English College Rome   x, xiii, xv, 2, 13, 16, 20, 60, 68, 87, 114–115, 123, 138, 146–147, 149
Enzie   43
Erskine, Cardinal Charles   14, 50, 57, 60–62, 168

Fabroni, Cardinal   147
Falconieri, Cardinal Alessandro   46–48, 64, 168
Farquharson, John   61
Ferguson, Alexander   45–46, 169

Fidecicchi, Mgr Augusto   123–125
First Vatican Council (1869–70)   13, 86, 101–102, 153–154
First World War   97
Fitzsimmons, John   132, 137, 170
Flanagan, Mgr Philip I.   109–110, 113–115, 118, 122–123, 125, 127, 128–135, 140–144, 164, 166, 170
Fleming, Abbot Placid   34
Florence   10, 92
Foley, James   40, 92
Fontainebleu   62(?)
Forbes, James   36–37, 99, 146, 148–149, 169
Fort Augustus   xv, 115, 165
Fortescue, Adrian   90, 105
Foylan, Bishop Michael   133
France   1, 4–10, 13, 17, 21, 23, 25, 31–32, 41, 60–62, 84
Franciscans   21–22, 24, 26, 135
Franzelin, Johannes Baptist   82, 102–103
Franzoni, Cardinal Giacomo Filippo   78, 168
Fraser, Bishop Robert   92–95, 105–106, 110, 112, 165, 170
Fraser, John   76
Fyfe, Thomas   45, 169

Gall, Robert   29
Gallagher, Daniel   78, 101
Gardiner, Paul   105, 144
Geddes, John   49–50, 56–59, 65
Genazzano   98
German College   2, 19, 87, 163
Germany   12, 19, 24–25, 35, 55, 97, 105
Gillis, Aeneas   47–48
Gillis, Alexander   76
Gillis, Bishop James   83, 158
Gillon, Canon Thomas   114, 141
Gillow, Richard   68
Gladstone, William   87
Glasgow   x, xii–xiii, xv, 43, 72–73, 78, 84–85, 96, 98, 103, 106, 108, 110, 111, 115–116, 119–120, 125, 129–130, 135, 137, 140, 142–143, 153
Glenlivet   47, 59, 73–74, 77
Godfrey, Cardinal William   111, 115, 142
Gogarty, John   126
Gordon, Adam   28–29
Gordon, James   36–37, 39, 41–42, 146–147
Gordon, John   74

Gordon, Robert   36, 110
Govan   86, 153, 157–158, 162
Gradwell, Robert   68, 99
Graham, Hugh   133
Grant, Alexander (rector)   76, 78–81, 83–86, 88–89, 92, 100–104, 106, 139, 155, 164–165, 170
Grant, Alexander (student)   66, 67
Grant, Abbé Peter   46, 49, 54–56, 58, 65
Grant, Peter (Blairs)   78
Gray, Cardinal Gordon Joseph   127, 134, 137
Gray, Bishop John   78, 104
Gray, John   xi, 92–94, 105–106, 108, 139
Greek College   3, 22
Gregorian University   xii, 14, 95, 113, 115, 132, 144
Gregory XIII, Pope (1572–85)   2–6, 11, 19, 145
Gregory XV, Pope (1621–23)   3, 8, 115
Gregory XVI, Pope (1831–46)   76–77, 80
Grey Graham, Bishop Henry   95, 106, 117
Griffin, George   76
Gritta, Lucas   46, 50, 169
Guthrie, William   49

Hamilton, Archibald   20, 39
Hay, Bishop George   50, 54–61, 65–66
Heard, Cardinal Theodore   134
Helminiak, Daniel   130
Henri IV, King of France   4, 7–8, 10
Henrietta Maria, Queen of England and Scotland   21, 23
Hinsley, Cardinal Arthur   120, 122
Hippisley, Sir John Coxe   60, 62, 66
Howard, Cardinal Philip Thomas   33, 36, 146–147, 149, 168
Huguenots   8
Humbert, Prince   161
Humble, Mgr James   131, 144
Hungary   2

Iceland   138
Imperiali, Cardinal   147
Innes, George   47, 49
Innes, Thomas   40, 47, 63
Innocent XI, Pope (1691–1700)   35, 37
Ireland   1, 6, 8, 16, 26, 145, 147–149
Irish College   12, 36, 56–57, 77, 100, 142, 149
Irvine, John (of Belty)   33

Irvine, John (of Cuttlebrae)   36, 39
Italy   2, 9, 11, 13, 25, 60, 97–98, 102,
    110, 119, 123, 138, 157, 160, 163

Jacobites   40–41
James VI, King of Scotland (I of England)
    7, 17
James VII, King of Scotland (II of
    England)   13, 25, 34
Jameson, John   39
Jamieson, Laurence   134
Jansenism   33, 45–49, 50, 63–64
Jervoise, Harry Clarke   87
Jesuits (Society of Jesus)   2–5, 7–9,
    12–14, 16, 19–32, 34–35, 37–38,
    40–41, 44–46, 52–55, 65, 68–70, 77,
    79, 81, 87, 100, 146–149, 160, 163
John Paul II, Pope (1978–)   137
John XXIII, Pope (1958–63)   127–128
Johnston, Wilfred   115, 141
Jubilee (Holy Year)   3, 5, 10–11

Keenan, Stephen   76
Kinsella, Matthew   126
Kyle, Bishop James   73–74, 79, 99–101

Langbank   131, 144
Latourelle, Rene   144
Lavelle, John   137
Ledochowski, Cardinal Miecislas   92,
    105, 109, 168
Leith, Alexander   29
Leith, Robert Gallus   48
Lennon, Mgr James   93, 106
Lennon, Peter   137
Leo XII, Pope (1823–29)   70
Leo XIII, Pope (1878–1903)   88, 100,
    103
Lercari, Monsignore   48–49, 64
Leslie, Alexander   38
Leslie, Andrew   28–29, 169
Leslie, Count Walter   34
Leslie, George   21
Leslie, Will   27–37, 43–45, 53
Leslie, William Aloysius   33, 35
Lismore   63, 71–72
Lithuania   10
Lochaber   96, 110
Lombard College   144
Lonergan, Bernard   127
Louis XIV, King of France   13, 35
Lovie, Walter   71

Loyola, Ignatius   9
Luzzi, Monsignor   75

MacBreck, James   30, 32
MacDermott, Canon Augustine   94, 139
MacDonald, Angus   69, 71–76, 99–101,
    169
Macdonald, Bishop Hugh   46–48
MacDonald, Bishop John   49–50, 68–69,
    78
MacDonald, Bishop Ranald   68–69, 70,
    71–73
MacDonald, Donald   66–67,
MacDonald, James   63, 66, 68
MacDonald, John (18th cent.)   49–50
MacDonald, John (19th cent.)   68–69
MacDonald, Neil   70, 99
Macdonald, Roderick   49
Macdonell, John   49
Macfarlane, Bishop Angus   86, 95, 106
MacGregor, Gregor   36
Mackay, William   80, 101
Mackenzie, Robert F.   142
Mackie, Andrew (sometimes MacGhie)
    33, 169
MacKillop, Alexander   76, 105
MacKillop, Mary   76, 91, 105, 137, 144
Mackintosh, Archbishop Donald A.
    96–98, 106–107, 165, 170
MacPherson, Paul   12, 14, 54, 65–67,
    70–71, 77, 79–80, 94, 99–101, 124,
    147, 164, 169
MacRae, Christopher   66–67
MacVarish, Duncan   90
MacWilliam, Alexander   89, 104
Madrid   14, 24–25, 28, 45
Magauran, Francis   112
Magill, Thomas   136–137
Malta   138
Manning, Cardinal Henry Edward   86,
    155
Marchetti-Selvaggiani, Cardinal Francesco
    120, 168
Marchioni, Francesco   55, 58–59, 61, 120
Marenda, Carlo   130, 144
Margaret, St   23, 33–35, 38, 40, 85, 131
Marifoschi, Cardinal Mario   54, 168
Marini, Hector de   32–33, 169
Marino   29, 50–51, 62–63, 79, 83, 87, 89,
    93, 97–98, 102, 104, 106–108, 112,
    131, 135, 162–163, 165–166
Maronite College   21

Marseilles 153, 155
Martin, Aidan 144
Martin, Gregory 2
Martinelli, Lorenzo 123
Martini, Francis 46
Mary, Queen of Scots 1, 4–6, 19
Marzi, Alessandro 55, 169
Massa, Vincenzo 53–54, 169
Mathieson, Donald 109
Mathews, Eugene 126
Maxwell, George 161
Mazarin, Cardinal Jules 23
McCaffery, John 125, 130–131, 143
McDonald, Archbishop Andrew Joseph 109, 116–117, 121, 124, 127, 130, 133, 141, 154, 161
McElroy, Christopher xii–xiii, xv, 137, 142, 170
McEwan, Mgr Hugh 132, 136
McEwan, Sydney 122, 142
McGregor, Gregory Killian 42, 48, 64
McHardy, James 73
McIntyre, Mgr John xii–xiii, 13–14, 104, 137, 170
McKee, John 144
McKenzie, Charles 76
McKerrell, Francis 81, 101
McLachlan, Bishop John 78
McMahon, John 133
McNeil, James 136
McRoberts, David 39–41, 65–67, 98–99, 103
Meany, John 91, 105
Meechan, Canon Michael 143
Meechan, Denis 125
Melfort, Abbé 49
Mercurian, Everard 3
Monaci, Philippo 87
Monte Porzio 87
Morandini, Francisco 118–119
Morici, Giovanni 46
Munro, Robert 31
Murdoch, Bishop John 77, 84, 102, 104
Mussolini, Benito 15, 119, 121–22, 124, 142

Namibia 138
Nantes, Edict of 8
Naples 7, 28, 36, 50, 52, 59, 60
Naselli, Giovanni 36, 37, 45, 148, 149
Neri, Philip 3, 10, 11
Netherlands 1, 3, 4, 7, 12, 25

Newman, Cardinal John Henry 84, 103, 140
Nicolson, Bishop Thomas 34, 35, 37, 39, 41
Ninian, St xv, 19, 93
Nolan, William 137

O'Kelly, Sean 130, 134–37, 166, 170
Ogilvie, John 21, 40, 116, 136, 164
Oratorians 3, 11, 21
Ostia 55, 122
Oxford 118

Pacca, Cardinal Bartolomeo 72–77, 98–100, 168
Pacelli, Francesco 120–122
Padre Pio 143
Padua 13, 22–3, 31, 35, 39
Pamfilii, Cardinal 147
Paolini, Bernardino 20, 169
Paolucci, Cardinal Fabrizio 147, 149
Papal States 8–9, 11–12, 44, 50, 62, 80, 84
Paris 2, 4, 5, 12, 16–17, 19, 21–25, 27, 29–32, 34, 37, 41, 43–49, 64, 68–69, 71, 96, 118, 123, 147, 149, 153
Passaglia, Carlo 81–82, 102
Passchendaele 97
Passionei, Monsignore 52–55
Paterson, Bishop Alexander 66, 68–75, 98, 100
Paterson, David 109, 112, 120
Paterson, John 71
Paterson, William 88
Paul of the Cross, St 50
Paul V, Pope (1605–21) 3–5, 20
Perrone, Giovanni 80, 82, 102
Persons, Robert 2, 4, 7, 8
Peru 138
Philip II, King of Spain 5–7
Philip III, King of Spain 7
Philip, Robert 21
Pinci, Valentino 122, 142
Pius IX, Pope (1846–78) 80, 83–86, 101, 154, 160–161
Pius V, Pope (1566–72) 3
Pius VI, Pope (1775–99) 44, 55–56
Pius VII, Pope (1800–23) 44, 62, 68
Pius XI, Pope (1922–39) 122
Pius XII, Pope (1939–58) 122, 125, 126
Pizzardo, Cardinal Guiseppe 15, 124, 125, 128–131, 144, 168

Plummer, Frances Elizabeth   84, 103, 164
Poland   10, 138
Pole, Cardinal Reginald   1, 16
Poletti, Luigi   85, 131
Pont-à-Mousson   4, 5, 149
Portugal   5, 7
Propaganda Fide, Congregation of   x, 8, 17, 22, 26, 40, 70, 92, 144

Quesnel, Pasquier   47
Quirinal Palace   11, 122, 161

Radet, General   62
Raffalovich, André   92
Ramsay, John   136
Ratisbon   x, 14, 20, 24, 34, 85
Reid, William   49, 64, 70, 99
Rice, Edmund   17?, 136
Richelieu, Cardinal Armand Jean de Plessis   23
ripetitore   108, 112–14, 117, 125, 132, 134, 136–37
Ritchie, John (1841)   80–82, 101
Ritchie, John (1874)   90, 101
Rivera, Cardinal Domenico   48–9, 168
Robertson, J. K.   115
Robson, Stephen   136
Rodini, Antonio   54–5
Rogers, Mgr Gerard   124, 132, 143, 166
Rolfe, Frederick   88–91, 104–05
Rooney, William   92, 104
Rossi, Augusto   143
Rossi, Gaetano   112, 143
Rouen   22
Ruffini, Mgr Ernesto   125

Sacripanti, Cardinal Giuseppe   37, 44–46, 50, 146–48, 168
Samalaman   72
Sant' Andrea degli Scozzese   83–84, 96
Sant' Andrea delle Fratte   137
Savona   62
Savonarola, Girolamo   10
Savoy   10, 126, 135
Scalan   46, 56, 59, 64
Scandinavia   xvii
Scots College Society   x, xi, 90, 108, 126, 133, 135, 138, 140, 143, 144, 165, 166
Scott, Bishop Andrew   77–79, 100
Scott, Sir Walter   94
Sebastiani, Michele   151
Second Vatican Council (1962–65)   xi, 13, 16, 98, 105, 127, 130, 132

Second World War   xi, 15, 142
Seminaries, Congregation of   15, 108, 109, 119, 120, 121, 123, 124, 128, 140, 141, 144, 164
Sempil, Abbé   48
Semple, Hugh   24, 25
Serafini, Avvocato   120, 168
Seton, Alexander   19
Sewell, Brocard   89, 104, 106
Sheary, John   136
Sheil, Denis   91, 105
Sheridan, John   112
Sicily   6, 10
Sinclair, Margaret   116
Sixtus V, Pope (1585–90)
Sloane, Alexander   55, 60, 61, 66
Smith, Alexander   48
Smith, Archbishop William   78, 105
Sobieski, Maria Clementina   50
Somme   96
South Korea   138
Spain   xvi, 2, 4, 6–8, 12, 14, 16, 24, 40, 44, 48, 60, 98, 101, 106, 119, 125, 130, 144
Spani, Carlo   130
Sperelli, Monsignore   36
Spinelli, Cardinal Giuseppe   49, 50, 52, 168
Spinosa, Andrea de   151
St John Lateran's (Roman basilica)   128, 129
St Peter's (Roman basilica)   11, 12, 17, 106, 107, 123, 142, 155, 156, 157, 158, 161
St Quentin   22
St Sulpice   68, 118, 153
Stack, Gerald   90, 104, 114, 140
Stephens, Edward   114, 139
Stewart, William   67
Stirling   6
Strachan, George   21
Strachan, John   32, 169
Strachan, Robert   39
Strain, Archbishop John   76, 86, 100, 112, 154, 156
Stuart, Alexander   92
Stuart, William   37, 45, 66, 148
Subiaco   98
Sweden   11

Tanzania   138
Tartaglia, Philip   136
Teilhard de Chardin, Pierre   127

ᴐmson, Bishop Francis   133
Thomson, John   53, 56, 59, 65, 147
Thomson, William   23
Thornton, Stephen   97, 107
Tivoli   87, 98
Tormey, John   137, 144
Tournai   4
Treanor, Patrick   134
Trent, Council of   8, 10, 16, 80
Turner, Placid   113
Tuscany   98
Tyrie, James   43, 47–49, 64

ultramontanism   80, 83, 86
Umbria   98
Urban VIII, Pope (1623–44)   3, 8, 22, 24
Urbani, Livio   46, 50, 168
Ushaw   110, 114, 138–39

Valladolid   x, xv, 14, 16, 41, 59, 98–101,
   106, 121, 129–131, 143–44
Vatican City State 13, 121
Victor Emmanuel II   160, 161
villeggiatura   xi, 112

Walsh, Bishop Francis   128
Watson, Robert   28
Wedderburn, John   23
Weld, Cardinal Thomas   75, 76
Westminster   86, 120, 155
Wilde, Oscar   92, 139
Winning, Cardinal Thomas   xii, 132, 135,
   137
Winster, Alexander   28, 31,–34
Winzet, Ninian   19
Woodford, Michael   136
Worms   19
Würzburg   21, 24